W9-DDN-338

The Allagash Abductions

Other books by Raymond E. Fowler

UFOs: Interplanetary Visitors
The Andreasson Affair
Casebook of a UFO Investigator
The Melchizedek Connection (A Novel)
The Andreasson Affair, Phase Two
The Watchers

The Allagash Abductions

Undeniable Evidence of Alien Intervention

Raymond E. Fowler

Foreword by Budd Hopkins

Wild Flower Press
P.O. Box 230893
Tigard, OR 97281

COVER DESIGN: David K. Brunn
David Brunn began designing art on the Macintosh when the machine was first
released in 1984, and he received his M.F.A. from the University of Oregon in 1986.
Dave creates his covers by using Adobe Photoshop on a Macintosh to "stitch"
together his own photographs. His inspiration, of course, comes from within.

Library of Congress Cataloging-in-Publication Data

Fowler, Raymond E. 1933-
    The Allagash Abductions: undeniable evidence of alien intervention
    Raymond E. Fowler; foreword by Budd Hopkins—1st ed.
            p. cm.
    Includes bibliographical references and index.
    ISBN 0-926524-22-4 (trade): $16.95 — ISBN 0-926524-23-2 (case):
$23.95
    1. Unidentified flying objects—Sightings and encounters—Maine—
Allagash River Watershed. I. Title.
    TL789.3.F678 1993
    001.9'42'09741—dc20
            93-17654
            CIP
Library of Congress Catalog Card Number 92-9999

First Edition: 1993

Address all inquiries to
Wild Flower Press
P. O. Box 230893
Tigard, Oregon 97281

Printed on recycled paper in the U.S.A.

This book is dedicated to
my mother, Doris H. Fowler,
who graciously shared her
childhood and adult UFO
experiences with me prior
to her death in 1988.

Raymond E. Fowler

About the Author

Raymond E. Fowler was born in Salem, Massachusetts, and received a B.A. degree (magna cum laude) from Gordon College of Liberal Arts. His career includes service with the USAF Security Service and with GTE Strategic Systems Division. He retired early as a task manager and senior planner involved with major weapons systems development.

Ray's contributions to ufology are respected by UFO researchers throughout the world. His investigative reports have been published in congressional hearings, military publications, newspapers, magazines and professional journals in the U.S.A. and abroad. The former USAF UFO projects' chief scientific consultant, Dr. J. Allen Hynek, called Raymond Fowler, an "outstanding UFO investigator.... I know of none who is more dedicated, trustworthy or persevering." Ray currently serves as national director of investigations on the board of directors of MUFON, the Mutual UFO Network, an international group that investigates UFOs.

He constructed and operates Woodside Planetarium and Observatory and offers star shows, telescope viewing and beginners' courses for children and adults on the subjects of astronomy, origins, vegetable gardening, freshwater fishing and UFOs.

Ray has presented thought-provoking slide shows on both UFOs and astronomy to hundreds of adult and children's groups throughout and beyond New England. These include programs for colleges, public schools, professional engineering societies, lodges, church groups, social clubs, Boy Scouts and Girl Scouts.

Table of Contents

Introduction...by Budd Hopkins

For those drawn to its study, the UFO abduction phenomenon is one of those subjects—like taxes, abortion and the CIA—which can easily generate more heat than light. Ray Fowler, we may be thankful, is one of that small group of researchers that resists the temptations and forgoes the pleasures of rigid belief. This book is proof of his scientific spirit and his solidly empirical method.

Unfortunately, many people approach UFO-abduction reports with fixed—often highly emotional—positions, and little respect for open-minded, scientific curiosity. Among the various groups with firm, a priori positions on the subject, the knee-jerk "debunkers" are most easily dismissed. These individuals combine the most rigid belief systems "UFO abductions are a scientific impossibility" with a total lack of interest in actually investigating such reports. They can be characterized, collectively, as ill-informed ideologues, their positions based on faith rather than data.

To illustrate this point: When Ray Fowler interviews someone who reports a possible UFO abduction experience, he has three options to explore. First, the individual is a cold-blooded liar. Second, he or she is suffering from some kind of psychological condition and may truly believe in an abduction that did not actually occur. Third, the witness is simply telling the truth as he or she best remembers it. The knee-jerk debunker, on the other hand, has radically limited himself; his belief system necessarily narrows the possibilities to the first two options only. Obviously, the quest for scientific truth is hobbled if its would-be adherents impose, in advance, such rigid limitations on the data. Unlike these blinkered debunkers, Mr. Fowler accepts a self-evident scientific imperative: an extraordinary, bizarre and compelling phenomenon demands an extraordinary investigation.

A major, but little-noted, obstacle to the objective study of UFO-abduction reports lies in the paranoid and/or religious baggage so many of us carry through life, coloring our vision and encumbering our sense of reality. Most of us, unfortunately, labor through our days carrying a dark and capacious satchel of fears—fear of the unknown, of death, of secret powers or hidden conspiracies. At the same time, though many of us are hesitant to admit it, we also carry at least a small hope chest stuffed with the need to believe that out there, somewhere, is a god or a force or a guardian angel secretly watching over us and protecting us from serious harm. Whether this inborn and touching human hope takes the form of traditional religious belief, mystical yearning or merely superstitious finger-crossing, its effect is the same. It is a kind of homemade scrim we erect to soften the hard edges of observed reality.

So it's natural that, when we encounter reports of apparently omnipotent alien beings equipped with a magical technology, we instinctively try to stuff these accounts into our pre-existent ideological luggage. The UFO occupants must be either malevolent body snatchers bent on our destruction or benign space brothers here to save us from our destructive human ways. (Some people have the ability to satisfy, simultaneously, their paranoid fears and their quasi-religious hopes by positing two alien groups—good guys and bad guys—at war with each other, with us as the ultimate booty. I have yet to see any evidence in support of this facile Manichaean cosmology.) The cool detachment investigators must bring to UFO-abduction research requires that we somehow bypass our own personal hopes and fears. We must handle interviews without bias or slant, conduct hypnotic regressions without leading the subjects and study all the evidence without censoring it to buttress our pet theories. We need to put aside our dark, paranoid trunks and our bursting hope chests; to prevent contamination, they should be opened only late at night, away from the investigation and in the privacy of our own homes.

All of this is by way of pointing out Ray Fowler's seriousness and objectivity. Though he is a man of devout personal religious beliefs, his books demonstrate that he is a committed, pragmatic scientist when studying the UFO phenomenon. His cool, non-ideological reporting of what *really* happens puts to

shame the two currently most popular, quasi-theological interpretations of the abduction phenomenon. In one outrageous,
paranoid vision of the UFO occupants, underground-based
alien devils abduct and kill our children to feast on their flesh
and vital bodily fluids—with the full cooperation of the United
States government, the president, the CIA, the Trilateral Com-
mission and, so far as I know, the American Red Cross and Am-
nesty International! Equally ludicrous is another popular and
opposite cult theology—the rosy-tinted myth that "ETs" are
simply misunderstood space brothers who, if *we* were only to
make the effort to understand *them*, stand ready to meet us and
chat with us (telepathically) in peace and light. In this view, if
we only stopped using the word "abduction," and instead stood
around at night flashing welcoming lights, the spaceships
would simply land and all would be well.

But Mr. Fowler and the men he writes about in *The Allagash Abductions* know that the feelings of "negativity" that follow abduction experiences are the direct result of alien
behavior; they can in no way be construed to be a human fail-
ing. Jack, Jim, Chuck and Charlie, "the Allagash Four," merely
tell what was done to them while they were under alien control.
They report that permission was not asked by their captors, detailed explanations were not given and both physical and psychological pain ensued. Neither the four abductees nor the
author seek to demonize the UFO occupants, but neither do
they try to excuse what is, by human moral standards, inexcus-
able behavior.

This point must be made as firmly as possible: It is a per-
version of the truth and an act of near-cruelty to blame UFO abductees for their "negative" reactions to alien encounters.
Though Ray Fowler does not address this problem directly in
his book, his cool, uninflected presentation gives any reader
plenty of information upon which to decide whether or not human reactions cause the aliens to behave as they do.

The Allagash Abductions provides a valuable link in the
historical chain of evidence and information about the UFO abduction phenomenon—a chain forged link by link ever since the
Betty and Barney Hill case first came to light in 1966. Mr. Fowler correctly states that the importance of the Allagash affair re-
sides in the four separate and mutually corroborating accounts
of the same event. He makes the inescapable point that, if these
four men were giving similar testimony in a trial of earthly abductors, conviction would be a foregone conclusion.

This book can be read with profit for many reasons. UFO
investigators will learn important lessons about how thorough
one must be in such cases, for Mr. Fowler is nothing if not thorough and persevering. Mental health professionals will sense

the power of the traumas resulting from these experiences and the depth of the desire of so many abductees to explore their half-forgotten memories. Researchers and scientists will be able to judge to what extent the Allagash encounters replicate earlier accounts of UFO abductions, with respect to physical wounds, reproductive procedures and other features commonly reported. Those who have experienced similar UFO encounters will find many points of commonality with Mr. Fowler's subjects, and consequently may feel an easing of their sense of aloneness and separation from "normal" society. Finally, the general public will find a clear narrative portrait of how a seasoned UFO investigator works, how hypnosis is utilized, and above all, what it is like to suddenly be lifted out of one's familiar world of lakes, canoes and campsites and placed into a world of helplessness, confusion and fear—a world of huge-eyed, non-human intelligences with their own indecipherable agenda.

Raymond Fowler tells his story simply, unobtrusively and competently. It is a story one will not soon forget. Despite its importance, however, we can be sure that the 1976 abduction of four young men in the Allagash Wilderness is only one of tens of thousands of similar incidents which, together, herald the most significant turning point in human history.

Budd Hopkins, New York, 1993

Preface

In November of 1949, *True* magazine published an article by Major Donald Keyhoe. According to the United States Air Force UFO Project Chief, it was "one of the most widely read and widely discussed magazine articles in history."[1]

Several months later, Major Keyhoe expanded the article into a bestselling book.[2] The article and book were entitled: *The Flying Saucers are Real.* Both provided compelling evidence that strange flying objects appearing in great numbers all over the world were of extraterrestrial origin.

At that time, how could I ever have guessed that I would be writing this book. It too would provide compelling evidence concerning the so-called "flying saucers." Neither Major Keyhoe nor I could ever have dreamed its subject matter forty years ago. Such evidence would demonstrate, beyond a reasonable shadow of doubt, that worldwide reports of humans being abducted by alien entities were really happening. *The UFO abductions are real!*

A lot of water has passed over the dam between these two books and their far-reaching conclusions. I was a teenager in those early days of UFO history and took an instant interest in "flying saucers." On July 4, 1947, I sighted an oval object in

---

1. Edward, J. Ruppelt, *The Report on Unidentified Flying Objects* (New York: Doubleday & Company, Inc., 1956), p. 64
2. Donald E. Keyhoe, *The Flying Saucers are Real* (New York: Fawcett Publications, Inc., 1950).

broad daylight while working on a farm in my hometown of Danvers, Massachusetts. At the time, I was completely unaware of the significance of a number of childhood experiences that later would prove to be related to what I had seen in the sky that day.

My interest continued and in 1963 I became a UFO investigator and later a State Director for the Washington-based National Investigations Committee on Aerial Phenomena (NICAP) headed by none other than Major Donald Keyhoe. By that time he had become the leading civilian spokesman on what the Air Force now called Unidentified Flying Objects (UFOs).

In 1967, I served as an Early Warning Coordinator for the Air Force-sponsored University of Colorado UFO Project. Still later, I became Director of Investigations for an international UFO investigation organization called MUFON, The Mutual UFO Network. During the years that followed, I became personally acquainted with Dr. J. Allen Hynek, former Chief Scientific Consultant to the United States Air Force's UFO Project. I became a scientific associate to the J. Allen Hynek Center for UFO Studies.

Almost three decades have passed since I investigated my first UFO sighting. During that time I have observed and documented in reports and six books what appears to be a slow but sure conditioning process initiated by the powers behind the UFO phenomenon. First there were the sightings of distant silvery discs and cigar-shaped objects. Then came the close sightings of structured craft buzzing witnesses on the ground and in the air. Next were UFO landings with physical traces left behind. Then, came the reports of abduction of human beings by the occupants of UFOs. These reports are the subject of this book.

In my last book, I presented evidence for the secret design behind UFO abductions. The book, entitled *The Watchers*, provided documentation of the third and last phase of my investigation of a classic abduction case which has become known as the Andreasson affair. Betty Andreasson, like so many other abductees, had been examined periodically by aliens over her lifetime from childhood. The aliens told her that she had been chosen to reveal their purpose to the world. In short, she was told that:

1. Mankind was going to become sterile.
2. They were physically related to man.
3. They were dependent upon man for the reproduction of their own species.
4. They were conducting a genetic engineering program with earth's life-forms for preservation purposes.

Data extracted from the abduction experiences of Betty and others also indicated that the tall blonde humanlike beings often seen with the small humanoid fetal-like creatures were their creators. Indeed, if we take what was told Betty at full face value, these same beings were responsible for the rapid development of homo sapiens from lower life forms millions of years ago.

Such revelations, if true, are mind-boggling. They would be the catalyst for far-reaching repercussions throughout the world. Therefore, it behooves us not to take them completely seriously until we know with some certainty that the UFO abduction experiences are grounded in physical reality. That is the purpose of this book. How does one go about proving that UFO abduction reports are real? One way would be to find one iron-clad case that provided overwhelming evidence that would not be denied in a court of law. This book documents such a case. It involves four highly credible persons who all shared the same conscious close-encounter with a UFO in 1976 during a canoe trip along the Allagash Waterway in the wilderness of Northern Maine. I have dubbed this case, the Allagash abductions. All four witnesses experienced missing time and relived a detailed and complementary UFO abduction experience under hypnosis. Two of the abductees are identical twins, which was of great interest to their alien abductors. Our inquiry revealed that each of the witnesses exhibited the typical benchmarks characteristic of other abductees, which included:

1. Alien interest in the reproduction system including the extraction of sperm from each of them.

2. A series of UFO and related paranormal experiences dating back to early childhood and right up until the present time: the May 20, 1988, abduction of one of the twins and his wife from their secluded Vermont home during our investigation.

3. Physical scars on their bodies that are typical of those on other UFO abductees.

4. The overnight appearance of a lump above the tibia of one of the twins which was removed by surgery and, unknown to the twin, sent to an Air Force installation for analysis.

The documentation afforded by this case alone would evoke a positive response from an unprejudiced jury that UFO abductions are real physical events.

Another way to demonstrate the real nature of UFO abduction reports would be to make a detailed study of hundreds of abduction cases. An analysis of these cases would then be initiated to discover whether or not a pattern exists that would establish their physical reality. The results of such a recently completed study are presented in this book. It revealed that such a pattern indeed exists.

In the following pages, you will relive the Allagash abductions and the other UFO experiences of the four percipients. All pertinent conversations and hypnotic regression sessions were recorded. You will be the proverbial fly on the wall overlooking every facet of an investigation that has been in process for over two years. In a very real sense, you the reader are a member of a unique jury. You have been called upon to listen to evidence supporting the strangest crime in history: the kidnapping and examination of people from all walks of life by alien beings from another world. The witnesses will now take the stand. Listen carefully to their testimonies without prejudice. Take careful note of the correlation of their testimonies with the testimonies of over two hundred other alleged abductees. Then you decide the answer to one of the most thought-provoking questions of our time: "Are the UFO abductions real?"

CHAPTER **1**

Help!

The Best Western motel loomed into view as I exited Route 128 onto Trapelo Road in Waltham, Massachusetts. It was May 6, 1988, and the motel was hosting the annual PSI Symposium sponsored by the Universalist-Unitarian Church. This year, the symposium was to be centered on the subject of UFOs. I was the keynote speaker for this evening and was arriving early to set up my audiovisual equipment.

Other speakers featured for the following day were Budd Hopkins and David Webb. Both Budd and David were well-known for their research of UFO reports involving the abduction of human beings by alien creatures. Interestingly enough, my presentation was on the Andreasson affair,[1] a classic example of a UFO abduction. My involvement with this case had already spanned more than a decade of investigation and was finally coming to a close. Eventually its results would be made public in a book entitled, *The Watchers*,[2] that would reveal the secret design behind UFO abductions. Little did I know, as I set up my equipment, that yet another unique abduction case awaited me in the wings of the auditorium. It would be the basis for providing indisputable evidence that *UFO abductions are real!*

---

1. Raymond E. Fowler, *The Andreasson Affair* (Englewood Cliffs, New Jersey: Prentice-Hall, Inc., 1979).
2. Raymond E. Fowler and Betty Ann Luca, *The Watchers* (New York: Bantam Books, 1990).

Jim Weiner wended his way to the motel. He had only one goal in mind. Somehow he had to meet and talk with me. At the time, Jim was undergoing treatment at Beth Israel Hospital for a brain injury sustained in a home accident. His condition was diagnosed as temporolimbic epilepsy. This condition had gone undiscovered until 1982. At that time, recurring chest pains and numbness in his side caused him to seek medical assistance.

During the course of his treatment, Jim was asked to report any unusual experiences that might be symptomatic of his condition. Jim complied and gave detailed accounts of several strange nighttime experiences that had plagued him since their onset in 1980. These included awaking to see strange creatures looking at him, levitating from his bed and temporary paralysis while something was done to the area around his genitals. During interrogations about these experiences, Jim told his psychiatrist that he felt they might be connected to a close-encounter UFO sighting experienced by himself, his twin brother and two friends. It had occurred during a camping and canoe trip along the Allagash Waterway in the wilderness area of northern Maine. His brother and friends had also been experiencing nightmares since the UFO experience.

Jim had just read *Communion*,[3] written by Whitley Strieber. In the book, Strieber had chronicled his UFO abduction and subsequent experiences that were strikingly similar to what Jim himself was undergoing. The psychiatrist, up to that point, had been analyzing such experiences as being possible effects of Jim's epileptic condition. However, as he explained to me later, the kinds of things that Jim was reporting to him did not necessarily correspond to the normal pattern exhibited by temporolimbic epilepsy. Jim's neurologist would tell me much the same thing. What was intriguing to them both was the fact that Jim's UFO encounter had been shared with three other persons. Jim's psychiatrist encouraged him to seek out a specialist who researched such UFO encounters. When local newspapers advertised the PSI Symposium on UFOs, he suggested that Jim attend and talk to such a person. Jim did and I was the specialist he sought.

After setting up my equipment, I headed for a table where I was to sell copies of my books and answer questions. I tried my best to be polite and cooperative as I attempted to make change, autograph books and talk to several people at a time. As always, there were all kinds of people with all kinds of interests. Some wanted help in writing books, others asked ques-

---

3. Whitley Strieber, *Communion* (New York: William Morrow, 1987).

tions, several expounded personal theories and many just wanted to share their personal UFO experiences with me.

Jim Weiner was in the latter category and was very persistent in having me hear him out. I must admit that initially I only half-listened to what he was saying. The third phase of investigation of the Andreasson case was taking all my investigation time. I was not about to take on another case. But my mindset changed when Jim mentioned several intriguing things: missing time, nightmares of alien beings and twins!

One of the trademarks of a UFO-abduction experience is a period of time that cannot be accounted for by witnesses. Most often, details of the abduction experience are buried deeply in the subconscious minds of abductees by their abductors. However, frequently portions of the experience surface via flashbacks of conscious memory and vivid, lifelike nightmares. In addition, the third phase of my investigation of the Andreasson case revealed a long-standing alien interest in genetics. It struck me that twins (natural clones) would be of great interest to aliens involved in genetic engineering. Suddenly, I became very interested in what Jim was trying so hard to tell me!

I immediately left the book table attended by someone at an adjoining table and found a quiet place to listen to Jim. The prospect of four witnesses, two of them twins, having a mutual UFO abduction experience was too much to pass by. If true, it would be a unique case in the chronicles of UFO history. A documented corroborative abduction experience would go a long way toward demonstrating the physical reality of such experiences

Our initial meeting was brief. I took down some notes along with Jim's address and told him that I would be in touch.

Incredibly enough, Jim and his brother Jack had kept in close touch with the two other witnesses over the years. Unfortunately, many times the whereabouts of persons involved in multiple-witness UFO sightings reported years after the fact are unknown. This was not one of those times. Charlie Foltz lived in the same apartment building with Jim. Chuck Rak lived near his twin brother in rural Vermont.

During the course of the investigation, I made it a point to learn as much about their individual backgrounds as possible. Many times one asks: "What kind of people are these abductees—psychotics? Hoaxers?" My answer has always been that most abductees are normal people from all walks of life. The small percentage of psychotics and hoaxers are usually weeded out during the investigative process. The following autobiographical sketches are provided for the reader's own judgment on this matter.

Jim and Jack Weiner were born on October 8, 1952. Their home was in a rural section of Allentown, Pennsylvania. They both enjoyed a happy though strict upbringing as chronicled by Jack in his autobiography:

> Our infancy was pretty normal for identical twins. All the stories you hear about twins are true. At least they were all true for us. We ate, slept, cried, moved, everything in unison. We shared every possible stimulus, developing the same likes and dislikes. We communicated with mental telepathy and our own language. There was no end to our discussions concerning our new environment. We delighted in sharing our new lives together, and that's what we did. Our childhoods were spent together. We were inseparable buddies.
>
> Since we lived in the country, we spent a lot of time outdoors with our big brother Tom. He quickly exposed us to a wide and wonderful world of cornfields separated by woodlots just teeming with all of the indigenous wildlife. To our Mom's dismay, our favorite thing was to bring some animal from the wild home for a pet. A pet could be anything from a handful of earthworms to a baby raccoon, infant deer, mice, a sparrow hawk, varied snakes and amphibious creatures. Dad was a master sheet-metal fabricator, so he made all the cages for our menagerie. He always emphasized that we do things ourselves and learn to experience things for ourselves. We kids were always included in his activities...berry picking...fishing.... It was our Dad who taught us to love and appreciate the natural world and always focus on the positive things in life.
>
> Our Mom was also the best. She cooked great, sewed, gardened...everything. Once...she fought off a fully grown black bear, that had gotten into our backyard garbage can, with a broom. She was feisty all right, but also very gentle and empathetic. That was one of the basic things about life that she taught us. Empathy, the ability to put oneself in the shoes of another so as to understand them better. Those many years with my family were the best that anyone could possibly hope for in a lifetime. My Mom and Dad provided the most loving environment possible and allowed us kids freedom to roam and learn by doing.
>
> Who could ask for a better life?

The twins spent their first eight grades in a Catholic parochial school. They attended a public high school.

Both went on to spend a year at a local community college before going separate ways to obtain degrees from different colleges. Jim attended Mansfield State College in Pennsylvania and earned a B.A. degree in psychology. Jack attended Massachusetts College of Art, located in Brookline, Massachusetts, where he earned a B.F.A. in graphic arts. Later he earned the certificate of Mastery in Ceramics at the Benjamin Franklin School of Artisanry which was affiliated with Boston University.

Chuck Rak was born on January 23, 1949. His childhood home was in Waban, an upper middle-class village of Newton, Massachusetts. Summers and weekends were spent at the family's 21-acre waterfront home located at Sandwich, Cape Cod, Massachusetts. His father was a psychiatrist, his mother a language therapist. Completing the family are two older sisters.

Unlike the twins, Chuck experienced a rough childhood. The divorce of his parents, an abusive father and an alcoholic mother, made life very difficult for him. Also unlike the twins, Chuck became a world traveler during his early teens. His father took him to England, Holland, Germany, Austria, Italy and Switzerland. He also visited his sister in different parts of the world when she was an employee of U.S. AID.

Chuck started to attend the University of Arizona but was forced to drop out because of parental financial disputes. He later attended Massachusetts College of Art for two and one-half years. It was there that he met and became friends with the twins and a fellow named Charlie Foltz, the fourth participant in the Allagash abductions.

Charlie Foltz was born on January 11, 1950, in Sharon, Pennsylvania. He experienced a happy childhood life in Brookfield, a farming community in Northeastern Ohio. Charlie worked on and around farms during most of his youth and helped his father install water pumps and tanks for private homes.

After high school graduation, he joined the Navy and became involved in their nuclear program with expertise in the disposal of radioactive waste from atomic submarines.

After his discharge in 1972, Charlie worked as an electric motor repairman and took night courses in art at Youngstown State University. Soon after, he transferred to the Massachusetts College of Art. There, he studied photography and art illustration and earned a B.F.A. degree. While in attendance, he became good friends with the twins and Chuck Rak.

As mentioned, their friendship and close contact with each other have continued to the present. Jim is now an instructor in the Computer Arts Department of the Massachusetts College of Art. He enjoys photography as a hobby. Charlie Foltz works for the federal government as a medical illustrator at the Veterans Administration Medical Center in Brockton, Massachusetts. Much of his spare time is taken up by volunteer work with children at the Shriners Burn Hospital and other Masonic activities. Jack and Chuck decided to get away from city life. They moved to adjoining towns in rural Vermont. Jack operates a computer art company out of his home. Chuck is self-employed as a portrait artist. His work often takes him to work at shopping malls, where he draws and sells caricatures. Both Jack and Chuck enjoy outdoor sports.

These witness profiles were researched as part of an overall investigation into their reported close encounter with a UFO. After Jim Weiner had asked me for help during our discussion at the PSI Symposium in May of 1988, I began an investigation that took two years to complete. Most of the inquiry took place in 1989 because I was already deeply involved in the third phase of my investigation into the Betty Andreasson Luca case and writing *The Watchers*.

My first step was to send the witnesses questionnaire forms to fill out. The forms were especially designed by MUFON, the Mutual UFO Network[4], to systematically collect data on UFO sightings. It took several months to get the forms filled out properly and sent back to me. I also requested and received individual written accounts of the UFO experience. I also obtained a list of names for character references and other investigative purposes. I wanted assurance that the witnesses were reliable persons and not hoaxers. In addition, I wanted documentation that such a UFO sighting had actually been *reported* by them in 1976. The following is a résumé of the results of these inquiries.

Character Reference Check

The first thing I did was contact Jim's employer—the director of the Computer Arts Learning Center at the Massachusetts College of Art. He told me that Jim had an "absolute sense of integrity" that caused him to go out of his way to help others. He added that Jim "provides a lot of service and doesn't really want attention or credit" and sometimes "doesn't even want any pay for it." The next person questioned was a hometown neighbor of the Weiner family who had known the twins for twenty years. He also vouched for their integrity. Jim Weiner's personal physician since 1983 stated that Jim's reliability was: "A straightforward issue. In all my encounters with Jim, I find him to be honest, caring and reliable. There has never been any indication that he is an attention-seeker or that he misrepresents the facts of any situation."

Also, a number of other persons were queried, including current neighbors of Jack and Mary Weiner. Schoolmates,

---

4. MUFON, 103 Oldtowne Road, Sequin, TX 78155.

friends and fellow employees who have known Chuck Rak and Charlie Foltz for many years were also questioned. All the witnesses were given good marks for honesty. None of the people questioned believed that any of the witnesses were the type likely to perpetrate a hoax for any reason.

Sighting Verification

To further rule out the possibility of a hoax, I asked many of the people whom I had called if the witnesses had ever mentioned the incident to them back in 1976. One of the persons I questioned was supposed to have gone on the ill-fated camping trip himself, but had to cancel because of a family schedule conflict. He related to me that the twins had told him about the UFO encounter upon their return from the trip. A friend of Chuck Rak also remembered being told about the UFO encounter right after Chuck returned from the canoe trip in 1976.

Several of the more recent acquaintances of the witnesses, including Jim's employer, also had been told about the 1976 UFO sighting. I also phoned the twins' mother and brother in this regard. Their mother told me that her sons had come back from the trip very excited about what they had seen. However, it was emphasized that she personally did not believe in the possibility of "visiting spaceships." On the other hand, she expressed a strong belief that they must have seen something out of the ordinary. The twins' older brother provided still further evidence that such a report originated in 1976.

Other confirmation came from the witnesses' trip diaries and from the Maine state ranger who had responsibility for the sighting area. It took a bit to track him down because he had since transferred to the Maine Department of Forestry. Although the four had reported the incident to an unknown subordinate, other campers alarmed by the glowing aerial object had filed reports directly with him at his office. The following are pertinent excerpts from my telephone conversation with him.

> Well, the funny part of it is, is that I don't remember names but I do remember the incident.... I don't remember them but I do remember the fiasco that we went through there.... They came in the office up there where I was the ranger at the time and reported that. I didn't see it, but, ah, we did call out to our radio dispatcher at the time, which done our emergency stuff and, ah, I do remember calling her and having her check with Loring Air Force Base, which was not too far from us to see if there was any aircraft missing or going down or anything. And there wasn't at the time. And that's the only thing that I remember. I do remem-

ber going through the radio procedure. That's the only incident that ever happened up there while I was up there. I guess we was there ten seasons."

The results of the thorough background check of both the witnesses and the circumstances surrounding their bizarre UFO experience were highly positive. The four witnesses that I surreptitiously refer to as "the Allagash four" appeared to be well-balanced and credible persons who shared an incredible experience. Each witness described the UFO encounter in writing, as requested on the MUFON questionnaires. I also obtained maps, photographs and diaries of their ill-fated canoe trip. Armed with this information, I was able to reconstruct in some detail the events that led up to their encounter with the wilderness fireball.

CHAPTER 2

Wilderness Fireball

August of 1976 found the Allagash four building their careers and skills as artists. Jack and Jim Weiner had graduated from college in 1975. Jack was working as a silk-screen artist in a Boston-based artists' loft. Jim joined Jack in Boston and was studying ceramics. Charlie Foltz was still studying at Massachusetts College of Art, and Chuck Rak, an avid lover of the outdoors, had moved from the city to a rural town in Vermont. His outdoor escapades include living in a tree house and taking a kayak tour of the Noatak River, north of the Arctic circle in Alaska!

During the preceding year, Chuck and a friend had traveled to Maine to canoe and camp along the Allagash Waterway. The beauty and challenge of the trip had so impressed him that he yearned to do it again. In August, he drove to Boston and visited Jack. He proposed that the twins join him for a trip to Maine to climb Mount Katahdin and canoe up the Allagash. Jack, reminiscing to me during my investigation, said that it sounded like a lot of fun and adventure so they enthusiastically accepted Chuck's proposition. Another person was needed to accompany them, who turned out to be Jim's neighbor, Charlie Foltz.

It had just turned midnight, August 20, 1976, when Chuck Rak's overloaded Chevy Vega hatchback left the quiet, narrow streets of Boston for Route 95. This multi-lane highway, stretching from Boston to Canada, would be their host for the next eight hours as they traveled through the wee hours of the morning to Mount Katahdin in Baxter State Park.

Mount Katahdin is the northern terminus of the Appalachian Trail, which runs between the states of Florida and Maine and is one of the highest peaks east of the Rockies. The summit looks down upon a vast expanse of lakes, streams and forests. This territory is Baxter State Park, which, with its more than 200,000 acres, comprises almost half the acreage in Maine. It is a region in which to commune with nature, to observe wildlife, to canoe on secluded streams and to fish for native trout in woodland lakes. Highways through the area are few and far between. Most roads are privately owned and maintained by the pulp industry. It is understandable that Chuck Rak wanted to share this natural paradise with his friends.

Four very excited but tired adventurers arrived at the gates of Baxter State Park at 8:00 A.M. Saturday morning with only four hours of sleep under their belts. They registered at the campground, unpacked and set up their tent for a one-night stand. Their goal was to stay awake during the day and get back on a normal sleeping schedule. Chuck and Jim went shopping for food and supplies, while Jack and Charlie hiked up Mount Katahdin as far as the timberline. By nightfall, sleep came quickly.

Sunday was spent climbing Mount Katahdin. They hiked precariously along a narrow ridge, appropriately called the knife's edge, to the 5,267-foot summit. In all, they hiked about eleven miles across extremely rugged terrain without mishap. Although they arrived back somewhat footsore, the perfect day of climbing served as an enthusiastic springboard for their eleven-day stint on the Allagash.

On Monday morning, they broke camp and headed North to Shin Lake, where Scotty's Flying Service was located. Scotty's long-time operation was so well known that it appears on the official state map of Maine. It was operated by a Navy veteran and his wife. They sold supplies, rented canoes and provided flights into the Allagash for those who dared to ply its waters.

Jack's notes best describe their trip to Shin Lake that day:

> Outside Chuck's overpacked Vega, the bright yellow sun punctuated a sky so electric blue that it made one want to scream. The car radio was blaring and our spirits were soaring as we headed for Shin Pond where our adventure into the Allagash Wilderness Waterway would actually commence. On the way, we stopped at a friend's camp to borrow their canoe as one of the two we needed for the trip.
>
> Shortly after, Chuck pulled into the parking lot of our destination. Within seconds, we all poured out of

the tiny car onto the warm gravel to stretch our legs and savor our mutual feelings of relief that we made it there safely, without incident and right on schedule.

On the dock next to the parking lot were several children using the dock as a springboard into the cool, clear water of the large pond. As we watched their antics, my thoughts drifted away to a time when I was very young and Jim and I used to play the same games down at the town swimming hole. I was almost ready to kick off my sneakers and jump into the water myself when Chuck's voice—screaming "Hey Jack! Get it together!"—jolted me from my melancholy and brought me back to the present.

A few quick strides got me caught up to the rest of the guys, who were already ascending the stairs to the office. The bells tied to the door jangled as we entered a homey office tended by the wife of the pilot who would be flying us into the Allagash. She was very organized and had everything pertaining to our business with them ready for us. A few minutes were spent discussing our flight plan and present water conditions. By this time, the four of us were raring to go, so we said our thank-yous and headed back outside to where our gear was being loaded onto the plane.

The plane itself was a small piper cub type with oversized pontoons. Our gear was packed into the plane, filling nearly all of the cargo space except for a small spot directly behind the pilot's seat for the third passenger. There was so much gear to take that only three people could fit into the plane at one time. Obviously, that meant two trips for the pilot, and we would have to split up into pairs. We flipped a coin, and it was tails! We won. Charlie and I would go first.

I climbed into the space behind the pilot. The tiny seat looked like it was made for a small child. But once I was settled in among the mountain of camping gear, it turned out to be quite secure and comfortable. I could see very well out the side window, so I was happy, knowing that I wouldn't miss the view.

A sudden bang accompanied by a dull thud told the pilot that all was loaded and ready. When the pilot pulled back on the throttle, the small plane shook from the vibrations of the powerful motor. Charlie and I waved to Jim and Chuck, who were jumping up and down and waving their hats frantically on the dock. It seemed like only seconds had gone by, and we were already at the far end of the pond and in position for takeoff. We both looked at the pilot, who sat relaxed as mud in his seat going over his final check list before giving her the gun. Charlie looked back at me with a huge grin. I could tell that his heart was beating just

as fast as mine because his face was bright red and his
eyes wide open. Then the whole plane shook. We were
in motion and rapidly gaining forward speed, kicking
up a towering plume of water behind us. My white-
knuckled hands grasped the back of the pilot's seat so
tightly that I'm surprised it didn't become a permanent
part of my anatomy. The vibrations ceased, and with a
feeling of going up in a fast elevator, the plane's pontoons were free of the water's friction. We were climbing steeply to avoid crashing into the tall pines that
surrounded the pond. Behind us, everything shrank
rapidly into the distance and the pilot leveled out at
about 600 feet. I swallowed hard to keep my heart from
popping out of my throat.

Outside, the view was outrageous. To the left of
the plane was the Mount Katahdin Range unfolding in
all of its majesty. Ragged, stony peaks penetrated right
up to a layer of patchy clouds that wafted above the
torturous terrain. They crowned the peaks with fluffy
pillows of bright oranges, golds and deep purples. Directly in front of us stretched countless acres of pine
forests dotted with shallow water holes. Some had
moose wading among the low scrub. They merely
raised their heads in a brief recognition of our passing
overhead.

Suddenly, Telos Lake came into view, and the pilot radioed the ranger station that he was going to
land. The radio crackled, and a clear voice with a
heavy Maine accent announced, "all's clee-ah, bring
'er in!" The plane went into a steep dive towards the silvery water and made a hair-raising landing, skidding
over the bumpy surface of the lake like a giant water
bug. It came to a halt across from our intended first
camp. We quickly untied the canoe from the pontoons,
unloaded our gear into it and paddled to shore. Behind
us, the plane made another spectacular takeoff as it
headed back to Shin Pond to get Jim and Chuck and
the other canoe.

Later, the reunited group rested and talked about the spectacular airplane rides. As Chuck noted, "The exhilaration of the
flight and the thrill that we had reached point of no return on
our two-week journey nearly kept us from noticing the increas-
ing hordes of mosquitoes enveloping our campsite!"

Suddenly, their reverie was interrupted by the sound of a
powerboat that seemingly appeared out of nowhere. Chief
Ranger Everett Cram killed the engine and beached to officially
register their presence on the Allagash Waterway. Still later, a
dinner of steak and fried potatoes topped off an exciting day.
They hit the sack early. Tomorrow promised to be a busy day.

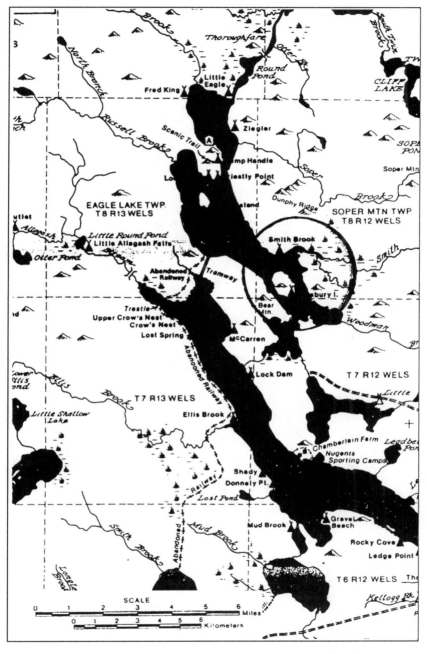

Figure 1. The Allagash Waterway topographical map.

Tuesday was spent canoeing against a northerly wind, between Telos and Chamberlain Lakes. Chuck and Jim pulled way ahead of the others, who later rendezvoused with them at the entrance to Chamberlain Lake. It was just after dusk when they landed on Mud Beach at the Mud Brook Campsite. (See Figure 1.) Several other campers tented nearby. The sky soon was ablaze from the light of thousands of twinkling stars.

Then it happened. A blazing light suddenly appeared in the eastern sky. Jim, who was currently studying ceramics, noted that "the light was most peculiar. It resembled that quality of light one sees inside a pottery kiln at cone 10, approximately 2,350° Fahrenheit." Puzzled, he reached for a pair of binoculars. From his notes we read:

There were some other campers on the beach tending a large beacon fire for their sons who were still out on the lake. One of the men at the fire suddenly remarked, "What is that bright star over there?" Directly across the lake we saw what at first appeared to be an intensely-bright star—three to five times brighter than the next-brightest visible star. I took out my binoculars and focused on the "star" and immediately realized that it was not a star. It was an object only a few miles away and approximately 200 feet above treetop level. It hovered perfectly still for a few seconds and then extinguished from the outside edge of the light to the center. I did not really think much about it, except that I had never observed a light implode like that before.

The incident was soon forgotten amidst setting up camp and planning for the next day's activities. Later, it would be recalled as a harbinger of another visitor in the sky—one that would change their outlook on life forever.

Heavy rains greeted the Allagash four on Wednesday morning, keeping them under cover. The weather restraint allowed them to eat a leisurely breakfast of ham, eggs and melon. Games of cards whiled the time away until the weather improved in the afternoon. Then they broke camp and started up the river towards Allagash Lake to do some trout fishing. They managed to canoe a third of the way upstream, but were forced to turn back because of heavy current. That night they camped at the intersection of the river and Chamberlain Lake. The Northern lights arced across the starry sky as they replanned their fishing trip. They decided they would head for Eagle Lake in the morning.

Thursday turned out to be a beautiful sunny day. The four canoeists plied their way across Chamberlain Lake to the lock that separated it from Eagle Lake. They portaged around the lock and paddled out onto Eagle Lake.

It was afternoon when they reached Smith Brook Campsite, the most remote spot on the lake. The area was deserted. After setting up camp they paddled to the mouth of Smith Brook to fish. Hopes were high that they would soon be hooking the beautifully-colored trout that haunt these remote waters. However, their hopes were dashed. An afternoon's fishing produced only inedible lake chub, which they threw back. At dinner, they consumed the last of their fresh meat. They had depended upon fish to replenish their food supply, so in desperation, they decided to try some night fishing. After dinner, they collected a big pile of logs and built a huge fire. Jim commented in his notes:

> The fire was so large that I was very worried that it would start a forest fire. The other guys told me to stop nagging them about it, but I was still concerned about it.

Such a beacon was absolutely necessary for them to find their way back to camp. The pitch blackness of a moonless night in the wilderness was such that the men couldn't see their hands in front of them.

Outlined against dancing shadows and leaping tongues of flame, only one canoe slid out onto the lake that eventful night. Charlie Foltz paddled from the front as bowman. Chuck took up the helmsman's position at the back. The twins sat beside each other in the middle and paddled with their hands.

They were halfway across the cove and about a quarter of a mile from shore when it began. Chuck was the first to sense it:

> I became aware of a feeling of being watched. I turned toward the direction from where I felt this and saw a large, bright sphere of colored light hovering motionless and soundless about 200-300 feet above the southeastern rim of the cove. Since I was in the rear seat and the object was over my right shoulder, there was a moment when I sat there with the paddle in my lap, knowing that I was the only one who saw it. Without taking my eyes off it, I drew attention to the object by exclaiming, "That's a hell of a case of swamp gas!" Charlie stopped paddling. The canoe's momentum slowed, and all eyes were on the object. For a while, we were all transfixed. I felt intense curiosity, as it was clearly nothing that could be explained. I became completely absorbed in observing the object to the exclusion of everything else.
>
> I could see a fluid pulsating over the face of the object as it changed color from red to green to yellow-

white. As my eyes became adapted to the intense brightness, I detected a gyroscopic motion, as if there were pathways of energy flowing equatorially and longitudinally from pole to pole. They divided the sphere into four oscillating quadrants of bright colored light. The color changes were very liquid and enveloping as if the entire object had a plasmic motion to it like a thick sauce does as it starts a rolling boil. I saw bulges of energy moving along the gyro pathways that seemed to trigger the motion and color changes. I could hear a discussion in the canoe about what to do. All I wanted to do was stay there and observe the thing.

Jack Weiner describes the shocking sight from his own perspective:

Jim and I were sharing the middle of the canoe. We both turned around and saw what Chuck was commenting about. At a distance of maybe 200 or 250 yards away, rising out of the woods, was a very large, bright, pulsing, spherical light. It was not making any noise at all! We turned the canoe so that it was parallel to the shore, so we could all get an unobstructed view of the light. When the light got just above the tree tops, it stopped rising and just hovered above the trees motionlessly. It obviously wasn't the moon or a star or anything like that. It also was not an airplane, helicopter or any other recognizable type of conventional aircraft.
It was very large, as big as a house, at least 80 feet in diameter, spherical in shape and pulsing light. There were changing patterns in it that reminded me of the science experiment that uses magnets and metal filings to illustrate the magnetic fields of magnets.
We all sat awestricken, wondering what it could be.

Jim Weiner describes what his impressions were as he glanced back to see what Chuck was yelling about:

I turned around and saw a huge, white/yellow, spherical object hovering just above treetop level at the southern shoreline. It was approximately the size of a two-story house in circumference, with no observable protrusions or windows. I do not remember seeing any colored lights. The object appeared solid and was absolutely silent. I immediately recognized it as the same light that we had seen from the campsite on Chamberlain Lake. The light resembled that quality of light one sees inside of a pottery kiln. It was extremely bright— like a miniature sun. It was impossible to see a solid edge on the object. It hovered silently over the treetops for what seemed about five minutes. We tried to rationally explain the object as a weather balloon but that strange light quality just couldn't be explained away. Well, I came up with the idea of signaling it with our flashlight.

Charlie's version takes over the eyewitness accounts at this juncture:

I looked at what I first thought was the moon rising over the trees. However, I realized that it wasn't the moon and was in awe of this sphere of silent light. It came to the edge of the tree line and paused momentarily. Then it moved along the shoreline about 15 to 20 feet above the trees. I was holding a large flashlight which I then flashed at the sphere—three short, three long and three short flashes.

Instantly, at the last blink of Charlie's flashlight, the huge, glowing object came to an abrupt halt and then began to slowly approach the stationary canoe. What happened next caused complete pandemonium. Jack picks up the account:

The moment Charlie signaled towards it, the light began to move silently towards us. It was agreed that we should sit tight and wait to see if it reflected in the water or affected the water once it came out over the lake. By this time, the light was only about 40-50 feet above the surface of the water and still bearing down on us steadily. We decided to get off the water and onto solid ground. We were afraid of falling out of the canoe into the swamp and drowning. We all started paddling—all except Chuck who was not paddling and seemed to be entranced by the light. The thing let out some kind of very strange light beam directed at the water and advanced on us. (See Figure 2.) Charlie yelled, "Swamp gas doesn't have beams!" as we continued to paddle frantically towards our campfire.

Chuck, as mentioned, suddenly became inanimate. He describes his feelings as the huge pulsating fiery globe closed on their tiny vulnerable canoe:

Charlie, who is a Navy veteran, started signaling it with a flashlight S.O.S. In a moment, the object emitted a cone-shaped beam of light from its low right underside that shone upon the water behind us and moved towards us slowly. I felt a bolt of panic possess the others in the canoe as I heard frantic splashing and felt the canoe lurch forward and away from the advancing light. I never took my eyes off the object, nor did I assist in the rush for shore. I felt no fear, only curiosity. I felt angry with my companions for wanting to flee.

Figure 2. The Allagash four see the light in the sky.

It was from this point on that the conscious memories of the four differed from one another according to each witnesses' vantage point. The next thing Charlie Foltz remembered was paddling for shore and standing at the campsite with the others watching the object move away.

> As we stood on the shore, I flashed the light once more, yet the sphere made no further response to us. It moved along the tree line until it reached the edge of the lake and then began to ascend at about a 45-degree angle away from us. As it rose, it approached two small clouds about a hundred yards in length and twenty yards in height, and a beam of light cut through the clouds like a headlight from a car would through fog. The sphere then just winked out and was lost as a pinpoint of light into the stars.

Chuck remembers staying in the canoe after the others had piled out in panic onto the shore. Transfixed, still holding his idle paddle, he could not take his eyes off the object:

> The object responded to the panic by slowly moving the light beam away from us. As the light beam veered away, I observed the object itself turning from a full moon to a thin sliver of a crescent with a corresponding axial shift in the light beam. This was the "wink-out" phenomenon we had observed with the other campers from Mud Beach two nights earlier. The object then headed in a southerly direction, towards Mount Katahdin, and within seconds, was gone behind a band of middle-level altostratus clouds.

Jack and Jim were able to consciously remember a bit more about the object and the abnormal beam of light that it emitted. First, Jack's perspective of the next set of events:

> As we continued to paddle, I looked back over my right shoulder and saw that the light was a large, spherical object pulsing with a kind of plasmic light that seemed to be boiling. It was just behind us, and I could see that we were never going to outrun the beam. It was advancing too fast. I remember thinking, "Holy shit! This is it! We'll never get away." The next thing I knew, we were on the shore getting out of the canoe. We were not in a hurry anymore. There was no mad dash for cover or anything. We simply got out of the canoe, walked to our left and quietly stood on the beach, looking directly at the object which was now a few yards away, about 20 or 30 feet above the water.
>
> I was transfixed on it! It was so close. And now the beam was coming out of the bottom of it like the object was sitting on the beam. It just hovered there, right in front of us, completely silent for what seemed like four

or five minutes. I remember feeling "out-of-myself"
while I was standing there looking at it. It felt like a big
hand had grabbed me by the stomach and was trying
to lift me. I felt sick to my stomach.

Suddenly the beam was pointing up towards the
sky. The object began to move up and away from us,
towards the southwestern sky. It seemed to blink out
and then reappear higher in the sky. It did that a couple of times and then shot into the stars and was gone
in just a second.

Jim also had some memory of the terrifying chase across
the cove:

There was no mistake that it was coming directly
to us. Jack and I both remember a vision of the object
hovering directly over us on the lake. Then I remember
standing on the lake shore, watching the object hover,
about 50 to 100 feet above the lake at a distance of 50
to 75 yards in front of us. It was again projecting some
kind of searchlight onto the lake's surface. Then the
search beam went upward into the sky, and the craft
vanished in that same implosion-like manner that I
had observed two days earlier. A second later, we saw
it moving away at a tremendous speed. It kept its light
beam in front of it and ascended in a step-like pattern
towards the southeast. In just a few seconds, it was
just a faint star that traveled in an arc from the southeast to the northwest, where it disappeared over the
horizon. It made absolutely no sound as it flew away.

All of the witnesses seemed to be in a state of suspended
animation as they watched the object leave the area. They felt
"strange" and "tired," to put it in their own words. Jim stated:

We all seemed to be in a state of shock, because
for a few minutes, we just stood there unable to move
or talk.

When the strange, anesthetizing effect wore off, Chuck got
out of the canoe and joined the others as they trudged dreamily
up the beach to their camp. Even in this state, they were dumb-
founded when they realized what had happened to the huge
bonfire that had been blazing minutes ago. Jim wrote in his
notes:

Then we suddenly realized that our campfire was
completely burned down to coals. When we left to go
fishing, we set very large logs on the fire to burn for a
good 2 to 3 hours. The entire experience seemed to
last, at the most, 15 or 20 minutes. Yet the fire was
completely burned down to red coals!

Jack added:

> Our fire was reduced to just a few warm coals, but we all felt so strange that we didn't start another fire. We just sat at our camp table until we fell asleep right there at the table. The next day we awoke, dazed. We could not believe what had happened the night before. We broke camp and continued on our way to the next campsite, where we signaled a passing forest ranger. When he arrived at camp, we told him the whole story, but he didn't believe a word of it. For the rest of our trip, we must have been in some kind of shock. I don't remember much of it from then on.

Indeed they didn't remember. Trip notes and diaries were kept faithfully until the UFO encounter gradually dwindled to nothing several days after the encounter. At that time, they had no memory of what happened during the time it took for their huge bonfire to burn down. (See Figure 3.) This would remain a puzzle for years, until Jim and Jack began to experience the strange dreams and paranormal phenomena that finally led Jim to me for help. We will examine one of these dreams shortly.

Let us first examine their encounter in the light of our present knowledge about UFO sightings.

UFO sightings have been broken down into specific categories, as summarized in the following chart:

NL - Nocturnal Light - Anomalous nighttime light
DD - Daylight Disc - Any UFO sighted in daytime
R/V - Radar/Visual - Simultaneous R/V UFO sighting
CE - Close Encounter - UFO within 500 feet
CEI [1st Kind] Only UFO sighted
CEII [2nd Kind] UFO and physical evidence
CEIII [3rd Kind] UFO and aliens
CEIV [4th Kind] UFO abduction by aliens

The first sighting of a bright, starlike object from Mud Beach might be classified as a Nocturnal Light. In retrospect, all thought that it was the same object that they had encountered two nights later at close range. They thought this because both objects shined brightly with the same weird, distinctive color and both exhibited an implosion effect.

On the other hand, the bright planet Jupiter also may have been the culprit. Astronomical records indicate that Jupiter rose in an easterly direction around 11:00 P.M. EDT on August 24, 1976. It would look several times bigger and brighter than the brightest star and would show a disk when viewed through binoculars. Its disappearance by imploding might have been

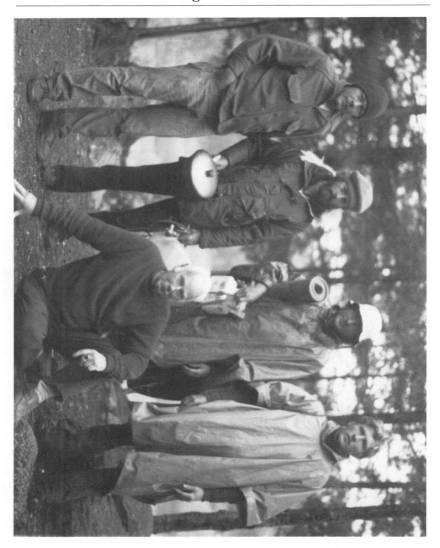

Figure 3. The Allagash four plus one. From left to right in back: Charlie Foltz, Chuck Rak, and the Weiner twins. Seated man came out of the woods, stayed for a while, left, and never gave his name.

caused by a cloud passing in front of it. That night did become cloudy when a rainstorm moved into the area. Then again, the witnesses think they sighted the bright object prior to Jupiter's rising. No other bright planets were visible at that time in either instance, nor was the moon.

Thus, although some uncertainty remains about the first sighting, there is no reasonable room for doubt concerning their second confrontation. They had experienced a genuine Close Encounter of the First Kind. Since this term was coined by the late Dr. J. Allen Hynek, it would be appropriate to compare their experience with comments on this category of UFO sighting. Hynek, astronomy professor at Northwestern University and former associate director of the Smithsonian Astrophysical Observatory, served as Chief Scientific Consultant to the USAF UFO Project. He defined a Close Encounter of the First Kind as:

> UFO sighting reports that speak of objects or very brilliant lights close to the observers—in general, less than 500 feet away. Cases in which the object was close enough to have shown appreciable angular extension and considerable detail, in which stereoscopic vision was presumably employed, and in which fear of possible immediate physical contact was reported.[1]

Needless to say, the Allagash case is a textbook example of this category of UFO sightings. Hynek also stressed the evidential value of the CEI in establishing the physical reality of UFOs:

> It is in the close encounter cases that we come to grips with the misperception hypothesis of UFO reports. While some brief can possibly be established for this hypothesis in the case of...sightings at a distance, it becomes virtually untenable in the case of the close encounter. The UFO reports...made by two or more observers who were capable of submitting a coherent, seemingly factual report, raise the question whether the reported perception can possibly be said to fall within the limits of misperception applicable to sane and responsible people.
> My own opinion...is that accepted logical limits of misperception are in these cases exceeded by so great a margin that one must assume that the observers either truly had the experience as reported or were bereft of their reason and senses. Yet the evidence of the observers' occupations, training, and past performance gives no indication of the latter circumstance.[2]

1. Hynek, J. Allen, *The UFO Experience* (Chicago: Henry Regnery Co., 1972), p. 86.
2. Hynek, *The UFO Experience*, p. 87.

I am sure that were Dr. Hynek alive today and had access
to this report, he would have concluded that the observers truly
had the experience as reported. However, perplexing questions
still remained. What happened to the four canoeists during the
period of missing time? Why couldn't they remember what happened? Why weren't they frightened when they observed the
UFO at close range after reaching shore? Why would they fall
asleep at the picnic table after the object left? Jim wondered if
a recurring dream experienced by his brother held the answer
to these questions. So did I, after hearing Jack describe the following nightmare to me in July of 1988:

> Two years ago, I started having these terrible
> nightmares that have recurred several times. I always
> awaken from them in a really hyper state of panic and
> uncontrollable fear, and I'm not right for several days
> afterward.
> In this nightmare, I am standing against a wall or
> some kind of upright table. It is in a place filled with a
> bright, hazy light. This light makes it impossible to see
> any boundaries of the space or any features of the
> space. I'm standing, but I can't move at all. I can't even
> speak, but I am fully awake and thinking.
> I am aware that Jim and Chuck and Charlie are
> sitting on some kind of bench or low table to my imme-
> diate left. I'm thinking—"Why don't you do something?
> For God's sake, help me! Please help me!"—but they
> don't even seem to notice me. They just sit there as if
> entranced.
> Then I notice some movement in the haze directly
> in front of me. The next sight sends me into complete
> panic. This thing comes toward me and then is stand-
> ing right in front of me, looking at me. I'm feeling really
> scared. All I can think about is getting out of there. I'm
> thinking, "I've got to get out of here! Don't hurt me!
> Please don't hurt me!" Next I realize that there is more
> movement coming out of the haze, and a second thing
> is standing there right in front of me. By this time, I'm
> beside myself with fright. All I can think about is get-
> ting out of there.
> The two things are looking back and forth from me
> to each other. Their heads are quivering like they're
> nodding at each other, but they don't make any noise
> at all. Then the one opposite me, on my left, reaches
> out and grasps my left wrist and begins to raise it up.
> It seems as though they are looking at my arm and
> then up to my armpit. I can see that the one on the
> right has some kind of metallic-looking tool or gadget
> of some kind in his hand. I don't like the looks of it. I
> think that they are going to do something to my armpit

with it—that they're going to put it in my armpit! At this point, I feel as if I'm going to be eaten alive, and I really become totally lost in absolute hysterical fear. Then I wake up. I'm totally soaked in sweat and waking with the worst case of the dreads that you can possibly imagine.

This nightmare always leaves me affected for several days. The first few times I remembered the nightmare, I could not remember what the things' heads or faces looked like, though I could remember from the neck to their legs. Then, last year, I again had this nightmare. This time when I woke up, I could distinctly remember all of them. I almost wish I hadn't, because I now know the why of those feelings of utter hysteria in the nightmare. They have large heads on a thin neck with two large metallic-looking eyes. By that, I mean that they are colored like those kinds of phosphorescent beetles that seem to change colors as they move. There were no eyelids! My impression is that they are insect-like, but there are no antennas or anything, and they don't have carnivorous-looking parts. Their hands are at the ends of their arms, but they are not like our hands. They are more elongated, with only four fingers.

That's it. I feel better, now that I've actually sat down and written it all out. I really hope you're who you say you are, because this kind of stuff is not the kind of thing that one likes to spread around too much. People think I'm nuts when I tell them this stuff.

I assured Jack and the others that I did not think they were crazy and thanked them for cooperating with the investigation. I remarked that such nightmares could be instigated by imagination or by real, buried memories surfacing from the subconscious mind. I explained that hypnosis had often been used to bring suppressed memories back to the conscious mind.

Jim's physician had already encouraged him to try hypnosis. Thus, Jim was willing to undergo hypnotic regression sessions with our local MUFON consultant. I asked the rest of the Allagash four to seriously consider this possibility. They expressed interest and were curious to see how Jim would react to hypnosis. Jim's first session was scheduled for January 21, 1989. Vacation, my busy schedule and the busy Thanksgiving and Christmas holidays preempted starting earlier. We all hoped this upcoming new phase of the investigation would lead to a solution to the mystery of the wilderness fireball.

CHAPTER **3**

"They're like Bugs!"

As the date of Jim's first session drew near, I realized I needed someone to assist me on this fascinating case. I enlisted the help of David Webb, one of the principal investigators of *The Andreasson Affair*. Dave, a solar physicist, is an expert on CEIII and CEIV cases.

MUFON consultant Tony Constantino was chosen to conduct the hypnotic regression sessions. David and Tony had probed my own UFO abduction experiences which were chronicled in my last book, *The Watchers*. Tony, unlike David, was a neophyte to UFO research, but was a qualified hypnotherapist well-versed in the art of regression techniques.

Hypnosis Session #1—Jim Weiner (January 12, 1989)

Jim arrived at Tony's house around 2:00 P.M. He appeared nervous and admitted that he was a bit apprehensive about being hypnotized. Tony spent some time getting acquainted with Jim. It was explained that hypnosis was just a technique used to place a person in a deep state of relaxation. He then turned on some soft background music and had Jim sit before him in a large easy chair. Jim was soon placed in a light state of hypnosis. (See Figure 4.) We began to interview him, taking special care not to ask any leading questions. The following, and other such excerpts throughout the book, were extracted from transcriptions of the recorded hypnotic regression sessions:

TONY: In 1976...you and three friends went on a camping trip of some type. Is that true Jim?
JIM: Yeah.
TONY: Do you recall preparing for that trip?
JIM: To go to Maine?
TONY: Yes.
JIM: I remember driving—driving up.
TONY: Do you see some of the landmarks?

Figure 4. Jim Weiner undergoing
hypnotic regression.

JIM:	Yeah, Route 95.
TONY:	Okay, do you recall arriving at the campsite?
JIM:	Yep.
TONY:	Do you recall some of the things you and your friends did to set up the campsite?
JIM:	Yeah.
TONY:	Can you mention one or two things that you had to do?
JIM:	Well, I remember flying into the lake on a pontoon plane. It was incredible. And we, we had to come two people at a time. When we got there, we set up our camp. There was a picnic table. So we put our tents up and made a tent out of a tarp and a rope that we would stretch between two trees. And, the, ah, I remember just after we got there that ranger came—Everett Cram and his sidekick, Mac. And they came to check us out.

Tony slowly but surely brought Jim through the initial phases of the trip until the campers reached Eagle Lake and the campsite located across from Smith Brook:

JIM:	We ran out of meat, so we decided we'd try fishing.
TONY:	Do you see yourself getting ready?
JIM:	Yeah, we built—we put logs on the fire cause we—it gets real dark up there at night. Black! So black. We were laughing because we were putting our hands in front of our faces and going, "My God, we can't see our hands!" You really can't see your hand in front of your face.
TONY:	And you had planned for that campfire to burn for approximately how long?
JIM:	Oh, a long time. We knew that we'd be out on the lake for at least an hour or so. It's a big lake. And we knew that the only way we'd find the shore was to have a big campfire.
TONY:	So now that the campfire is built, do you see you and your companions getting into the canoe?
JIM:	Um, we didn't go far. I remember that Chuck Rak was on one end of the canoe. Charlie Foltz was on the other end and Jack and I were in the middle. And we had...we didn't bring much with us. Just flashlights and our fishing rods. And I— I can clearly remember shining the flashlights

into the water. It was so clear. It was like a swampy area with submerged trees that were sticking up out of the water. And, ah, I remember shining the flashlights down into the water and seeing the trees under there and the water was really cold. But anyway, we didn't seem to be out very long at all.

TONY: And then what happened?

JIM: Well, Charlie's face lit up. I remember seeing his face and thinking, "Oh, shit, here come the, the, ah, ranger!"—'cause we weren't supposed to be out at night fishing. And he said, "What, what the hell is that?" And, ah, I was facing him and I had to turn around and see. And I remember looking at the end of the lake. Just above the trees is this big, white sphere and it—I knew immediately that it was what we had seen two days before. It had that same weird quality of light. It was almost like a sun. It was a whirling light. It reminded me of, ah, the inside of a pottery kiln when you can see the heat boiling around inside of it. Ah, and it just floated above the trees. It didn't go anywhere. It just sat there. It didn't make any noise at all. Nothing. And there's no noise up there at night. All you hear is a loon. No crickets, no frogs, no cars, no noise. It's absolutely silent.

TONY: And then what happened?

JIM: Well, we watched it and we tried to think of what it could be. The first thing that came to our minds was a big weather balloon. But it was too—the light was wrong. No weather balloons have that kind of light. And I said, "Let's shine the flashlight at it." And so, Charlie Foltz shined his flashlight. I'm pretty sure he did a dot-dot-dot, dash, dash, dash—an "S.O.S." He only did it once or twice and then, all of a sudden, this beam came out of the thing! It lit up our canoe like a candle. Then it started coming towards us! And I remembered it coming out over the edge of the trees, and we could see its reflection on the, the lake—cause the lake at night turns into a sheet of glass. There's no ripples. There's no wind. And it's—it started coming right towards us with this light. And, ah, I remember it was like somebody pressed a button on my nose, and I just felt complete terror! Jack did too.

DAVE: Jim?

JIM: Hmm?

DAVE:	This is Dave. I have a question. You mentioned it looked like a tube? What were the boundaries of it like?
JIM:	It was like—I remember it reminded me of a hose. The rubber part of the hose was where the bright light was and inside of it was dark. It wasn't black, but seemed darker. And I remember having a, almost like a flash or a vision of this thing right on top us. And it scared the hell out of me. I had this, this, ah, fear that we'd tip over and drown cause the water was real cold and all of these submerged trees, and Jack did too. And I remember paddling. I remember the front of the canoe being out of the water and paddling. And when we...when we got to the shore, we turned around and the thing was right there in front of us. I remember thinking to myself, you know? If I had a stone in my hand, I could hit that—so it had to be close. And the light was shining down on the water, and it was real close to the water. And, ah, then it went up into the sky, and it blinked. It winked. It imploded. It seemed like the light imploded on itself. Almost like an iris when it shuts on itself. And, at first, I thought it had disappeared. And then, when I looked, I realized that it was moving away really fast. That thing was flying! And it went up in a stair-step motion, like when you throw a Frisbee and it flies at a certain level and then, um, hits a, a layer of air or something so it suddenly goes straight up and then keeps going.

It was obvious to us that the period of missing time somehow had to be sandwiched between sighting the object and reaching shore. The beam of light hitting the canoe seemed to be the dividing point between memory and amnesia. We decided to concentrate on this segment of the terrifying encounter. Tony brought Jim back to where the beam engulfed the canoe:

JIM:	I remember the light coming down and it hit the boat and it went like this, back and forth (moving his hand back and forth). But, it never left, never left the boat. And then the next thing I remember is paddling. I don't remember anything between that.
DAVE:	Tell me more about the inside of this tube of light. You said it was dark.

JIM:	Yeah, that's all I seem to remember. I just remember it really impressed me. It was a tube. I never saw anything like that before.
TONY:	Why would it be dark inside?
JIM:	I don't know, but it was. I could see it was. It was darker.
TONY:	Is the light always connected to the larger globe of light?
JIM:	Yeah.
DAVE:	Ah, you were enveloped by this light? When you said the boat was covered by the light?
JIM:	It, it wasn't as big as the whole boat (a 16-foot canoe). It was, ah, a, a, beam and it went back, like back and forth like a search beam.
TONY:	Did it always focus on the canoe and the occupants?
JIM:	Well, it, it panned us first.
TONY:	How?
JIM:	It went across the canoe and then it, it locked right on to us. That's what, that's when we became terrorized.
RAY:	When you got back to shore, what was your bonfire like?
JIM:	It was low.... The fire was just coals.
RAY:	How long would it take the bonfire to get down to that?
JIM:	A heck of a lot longer than that. Some of those logs were eight, ten inches in diameter. It should have burned at least an hour.
RAY:	If there were time unaccounted for, why can't you remember?
JIM:	I don't know. I, I'd swear I remembered everything that happened.

During this initial light hypnotic induction, Jim's recall seemed no more unique than what it would have been in a normal waking state. He spoke in the past tense, indicating that although he was recalling the incident, he was not mentally reliving it.

Both Tony and I felt it was time to place Jim in a deeper state of hypnosis. Past experience had revealed that Jim was responding normally to hypnosis. Most abductees under light hypnosis have reacted in the same manner. However, when progressed to a deeper state, abductees usually experience a breaking point. At this juncture, buried memories suddenly flood the conscious mind like waters bursting through a mental dam. Thus, using verbal instructions and background music, Tony eased Jim deeper and deeper into the hypnotic state. Shortly after the questions commenced, a profound change overcame Jim. He remembered more. His facial and body demeanor suggested agitation, as did his comments:

TONY:	What do you remember that you can tell us about that night?
JIM:	Ohhh! (Becomes agitated.)
TONY:	Just relax.
JIM:	It's hard.
TONY:	Just allow it to happen. Just allow it to happen. Every time you breathe out, sink more deeply into the chair.

Tony continued to ease Jim into an even deeper state of relaxation. Jim's facial muscles loosened. His head drooped forward and his body sunk deeper and deeper into the chair. Then Tony continued his questioning:

TONY:	You sense that there is something you should remember?
JIM:	Yes! (Again becomes disturbed.)
TONY:	Just relax. Just relax.
JIM:	I have a sense that there is something I should remember, but it's almost like...a block...a feeling comes back.
TONY:	What kind of a feeling?
JIM:	Of fear! I can feel my heart pounding (becomes very perturbed and Tony again steps in to calm Jim).
TONY:	And tell us why your heart is pounding?
JIM:	I'm afraid of that light (breathing heavily).
TONY:	Just relax. It's so pleasant, it's so peaceful. Why are you afraid of that light?
JIM:	It's not normal! It's on us. Jeez, it's a big light! It's around us. That's why I'm so scared. I don't even see Chuck (Jim now is visibly shaken and hyperventilating.)
TONY:	Where is he? Just relax. What happens to Chuck? Just relax. Can you see the canoe?
JIM:	No, it's just inside (exhaling violently).
TONY:	Inside where? Just relax. Inside of what?

JIM:	The tube!
TONY:	Just relax. You do not see Chuck but do you see a canoe where it should be? Do you see the spot where he was sitting? Just relax.

Long pause before Jim literally forces out an answer.

JIM:	I see the inside of the tube!
TONY:	And where are you when you see the inside of the tube?
JIM:	I think I'm still in the boat, but I don't see the trees anymore.
TONY:	What is it like inside the tube?
JIM:	It's sparkling—No, it's not a sparkle, it's...(lets out a long deep breath of air). It's a, it's kind of a, it's moving. It's, it's, it's moving.
TONY:	Does it move left to right or up and down?
JIM:	No, the walls, the walls move.
TONY:	Towards you or away from you?
JIM:	Nope, just in, in themselves. Like, when, an, not exactly like but when you blow smoke through a, through a light beam, you know? You can see it. Oh! I know how. Like when dust, when you see dust, when you see dust particles in a light beam.
TONY:	Do you see Jack?
JIM:	Jack's behind me.
TONY:	Are the four of you in the canoe?
JIM:	I think it's just two of us.
TONY:	Where are the other two?
JIM:	They're not there.
TONY:	They're not in the canoe?
JIM:	No. Ohhh. I don't like that feeling!
TONY:	What are your physical sensations? What's happening to your skin? To your fingers? What's happening to your body?
JIM:	(Does not answer, gasps for breath.)
TONY:	Two minutes after the light enveloped you—what happened? Just drift back slowly.
JIM:	(Does not answer, blows out air.)
TONY:	What happens two minutes after the light enveloped you?
JIM:	(With a forced whisper.) I can't remember.

Tony tried over and over again in an attempt to discover what happened after Jim and the others were enveloped by the hollow beam of light but to no avail. Finally, Jim remembered looking up the tube:

DAVE:	What is it like?
JIM:	It's dark up there (long pause, groans). Boy! It's a frightening feeling.
RAY:	It's dark at the other end of the tube?
JIM:	That's what I seem to remember. I don't…(Jim's body begins shivering all over). I know whatever's at the other end there, I'm not going to like.
TONY:	Do you ever see what's at the other end?
JIM:	Boy, I, I can't remember.
RAY:	Why can't you remember?
JIM:	I don't want to remember that.
TONY:	Remember what?
JIM:	I don't want to remember what's at the other end there!
TONY:	Why do you say you don't want to remember if you can't remember?
JIM:	(With trembling voice.) I can't remember. I know there's something there though. I knew—I know there's something on the other end of that tube. That's why I don't want to go there. That's why, that's why we didn't want to go there.

It soon became apparent that we were not getting any further with Jim. We could not break through the mental block that prevented him from remembering what happened next. Since the current method of questioning wasn't leading to further answers, Tony decided to employ a technique that had proved successful in the past:

TONY:	Just relax. I'm going to ask that you visualize something. I'm going to ask that you visualize that you're back in your room—that you have a gigantic TV screen. Do you see that?
JIM:	Um-hum.
TONY:	Can you draw a line down the middle?
JIM:	Yep (draws an imaginary line).
TONY:	Can you see it?
JIM:	Um-hum.
TONY:	You can see that the left hand side of the screen lights up with a big "No" on it?

JIM:	Right.
TONY:	Now, the right hand side of the screen lights up with a big "Yes" on it?
JIM:	Um-hum.
TONY:	Now when I call you your first name, if I call you the wrong name, the "No" will light up.
JIM:	Um-hum.
TONY:	If I call you your right name, obviously, the right side of the screen will light up.
JIM:	Um-hum.
TONY:	Is your first name David?
JIM:	No.
TONY:	Did the left side of the screen light up?
JIM:	The "No" side.
TONY:	Is your name Jim?
JIM:	Yes.
TONY:	Did the right hand side light up?
JIM:	Right.
TONY:	When I ask you questions, tell me whether it's the left side or the right side that lights up. Would you do that?

Tony proceeded to ask Jim a battery of questions. This technique is used to elicit answers from the subconscious memory rather than the conscious memory. Under hypnosis, answers are by subconscious reflex instead of conscious reflection. The trick is to quickly ask many general questions that have obvious answers and then suddenly interject questions that involve blocked memories. Several interesting answers were elicited from the latter kind of questions as excerpted below:

TONY:	Do all the strange occurrences in your room [at home] have anything to do with that sighting in 1976?
JIM:	Yes.
TONY:	Do you know what happened at the other end of that tube?
JIM:	(Sighs loudly.) Yes.
TONY:	Which side of the screen?
JIM:	Something happened there.
TONY:	Which side of the screen lit up?
JIM:	The right side.

TONY:	The "Yes" side?
JIM:	Yeah, that's the side that lit up but it's—I can't tell you what happened on the other side of that tube!

All of the questions above were preceded by general questions asked in quick order. The last question was the first real hint of a typical component that has shown up time and time again in UFO abduction experiences. During the abduction, the aliens induce a strong posthypnotic command upon the abductee's conscious mind. The abductee is told that he can't tell anyone about the experience. He must forget about it. Knowing this, Tony continued to press hard against a potential alien-induced mental block:

TONY:	Do you know what happened on the other side of that tube?
JIM:	(Starts breathing heavily and will not answer.)
TONY:	Okay, Okay. Tell me what side of the screen lit up if something happened at the end of the tube?
JIM:	(Breathing heavily.) Yes.
TONY:	Does it have to do with you?
JIM:	(Pants heavily, refuses to answer.)
TONY:	Does it have to do with your companions?
JIM:	Jack! They hurt Jack.
TONY:	Repeat that!
JIM:	They hurt him.
TONY:	How did they hurt him?
JIM:	They did something—I know they hurt me.
TONY:	Repeat that!
JIM:	They hurt me in my bedroom (Jim refers to another experience to be discussed later).
TONY:	When they hurt Jack—Did this occur in the canoe? Yes or no?
JIM:	No.
TONY:	Did it occur at the end of the tube?
JIM:	(Becomes more agitated, refuses to answer.)
TONY:	What do you mean—they did something to him?
JIM:	They, they hurt him somehow.
RAY:	Where?
JIM:	His body.
RAY:	What part of his body?

JIM:	His arm. He was moving his arm.
RAY:	Who was moving Jack's arm?
JIM:	Ohhh!
RAY:	What was moving Jack's arm?
JIM:	Some *thing*. There was, there was more than one. There was—
RAY:	How many?
JIM:	Three, four.
RAY:	How could you tell there were three or four?
JIM:	I could see.
RAY:	See what?
JIM:	I could see—their—see the legs.
RAY:	What did they look like?
JIM:	They had suits.
RAY:	Um-hum, describe!
JIM:	Ohhh! (Sighs and begins blowing out air.)
TONY:	Just relax. Is this in the light tube?
JIM:	Somewhere else. In a room.
TONY:	Where was the room?
JIM:	Had to be inside there (i.e., in the UFO).
TONY:	How did you get there?
JIM:	I don't know. I don't remember moving in the tube. I remember looking at the end—looking at the other end, and I...(cannot talk, very agitated).
TONY:	You said Chuck was gone. Was it you that had gone?
JIM:	Chuck was gone. I remember looking up that tube.
TONY:	Did anything happen to Chuck?
JIM:	I don't remember Chuck.
RAY:	What happened to Jack?
JIM:	They were looking at his arm.
RAY:	Who are they?
JIM:	These things.

Again, we seemed to be at an impasse. We decided to concentrate on getting a better description of the entities that Jim called the *things*:

RAY:	What things?

JIM:	They had arms and legs. I can't remember their faces though.
RAY:	Do you want to remember their faces?
JIM:	Oh yes, but I can't.
RAY:	What did their fingers look like?
JIM:	They had gloves.
RAY:	How many digits on the gloves?
JIM:	(No answer.)
RAY:	Count. You're looking at them right now. Count. How many digits?
JIM:	It was like they had, ah, connected fingers somehow. Three or four.
RAY:	What color were the gloves?
JIM:	Shiny—blue-gray comes to my mind.
DAVE:	Remember any, ah, body? Skin?
JIM:	No. Clothing. I remember the suits (takes deep breath and exhales). And there were three, four and a bench....

When Jim inadvertently mentioned seeing a bench, I remembered that his brother Jack had dreamed about seeing this bench with Chuck and Charlie sitting on it. To see if he would agree with Jack, I asked him if anyone was on the bench:

RAY:	Who is on the bench?
JIM:	(Breathing heavily.) My God! I think Chuck and Charlie are there—sitting on the bench.
TONY:	And where were you?
JIM:	I don't know. I wasn't near Jack. I was standing away from Jack. I was watching.
RAY:	Why didn't you help Jack?
JIM:	I don't know. It was like, ah, all I could do was watch. I remember they were around Jack. Three, four—seems like a dream—like everything was happening in slow motion. But I remember them going like this (demonstrates with his arm). They were moving it and I, I got the impression that they were going to hurt him.
RAY:	What was done to the two who were on the bench?
JIM:	(Sighs.) Just sat there.
DAVE:	What was the bench sitting on?
JIM:	It was attached to the wall.

DAVE:	Did it have legs?
JIM:	No, it was—like molded—it was molded out, not into the wall but out from the wall.
DAVE:	How far were they from you—Chuck and Charlie?
JIM:	Ah, four, five, six feet. Somewhere in there.
DAVE:	How far is Jack from you?
JIM:	Not far—six, seven feet.
DAVE:	Is there anyone else around you—closer than that?
JIM:	There's someone standing over here (points). There was (pause) an opening. There's an opening over here (points). Ah, (slurs his words) S-s-s-, then one of those things were there in the opening.
TONY:	What does he look like?
JIM:	Like—almost like people but they weren't people. They were skinnier. Thinner. Almost like a, like a—an exoskeleton but it wasn't bony. It's like—just a blank when I try to see their heads.
DAVE:	What color suits are they?
JIM:	Bluish-gray.
DAVE:	What was the texture like?
JIM:	Sheenish. Like the kind, ah, skiers wear.
RAY:	How tall were they?
JIM:	I'd say five feet somewhere.
RAY:	Were their eyes pleasant to look at? (A ploy to shock Jim into remembering their faces.)
JIM:	I don't remember. That's the thing that puzzles me the most. Jack remembers the faces, (in his dreams) and he's even told me, but I don't remember anything. I just seemed to have blanked it out. I think that I'm just so completely flipped out by the whole thing that I could only fight to concentrate on what was just right in front of me. I must have picked Jack's arm and used that to keep my sanity.

The hour was getting late, and Jim had been under hypnosis for over two hours. Tony signaled that we should bring the session to a close. However, before doing so, he gave Jim a post-hypnotic suggestion to remember what he had seen in detail so that he could draw it for us later.

Jim opened his eyes and just sat there for a while staring into space. He looked like he had seen a ghost. We laughed in an effort to break the ice. He looked at us very soberly and said, "It was tough. It was tough getting by that feeling." I knew exactly what he meant. I had encountered tremendous pressure not to remember my experiences when I had undergone hypnosis.

Jim found the recalled memories extremely disturbing. He was full of questions about UFOs. We assured him that we would talk to him about the subject after the investigation was over. It was important not to fill his mind with information that might taint his future testimony. We also urged him to refrain from reading UFO literature and from divulging any information about the session to the other witnesses. Jim realized the importance of doing this and promised that he would remain silent for the time being.

When we felt Jim was fully awake, I drove him to the local railroad station to catch the next train to Boston. His brother had originally dropped him off but was not allowed to sit in on the session for obvious reasons. I left Jim standing on the train platform looking like he was in another world. In a real sense, he was. I knew from personal experience that such revived memories would be a unique burden for him to carry for the rest of his life.

It would be a month before we would conduct another hypnotic regression session with Jim. This gave Dave, Tony and me time to evaluate data and prepare for the next meeting. Tony felt, as I did, that his initial induction of Jim produced simple recall but that when he deepened the trance, Jim had reached a stage of real time regression. In his evaluation he commented on this and stated:

> Jim spoke in the present tense—"I don't like this at all,...I can see...." All this suggests a true regression as opposed to his previous pseudo-regression....It was a worthwhile meeting, and I look forward to others. I am intrigued, fascinated and mesmerized by this entire experience, and a bit frightened; still, I want to continue working with you.

I was struck with the emotions that Jim manifested when reliving the experience. He literally displayed the fear, apprehension and agitations that such an experience would certainly provoke. I was also struck by the fact that Jim could or would not see the heads of the aliens. Jim's brother also was unable to see the alien's heads in the first of his recurring dreams. It was not until the last few dreams that the frightful faces materialized. One wonders whether the aliens programmed them not to see their faces or whether the sight of them caused self-imposed amnesia. One thing was certain. We were no longer investigating a CEI. The results of the first session had dramatically upgraded this unearthly episode. It was a CEIV— A Close Encounter of the Fourth Kind. We were now dealing with the abduction of human beings by alien operators of a UFO!

For the benefit of those not acquainted with the content and implications of such experiences, I again quote one of the world's greatest authorities on UFOS. I believe Dr. J. Allen Hynek's insights will help place the astonishing details of this case in their proper perspective:

> We come now to the most bizarre and seemingly incredible aspect of the entire UFO phenomenon. To be quite frank, I would gladly omit this part if I could without offense to scientific integrity. Unfortunately one may not omit data simply because they may not be to one's liking or in line with one's preconceived notions. We balk at reports about occupants even though we might be willing to listen attentively to accounts of other UFO encounters. Why? Why should a report of a car stopped on the highway by a blinding light from an unknown craft be any different in essential strangeness or absurdity from one of a craft from which two or three little animate creatures descend? There is no logical reason, yet I confess to sharing a prejudice that is hard to explain. Is it the confrontation on the animate level that disturbs and repulses us? Perhaps as long as it is our own intelligence that contemplates the report of a machine, albeit strange, we still somehow feel superior in such contemplation. Encounters... with an intelligence of different order from ours, give a new dimension to our atavistic fear of the unknown. They bring with them the specter of competition for territory, loss of planetary hegemony—fears that have deep roots. Our common sense recoils at the very idea of humanoids and leads to much banter and ridicule and jokes about little green men. They tend to throw the whole UFO concept into disrepute. Maybe UFOs could really exist, we say, but humanoids? And if these are truly figments of our imagination, then so must be the ordinary UFOs. But these are backed by so many reputable witnesses that we cannot accept them as simple misperceptions. Are then, all of these reporters of UFOs truly sick? If so, what is the sickness? Are these people all affected by some strange virus that does not attack sensible people? What a strange sickness this must be, attacking people in all walks of life, regardless of training or vocation, and making them, for a very limited period of time—only minutes sometimes—behave in a strange way and see

things that are belied by the reliable and stable manner and actions they exhibit in the rest of their lives. [1]

Hypnosis Session #2—Jim Weiner
(February 25, 1989)

Jim was less apprehensive when he arrived at Tony's for
the second session. His curiosity far outweighed any anxiety he
had regarding hypnosis or his UFO experience. Thus, it took
less time for Tony to place Jim in a light trance.

Tony brought Jim back in time to where he was on board
the UFO, watching the aliens examine his brother Jack. Again,
Jim noticed Chuck and Charlie sitting on a bench, each with "a
dumb, expressionless look" on his face. Jim could only see
things clearly that were straight ahead of him. He could not
move his head. It was readily apparent to us that all witnesses
except Jack had been placed in the state of suspended animation that is characteristic of abduction reports.

Jim noticed other things when asked to use his peripheral
vision. He described a diffuse light emanating from a fixture
above that looked as if it were made of white plexiglass. The fixture was inset at the middle of a shallow, rounded, metallic,
gray ceiling.

Despite our new findings, we again reached an impasse
when attempting to move Jim ahead in time. Tony gently and
slowly deepened Jim's current level of hypnotic trance in an attempt to break through the memory block. It worked. Previous
to this point, Jim was not able to move ahead in time. His mind
was like a needle stuck in the grooves of a mental phonograph
record. It kept playing only one scene—the aliens examining
Jack's arm. Now, almost like magic, the needle jumped out of
the groove and time moved on:

TONY: What else happened with you, your two friends
          and Jack? Now you see them, don't you?
JIM: Yep.
TONY: Working Jack's arm?
JIM: Um-hum.
TONY: And what do they do next? Just relax and allow
          it to flow up from those memory banks. What do
          they do next?
JIM: They're looking at his throat. They got his head
          way up and looking at his throat, and they're

---

1. Hynek, *The UFO Experience*, pp. 138,139.

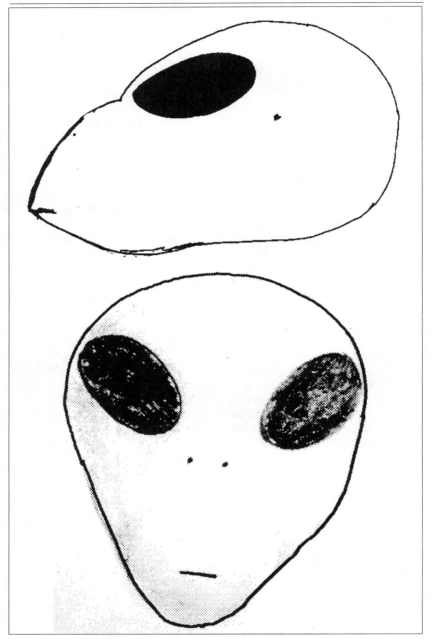

*Figure 5. Jim Weiner's recollection of
the faces of his abductors.*

touching it with their hands like they're, ah, studying the musculature. They're turning it this way (demonstrates with his hands) with their hands by his chin.

TONY: Just relax. Just allow it to flow out. And how long do they do that?

JIM: Just a couple of seconds.

Jim then felt that the aliens were communicating with each other about Jack. He could not hear anything, but their motions and mannerisms seemed to indicate this. It was then that we realized he now could see their faces:

JIM: They're like bugs! They've got, ah, bug eyes. Their eyes aren't eyes—aren't on the front of their heads. They're more temporally located. (See Figure 5.)

TONY: Just relax. Just relax.

Jim proceeded to describe the aliens in some detail. The eyes did not have pupils and did not blink. They were blackish-brown in color. The faces were a light color with no nose. There was a trace of a mouth. There were just holes for ears. They all wore tight-fitting, bluish-gray suits made of a shiny, reflective material. Jim explained that it was hard to tell if their gloved fingers had three or four digits because two of the digits seemed connected together forming one fatter digit. After obtaining a description of the aliens, we turned our attention once again to the aliens' examination of Jack:

DAVE: Does he (Jack) look awake? Are his eyes open?

JIM: Yeah, his eyes are open and he's looking at them. He's got this (pause), I mean it's kind of a look of astonishment. I think that he's—he can't really believe what's going on, and he's a little frightened about what they're doing to him. He seems to be a lot more aware than I am. I feel like I'm, um, dulled—like everything is very—[it's] very difficult to maintain awareness.

TONY: Just relax.

Tony proceeded to place Jim into yet a deeper state of hypnosis and continued his questioning about Jack:

TONY: What else do they do?

JIM: (Becomes agitated.) They, they looked at his eyes (pause). They've got something—they're looking—they have something in their hands!

TONY: With an instrument or with their hands?

JIM: No, they've got—they've got instruments.

DAVE: Can you describe these?

JIM: One is a kind of a prod of some sort. Ah, thin, long, eight—ten inches. Oh! They're touching his eyes with it (pause). But it doesn't seem to hurt him.

RAY: Is it connected with something, or is it just a separate instrument?

JIM: It's, it's hand-held. They're holding it in their hand.

DAVE: What about the one they used on his eyes?

JIM: They held that too. It's like a little flashlight, or, or some, something.

DAVE: Did you see light coming from it?

JIM: Yeah, blinking. A little blinking light.

DAVE: What color is the blinking light?

JIM: It was a whitish color.

Jim then mentioned that his brother was removing the rest of his clothes. He was already naked from the waist up:

JIM: They're taking down his pants, or rather, he's doing it. And (pause) they've got him completely naked! He's got the most incredible incredulous look on his face—like he's astounded at what—what's happening.

RAY: Can you describe in detail what they do?

JIM: Yeah, they're looking at his genitals, feeling his testicles and his penis and the insides of his thighs.

DAVE: What are they feeling with?

JIM: Their hands. They're looking at the hair on his legs 'cause they're going like this. (Demonstrates with his own leg.) They're looking at his knees and they're making him rotate his feet, his, his legs and his feet, and they're looking at his toes.

DAVE: How many are looking at him at this time?

JIM: These, this—there's three or four out there. There's, there's, ah, one on his left—there's four. There's one on his left. There's one kind of to his right but a little behind him and two others in front.

TONY: Just relax.

JIM: They're looking at his rear, and, ah (pause) they seem to be more interested in his genital area than anything.

Jim continued to describe the aliens examining his brother's nude body. We asked if he could hear, smell or sense anything going on. He heard a very low humming sound but could not smell anything unusual. The temperature was warm and it felt humid in the room. Then, suddenly Jim's countenance changed as he watched (in his mind's eye) the aliens escort Jack out of the room. He breathes out a long sigh:

JIM: They're taking him over in this other place. He doesn't like it. They're kind of ushering him. They've got their hands on him so...

DAVE: How?

JIM: They're holding his arms.

DAVE: How many? How many of them?

JIM: The—one on each side.

DAVE: Is he walking?

JIM: Yep. Yeah (begins panting). They took him out!

DAVE: Where, where are his clothes?

JIM: They're still there on the floor.

TONY: What do you and your friends do once he's gone?

JIM: I think—we're waiting. I keep looking at these things (aliens) and (sighs) I can't believe it. I can't believe these things are there. They're like big bugs!

DAVE: What happens during that time?

JIM: He's, he's gone, and ah, those other ones, they're still next to me.

Jim instantly became agitated and began panting. He looked terrified:

DAVE: What happens?

JIM: I, I think it's my turn.

TONY: Your turn for what?

JIM: (Breathing heavily.) I think they want to look at me.

TONY: Just relax, just relax.

Jim was hyperventilating. Tony immediately came to his rescue and spent some time calming him down before proceeding with the session. When the session continued, Jim described being examined and prodded with instruments by the aliens in the same manner.

DAVE: Did they say anything to you?
JIM: No, no, but they're doing the same thing. They're—they, they, they know that Jack and I are the same—that we look the same and the other two don't and that's what they're interested in. They, they got my shirt off. They made me take it off.

This was the first inclination of communication between the aliens and Jim. It was not verbal. It seemed to be a strong telepathic impression. Again, this kind of communication is typical of other abduction reports:

DAVE: How did they make you?
JIM: Ah, I just got the impression that if I didn't do that, I was going to be in trouble.
DAVE: Did they say anything to you?
JIM: No, but I know that's what they want me to do, so I figured that I might as well do it and maybe, they'll—they won't hurt me. They didn't really hurt Jack, so why should they hurt me?

The shiny-suited entities continued to examine Jim. They poked his ribs with a prodlike instrument and again communicated with him:

JIM: They're doing the same thing with my arms that they did to Jack.
DAVE: What happens next?
JIM: Ah, I, I get the impression that I'd better take my pants off. Yeah, yeah, they're—I, I better get my pants off.
TONY: And then what do they do? What happens next?
JIM: They're looking—they're checking out my genitals (agitated).
TONY: Just relax, just relax.

JIM:	It's, it's kind of embarrassing because I'm so—this is so weird—ah, it's like my penis wants to shrink inside of me.
TONY:	Just relax, just relax.
JIM:	But, ah—(let's out a big breath). Jeez! (Starts gulping for air.)

Jim was breathing so hard that he could not talk to us. Tony again stepped in and calmed him:

TONY:	Just relax with each breath that you exhale. Just feel all those burdens lifted from your shoulders. You're with friends and it's warm and safe here. Just pleasant to relax.... Just let go. What happens next? Just relax, just relax.
JIM:	(Calms a bit but breathing heavily.) They want me to go over there but I don't want to go over there!
TONY:	Go over where, Jim?
JIM:	Over, over (voice trembling with fear) where—through that thing—that opening down that hallway.
DAVE:	Are Chuck and Charlie there?
JIM:	Yeah, they're over there (points at the bench).
DAVE:	Have they moved?
JIM:	No, but I don't want to go over there. I don't wanna.
TONY:	Just relax, just relax.
RAY:	Do you go?
JIM:	Yeah, I don't have much choice.
DAVE:	Are you naked?
JIM:	Yeah, not cold though.
RAY:	Keep on describing in detail what happens next.

Jim did not answer. He was in a terrible state. This was one of those times that I wondered if we really had the right to put people through ordeals like this even though they fully agreed to it as willing participants:

RAY:	Describe your surroundings!
JIM:	They've got those—it's like—I know that's where they, they—that's were they want me to go.
DAVE:	How many? How many are there?

JIM:	There's two of 'em. Two. One on either side and they're holding me. They're holding me up (sighs). I feel like, ah, I'm going to faint.
TONY:	Do you go through the opening?
JIM:	I, they, I'm in front of it. It's, it's, it's dark in there. It's, ah, it goes somewhere else. There's another room. It's the, ah, hallway that's dark.
DAVE:	What's the hallway look like?
JIM:	It's, ah, it's not long, it's short but it's (pauses and then shouts). I'm not going in there! No! No f---ing way! Uh-h-h, just leave me alone!

Tony had all he could do to keep Jim's emotions in check. Jim kept shouting that he did not want to go into the dark hallway that led to another illuminated room. Finally, Tony calmed him down enough to resume our questioning:

JIM:	(In a subdued but determined voice.) I, I, just don't like those things touching me.
DAVE:	What does it feel like when they touch you?
JIM:	Like bugs. I don't like bugs.
DAVE:	This is a curved hallway or straight?
JIM:	It's straight, but the surfaces are—the right surface is curved and, ah, I'm not going there. I just, just—No! I, I just want to get dressed.

Tony decided it was time to employ another technique used to help a regressed person through a traumatic experience. He had Jim imagine that he was looking at TV in his favorite chair at home. The trick was to have Jim imagine that he was watching what was happening to him on TV rather then actually reliving the experience:

TONY:	Just describe to us in as much detail as you can what happens next as you see it on the television screen.
JIM:	Ehhh? (With a surprised expression.) They poked me—they poked me with something to make me go down there. Bastards!
DAVE:	Where did they poke you?
JIM:	In my left side. It poked me in my ribs hard. They made me go there! Those—(voice drops to a whisper) those f---ing miserable bastards!
DAVE:	What did they poke you with?

JIM:	That big thing, that, that pointy thing (i.e., with the prod they had used to examine him).
TONY:	And what happens next Jim?
JIM:	There's another room there (pause). It's a little room like, ah, smaller than the other one. Like an anteroom of some sort and there's, ah-h-h!
TONY:	Just relax.
JIM:	There's a table. A flat table.
TONY:	What's it made of?
JIM:	Some kind of, some kind of thick, thick metal or plastic. They, they, they're, they're gonna—they're making me lay down on that! Where's Jack?
TONY:	Just relax. Are you lying on the table?
JIM:	Yeah (the TV technique had calmed Jim).
DAVE:	Can you look around the room and describe it?
JIM:	There's a divider. There's—it's just not a single room. You come in on your right this way (motions with his hand) and just go off to the side. There's the table and over here, there's a wall. But there's an opening over here, and it goes around 'cause I can see the opening, and then there's a wall that goes this way (motions with his hands).
RAY:	Are there any instruments or any other, ah furniture in the room?
JIM:	No. There's this table.
DAVE:	What color?
JIM:	It's, ah, a light grayish color, and there's a light up above it. And, ah, I'm on, they got me on the table. I can't believe those bastards poked me in the ribs! I can't believe that.
RAY:	What happens next?
JIM:	They, ah (starts to breathe heavily again) they're, ah, fiddling around with my genitals. I think they're trying to get me to have an erection. But, hah! Those bastards. They're not going to get it. It's like my penis is shrunk down inside of me. It's, it's like they're trying to, they, ah, you know, I think they want a sperm sample.
RAY:	How are they trying to get it?
JIM:	They're trying. They're fiddling around with my penis trying to.
RAY:	How would they collect it?

JIM:	I don't know. I don't see anything in their hands, ah, just that pokey thing. I, I feel really threatened. I get the impression that if I don't get an erection soon I'm going to be in trouble.
RAY:	Um-hum, so what happens next?
JIM:	So I, I'm trying to think of things that will give me an erection, some—anything—naked women—having sex with my girlfriend, anything—if my girlfriend ever knew that! Maybe if I give them what they want they'll let me go. I'm telling them [I] can't do this lying down—can't do this lying down. Just let me sit up. Just let me sit up, and I'll do it (exhales loudly). So I, they let me sit up (pauses) and then they have a, some kind of container, ah, sil—silvery metal. So they're gonna, they're gonna let me ejaculate in it (pauses). And—(panting) that's what I'm doing. I'm giving them their damned sample!
DAVE:	Can you describe the container?
JIM:	It's not big. It's just a small—(breathing heavily)—just, ah, like a bottle. But it's, it doesn't—it's rounded on the bottom. There's no—it's, it's not freestanding. It reminds me of a, a, a, air, an air gun can—canister. Like the kind they put in air guns, only bigger and it's silver. Silvery.
RAY:	What are the dimensions?
JIM:	Oh-h-h, five, six inches in length. Looks to be, ah, an inch and a half diameter. But it's got a smaller neck. It's, it's smaller at the neck where it goes to my penis.
RAY:	It fits right over your penis?
JIM:	Yeah. So I gave 'em, I gave them their sample. The rotten bastards. I'd been a lot nicer about it if they hadn't poked me in the side. I just want to murder—
RAY:	What do they do with the sample?
JIM:	They took it away. The—one of them walks, walked away. They took their sample.
DAVE:	Where does he go with the sample?
JIM:	In that other room. He went around, went around the, the thing—the divider.
RAY:	What happens next?
JIM:	I'm glar—glaring at them. I'm really pissed off. I want to murder 'em! How can they do this to people? I betcha that's what they did to Jack, too. Those rotten bastards. They got no feeling. No, no emotion.

TONY:	And then what happened? What do you see on the imaginary television screen? You've been sitting on the table for a few minutes now. And then what happened? Do they finally help you off the table?
JIM:	Yeah, they let me go back.
TONY:	Back where?
JIM:	Back to the other room.
TONY:	Where your clothes are?
JIM:	Yeah. They let, let me put my clothes on. I want, I said, "I want to put my clothes on now. Leave me alone!"
DAVE:	Was it the same two [aliens]?
JIM:	Yeah. He came, the other one came back (the one who had left with the sperm sample).
RAY:	Is Jack in there?
JIM:	No, he's not here yet.
DAVE:	Are Chuck and Charlie there?
JIM:	Chuck and Charlie are there.
TONY:	Same position? (i.e., sitting on the bench)
JIM:	Yeah.
TONY:	Does Jack come back in a short while or...
JIM:	Yeah, he came back.
RAY:	Has he got clothes on?
JIM:	No, he's naked.
TONY:	Does he put his clothes on?
JIM:	He (an alien) he let him (Jack) put his clothes on.
RAY:	What happens next?

Jim would not answer. He again became extremely agitated. Tony once again reminded Jim to watch the imaginary TV screen to spare him from reliving severe trauma. At first, Jim only remembered himself and Jack putting on their clothes and then being back in the canoe, paddling for shore:

RAY:	So when you leave, how do you leave?
JIM:	Eh-h-h, they're (aliens) around us (the four). Eh-h-h. The only thing I remember is being in the boat.

Tony continued to bring Jim back to the point in time when he and Jack put on their clothes while being surrounded by the aliens. Every time he was asked what happened next, Jim suddenly found himself in the canoe, paddling with the others. We could not get through the mental block, so we let Jim relive the paddle to shore and watch the glowing craft hover before streaking away. However, under hypnosis, Jim remembered something that he had not mentioned previously. For just a moment, the pulsating plasma-like light that flowed around the object dimmed. Jim got a good glimpse at the UFO's configuration. We asked him to sketch it while under hypnosis:

RAY: I'll tell you what. Remaining in the deep state of
               relaxation that you are in, you can open your
               eyes and you can draw that for us. Here's paper
               and pencil. You can also draw the light on it, and
               you can also draw the tube.

JIM: So it was this kind of a shape (comments while
               he sketches). But it was more (paused while
               sketching) like a nut. (See Figure 6.)

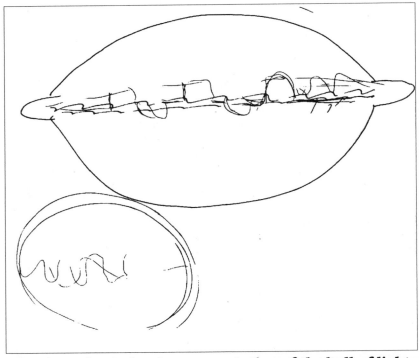

*Figure 6. Jim Weiner's representation of the ball of light,
made while under hypnosis.*

Jim drew a walnut-shaped object with two hemispheres, one inverted upon the other, with a glowing ring around its midsection.

JIM: This whole area in here (the ring) seemed to have like a pink, a pinkish-white.

RAY: Was it absolutely stationary, or was it moving in any way (i.e., when it dimmed momentarily to reveal its shape)?

JIM: No, it was stationary and, ah, I distinctly remember it being a little rounder this way (modifies the sketch to make the object a little rounder). It was difficult to make out because it was so dark (it was barely reflecting the glowing ring around it). And then it went light again. It lit up. And then it went, it, ah, it imploded. Almost like when you see an iris [on a camera] close.

Jim again described how the object left and how odd it was for them to be watching it so calmly when, moments before, they had been paddling away from it in fear. At that time, he and his friends had no memory of the abduction. All they could remember consciously was the beam of light hitting the canoe and themselves paddling for shore.

Time was not on our side, and Tony indicated that the session would have to come to a close. Out of curiosity, I snapped a quick question at Jim:

RAY: When did you see these creatures again?

JIM: In Texas.

RAY: What year was that?

JIM: I think it was 1980.

I remembered Jim telling me about a series of lifelike nightmares involving bedroom visitations by alien creatures and paranormal happenings. We decided that time must be set aside to examine such incidents in the lives of the Allagash four.

Tony took his time bringing Jim back to a normal state of consciousness. We all felt embarrassment and empathy for him as he slowly stirred in the chair and blinked his eyes open. It was hard for him to accept the grotesque memories that had just taken up permanent residence in his conscious mind. On top of this, we had requested that he not talk about them. I was really concerned about him as I left him at the railroad station.

He was pale and distraught. Perhaps this is one of the reasons aliens dull memories of abductees. In a sense, it is an act of mercy.

Aside from our empathetic reactions, we were very pleased with the results of the regression sessions. Sometimes it takes many sessions to break through such a memory block, and sometimes there are occasions when we fail to make any break. Regression attempts are aborted when abductees experience physical pain when hypnotically questioned about hidden memories. In some instances, we fail to break through a memory block because the abductee is simply not responsive to hypnosis. This was not the case with Jim, as Tony noted in his evaluation of the second session:

> Frankly, I'm quite elated with what we've been able to uncover through our somewhat slow but careful and gentle questioning. Jim continues to be a good, solid subject—friendly, cooperative, patient and good-natured. I like our approach of a somewhat light stage, which we later deepen. This worked well the first time we worked with Jim and seemed to work well this time also.
>
> As you recall, I numbed the back of Jim's hand and then stimulated that area with a pin. Jim felt no pain but did feel pressure. This indicated at least a level four (out of a possible six) stage of relaxation—a medium stage. Yet his talking in the present tense would indicate a level five stage of relaxation, bordering on the deep stage of relaxation. These stages/states/levels are not carved in granite and are only indications, differing from individual to individual.
>
> Other indications of a medium-to-deep level of relaxation are his pointing to where others are standing/sitting, his head turning in the direction of something/someone he may be describing, his using his fingers to describe/indicate the size of something, his heavy breathing and obvious physical agitation when they want to examine him "...as they did Jack."
>
> I am also impressed with the rather wide range of emotions Jim displayed: from fear ("not want to be there") to anger ("He didn't have to poke me," etc.) to some humor ("If my girlfriend ever knew that...") to awe.
>
> Based on all of the above, I conclude that Jim was experiencing a true regression, wherein he relived his experience, rather than a pseudo-regression, wherein he would merely be remembering it. In stating this, of course, I'm also stating that as a lay (MUFON) consultant in hypnosis with admittedly limited experience in this area of (UFO-related) hypnosis, Jim is reporting/

reliving experiences which *actually occurred.* (Italics are mine.)

From my perspective, as a UFO investigator, Jim again had relived yet another typical component of the UFO abduction experience: *the taking of a sperm sample.* I wondered if the other three would be subjected to the same procedure. One thing was sure: this was just another example of alien interest in the reproduction system of human beings. Past studies indicate that aliens are carrying on a large-scale operation dealing with genetics. Later, we will discuss this subject in some detail, but now, let us move forward to the next hypnosis session. We decided that Jim's brother, Jack, would be next to relate his experience to us under hypnosis.

CHAPTER 4

"Don't be Afraid"

Two months passed before weather and schedule cooperated in allowing us to conduct the first hypnosis session with Jim's brother, Jack. Jack, unlike Jim, did not live close to me. He and his wife, Mary, lived in a cozy but isolated mountain home in southern Vermont. The trip from there to our meeting place in Beverly, Massachusetts, could take between three and four hours each way, depending upon weather conditions. We appreciated the sacrifice of time and energy that was spent initially and in the following months. All members of the Allagash four were determined to find out what had happened to them during those missing hours on Eagle Lake. Little did they know that the wilderness fireball was just one of a number of such encounters in their lives. Our probe would reveal both past and ongoing interfaces with aliens from another world.

When Dave and I arrived at Tony's home, Jack and his wife were already there. It didn't take us long to see that Jack's temperament was very different from that of his brother. Jim was more calm and reserved. Jack was excitable and very talkative. This was especially the case when he was being presented with the prospect of being hypnotized. Jack wanted his wife with him during the session for moral support. He was not aware of what Jim had relived under hypnosis. However, he did know that whatever occurred had been traumatic for his brother. Obviously he was very apprehensive.

I watched and listened as Jack talked incessantly and nervously shifted around in his chair. Dave and I wondered if Tony could hypnotize such a high-strung person. Nevertheless, Tony took it all in stride. He spent time to calm Jack down a bit and gain his confidence. As Jack sat back in the hypnotist's big easy chair, he himself doubted whether he could be hypnotized. He was wrong. Tony was able to place him in a deep state of hypnosis with little effort. (See Figure 7.)

Hypnosis Session #1—Jack Weiner (April 15, 1989)

Jack, like Jim, described the same general events that led the four to go fishing out on Eagle Lake at night. Tony brought him slowly up to the point where they sighted the UFO. We'll pick up the conversation from there:

TONY: What time is it?
JACK: It's after nine—and it's dark. We're fishing (sighs and grins). It's beautiful. It's beautiful out there. Then Chuck says, "Hey look at that! What's

Figure 7. From left to right: Tony Constantino, Ray Fowler and Jack Weiner

that?" And we look and there's a bright light. It's a bright light and it's coming out of the trees.

TONY: Through the trees or above the trees?

JACK: Above the trees. It's coming up and we're looking at it, and we don't know what it is. But we know that it's what we saw the other night, 'cause it twinkles and it moves, and we know that it was the same, but we don't know what it is.

TONY: What happened next?

Jack answered Tony by describing how he and his companions went through what UFO investigators term the escalation of hypotheses. This is a typical process of witnesses going from a simple, quick explanation, step by step, to the realization that no conventional explanation could suffice for what is being observed:

JACK: Well (pauses) we're talking about it. We're, we're trying to—we're wondering if it, it's a plane, but it's not a plane. And then we wonder if it's a helicopter, but it's not making any noise. And then we don't know what it is because it's hovering. And then (pauses) Charlie takes his flashlight and blinks at it, and now it starts to move. It's moving towards us! And we say, "Now we've done it! Is it swamp gas? It's swamp gas." And then we say, "Let's wait." And it's still coming towards us. It, it's coming out over the water, and it's reflecting in the water now so we know it's there. And we look to see if it moves the water. It's not moving the water. We're scared and we don't want to be there, so we start to paddle! We're paddling, and it's right behind us. It's still coming towards us, and we're saying, "Swamp gas doesn't have *beams*."

TONY: What beams Jack?

JACK: There's a beam. A beam of light comes out of it.

TONY: Can you describe the beam Jack?

JACK: It's thin. It's thin where it comes out of, but it's wide, it's wide when, when it is on the water, and it's bright, and it's hollow. It's a hollow beam.

TONY: How do you know that Jack?

JACK: Because you can see. You can see that it's hollow. It makes a ring on the water and it's coming towards us (sighs). (See Figure 8.) I'm looking over my shoulder at it, and it's right there! It's

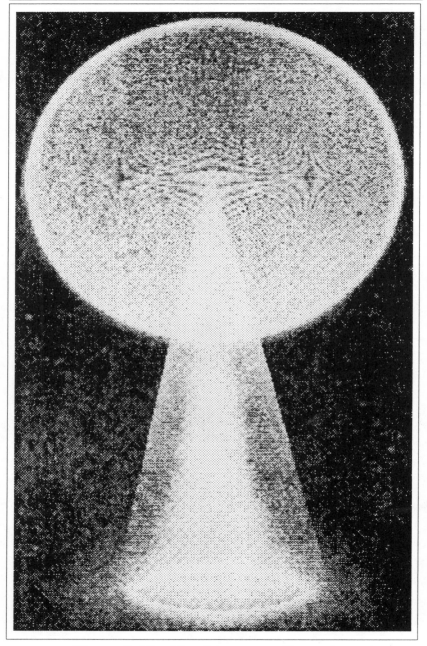

Figure 8. The blue beam over the water.

right behind us, and I'm paddling with my hand and the beam is right behind us!

Now Jack was in a total panic. His facial muscles were contorted. His chest bulged in and out as he gulped in and breathed out deep breaths of air. Tony immediately took steps to calm him:

TONY: Just relax. Just relax.
JACK: Then (pauses and relaxes in the chair) then (pauses) we're at the beach.

This was amazing. Like Jim, Jack had no recollection of an abduction experience. When the beam overtook the canoe, the next remembrance of both twins was suddenly being on shore calmly watching the object without any fear. We decided to let Jim describe what his conscious mind remembered from shore first. Then we would attempt to break through the memory block of being abducted from the canoe:

JACK: We're at the beach. We're in the canoe and it's still there—the, the thing, the light. We got out,

Figure 9. The big ball of light.

and we walk, and we stop, and we're standing, looking at it. And it's just there, and it's right there!

DAVE: What did it look like?

JACK: It's a big ball of light. It's, it pulses. It's, it's as big as a truck. As big as a—as a tractor-trailer truck. It's so close I could throw a stone and hit it. That's what I'm thinking. It's so close. (See Figure 9.)

RAY: What happens next?

JACK: I'm looking at it, and I see a line, a line on it. A squiggly line and I'm looking at this line, and I feel funny when I look at it like I'm going to throw up.

All of us jumped on this new piece of information. Jim had not mentioned this aspect of the glowing object. Not only that, but the physical effect caused by looking at it was intriguing. It would be something for MUFON consultants to ponder over during their analysis of this fascinating case:

TONY: Where is the squiggly line?

JACK: It's in the middle of it and it's, it's weird. It doesn't look like anything, and there's, there's energy. There's energy coming out of the lines, and when I look at it, it makes me feel strange— like I'm floating, and I'm going to be sick, and so I don't want to look at it.

DAVE: What color is the light?

RAY: Is the squiggly light brighter than the big ball of light?

JACK: No, it's darker. It's orange, like an orange, and it moves. It's moving. It's like, um, magnets and filings. It looks like the patterns that magnets make filings look like except they move. That's what's coming out of the lines.

RAY: How does it move? Left to right? Right to left?

JACK: It moves from the line out and around it, around the light (i.e., around the equator of the glowing UFO).

Tony stopped and calmed Jack. The psychosomatic effect upon Jack was making him literally feel sick to his stomach. It was decided to move him on in time, as he seemed locked onto the radiating line around the object.

Jack described the object's departure as his brother did—
in the same step-like manner—as it disappeared among the
stars:

TONY: And what happens next?
JACK: Then we walk back to camp, and we sit down.
             Charlie checks the fire and says, "Holy shit, the
             fire's out now. What do we do about the fire?"
             And we say, "Nothing." Let's go to sleep. We're
             just tired, very tired, very tired, and we go to
             sleep.

Surprisingly, Jack was already in a fairly deep state of hypnosis. He was a good subject. However, before making another
attempt to restore Jack's memory, Tony placed him in an even
deeper trance. Then he brought Jack back in time to where the
beam from the UFO was overtaking the fleeing canoe. Again, as
in so many other cases, the deepened state of hypnosis un-
locked the doors to Jack's subconscious memory. He was no
longer just telling us what happened. He was at Eagle Lake, reliving the terrifying ordeal:

JACK: The beam—it's going to get us! It's right there
             right behind us. I know there's no use. It's no
             use paddling. The beam! (Pants heavily.) It's got
             us! It's there. We're in it!
TONY: How do you know that you are in it?
JACK: Because we can't see out.
TONY: Look up Jack. What do you see?
JACK: It's got (pauses) something in it moving. Like
             smoke—like smoke is in a room and there's light
             in there.
DAVE: Can you see Charlie?
JACK: Charlie's in the front of the canoe. I can see him.
             He's looking up.
DAVE: Is he in the beam too?
JACK: Yes, it goes around the canoe. It's all around the
             canoe. Everything is lit up. It's so bright!
DAVE: Where's Jim?
JACK: Where's Jim? Jim is next to me. Jim is next to
             me. I'm holding him.
TONY: Why are you holding him?
JACK: Because I'm afraid if I let go I'll lose him, or
             something's going to happen.

RAY:	What does happen next?

As soon as I asked that question, Jack grimaced and began breathing heavily. He could hardly talk, as he puffed out air hysterically:

JACK:	Next? (Pauses, breathing heavily.) Something happens. Something changes. I feel—the feeling changes. There's something different—it's—something's happening (pauses, puffing out air). Ohhh—Whew-w-w—Charlie's screaming!
TONY:	Why?
JACK:	Chuck! Chuck! (Long pause, breathing heavily.) Chuck's gone!
TONY:	Where did Chuck go?
JACK:	I don't know. He fell out—maybe he fell out. No, no, he didn't fall out.
RAY:	Does anybody else disappear?
JACK:	No, I see Charlie's face.
TONY:	And where do you see his face?
JACK:	In the front of me. He looks horrible. His eyes are open. His mouth is open.
RAY:	What happens next?
JACK:	We're looking, we're looking for Chuck, but he's not in the water. We don't know what happened. Now, we're—Oh-h-h!
TONY:	That's all right.

Tony stepped in at this point to calm Jack. His extreme agitation was unnerving to all of us. We did not want to see him suffering like this. Tony was only partially successful. Jack would start to describe and then suddenly slip back into reliving what was happening:

JACK:	I feel funny (pauses). I feel funny. I don't feel like I'm here (pants). I don't feel like I'm supposed to feel (pauses) like something's happening, and I'm really scared (pants heavily). Something is happening.
TONY:	Are you still looking up, Jack?
JACK:	No.
TONY:	Where are you, Jack?
JACK:	I don't know (very agitated).
TONY:	What do you see, Jack?

JACK:	Oh! Lights in front of me, and there's Jim (suddenly becomes frantic). I can't move!
TONY:	Is he sitting or standing?
JACK:	He's sitting.
TONY:	What is he sitting on?
JACK:	A bench.
TONY:	What's supporting it?
JACK:	I don't know. It comes from behind them. It doesn't have legs.
RAY:	Who else is with Jim?
JACK:	Chuck and Charlie. Chuck and Charlie. They're all on the bench. I don't know why they won't help me.
TONY:	Are you standing or sitting?
JACK:	I'm standing.
TONY:	Can you move?
JACK:	No.
TONY:	Why?
JACK:	I don't know.
DAVE:	Can you breathe?
JACK:	Yes, and I can move my eyes, and I can't move.
RAY:	What else do you see?
JACK:	Jim, Charlie and Chuck.
RAY:	What else?
JACK:	(Pants heavily.) Why won't they help me?
DAVE:	How far away are they?
JACK:	Not far. Close enough—close enough that they could help me, but they're not helping me.
TONY:	Look up as high as you can. What do you see?
JACK:	Just light.
TONY:	Look down as far as you can. What do you see?
JACK:	My feet (speaks in a surprised tone). My toes!
TONY:	Where did your shoes or boots or socks go?
JACK:	I don't know.
DAVE:	Are you naked?
JACK:	(Breathes heavily, pauses.) I'm naked.
TONY:	Where have your clothes gone?
JACK:	I don't know.

Further questioning indicated that, beyond a certain distance, Jack could only see hazy light. His friends appeared to be in some kind of immobile stupor, and he could not move a muscle except for his eyes. Then he noticed something moving through the haze towards him:

JACK:	Something's moving.
TONY:	What's moving?
JACK:	Something.
TONY:	How do you know?
JACK:	Ohhh! I can see 'em now!
TONY:	What do you see, Jack?
JACK:	(Puffs out air.) I don't want to be scared. Ohhh, (whispers) I don't want to be scared.
TONY:	Relax. Tell us what you see?
JACK:	Oh! Something's coming toward me. Oh-h-h! Oh-h-h! (Breathes heavily.) It's something. Is it going to hurt me? Oh-h-h!
TONY:	What do you mean by something?
JACK:	It's not like me.
TONY:	What does it look like?
JACK:	Shiny.
TONY:	Start at the top and work down. Describe it. Describe what you see.
JACK:	Well-l-l, it's my height. It doesn't smile.
TONY:	How do you know that?
JACK:	It doesn't have a mouth (i.e., like a human mouth). It doesn't have a nose.
RAY:	How does it look at you?
JACK:	It has eyes.
RAY:	What do they look like?
JACK:	They're not like ours.
RAY:	How do they differ?
JACK:	They don't blink. They don't have eyelids. They're big!
RAY:	What shape?
JACK:	They're long and round and they look like eggs—eggs—they look like eggs. They're funny. They're, they're (pauses) I, I don't believe it. I can't believe it. They, ohhh, God! They look shiny, scary, still looking at me. They won't help me (breathes heavily). Oh! There's another one! There's another one coming.
TONY:	Is it the same? Is it different?
JACK:	It's the same...large round heads.

TONY:	What's on top of their heads?
JACK:	Nothing. They've large eyes on the side of their heads. There's no nose (pauses) and their mouths (pauses) their mouths are on the bottom (pause) like turtle mouths. Ohhh, they have a neck. They have shoulders. They're small and thin and their clothes are funny. I can't see their joints. When they move, their joints don't move right (sighs).
RAY:	Do they have arms?
JACK:	They have arms.
RAY:	What do they look like?
JACK:	They're thin—thin and shiny arms, and they're not like mine (pants). Now there's two of them. (See Figures 10 and 11.)
TONY:	How do they (the arms) differ?
JACK:	They don't have fingers.
TONY:	What do they have?
JACK:	They have (pants) things like fingers.
TONY:	How many?
JACK:	Four. Four. Four fingers.
RAY:	Any thumb?
JACK:	No thumbs. I can do it. I can do it. I can do it (demonstrates with his own fingers). I can do it. They look like this. That's what they're like. (See Figure 12.)
RAY:	All the same size fingers?
JACK:	All the same.

Jack stated that the aliens' hands were gloved and that they wore shiny coveralls. Their feet were covered with the same shiny material, which was highly reflective. Then one of the creatures touched Jack:

RAY:	Where do they touch you with their fingers?
JACK:	On my wrist, my left wrist. It touched me.
TONY:	Why?
JACK:	They were looking at something.
TONY:	What does it feel like when they touch you?
JACK:	I don't want to know what they feel like. Oh-h-h! Like caterpillars.
RAY:	What do they do next?

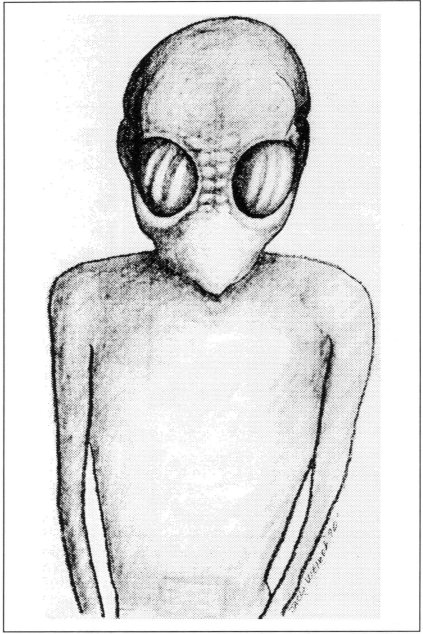

Figure 10. Jack Weiner's drawing of one of his abductors, front view.

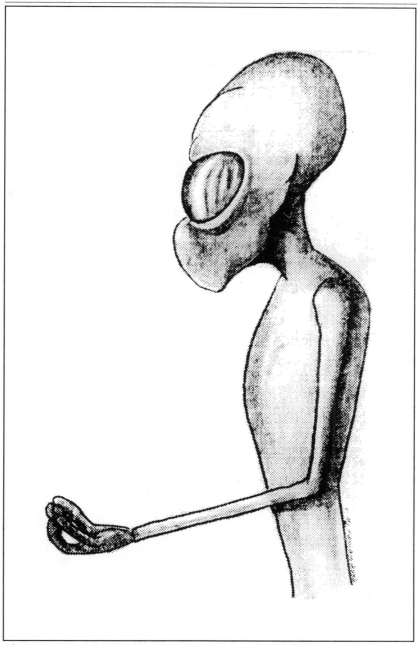

Figure 11. Jack Weiner's drawing of one of his abductors, side view.

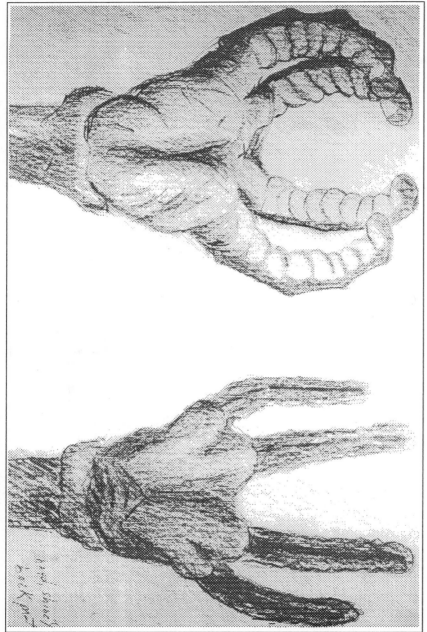

Figure 12. Jack Weiner's drawing of one of his abductor's hands, palm view (top) and back of hand (bottom).

JACK:	(Breathes heavily.) They lift my arm...I DON'T LIKE IT!
TONY:	Just relax, just relax.
RAY:	What do they do to you next?
JACK:	They're looking at it (nervously). They're going to do something to me...One of them has something.
TONY:	Describe it.
JACK:	It's something in his hand (breathes heavily). It's metal. He's going to do something with it! Oh-h-h!
TONY:	It's okay for you to share this with us. Just relax, just relax. What's he doing Jack?
JACK:	They touch me (sniff) with this thing...under my arm...feels funny...they're pushing it. It's not so bad (pauses). Feels (pauses) feels like a scrape. A scrape.
DAVE:	How often do they do that?
JACK:	Once (pauses). Then they stop.
DAVE:	Can you describe the instrument—its shape?
JACK:	Yes. It's metal. It fits in their hand. It's a few inches long. It's shiny. It's got something on the end. It's not bad.
TONY:	What shape is it at the end?
JACK:	Scooped. Scooped and flat.
RAY:	What diameter is it?
JACK:	It's the diameter of a (pauses) like a pen.
RAY:	What, what shape is the handle—whatever they're holding it with?
JACK:	It's formed—it fits in their hand. It fits their hand, and there are things on it. Things that—it pushes, pushes and I feel pressure (begins panting). I don't want it to go in me! Oh-h-h! (Pauses). No, it scrapes. It scrapes. (See Figure 13.)

The alien used the instrument on Jack. It scraped his legs, the insides of his thighs, the backs of his knees and his calves. All of this time, Jim and the two others sat on the bench staring blankly into space. If we are to accept the accuracy of Jim's memory, there was a time when he stood, for a while, and watched Jack being examined before he was put on the bench. It is important to realize that such experiences are buried deep within the subconscious and only portions are remembered at a time. Neither Jack nor Jim remembered how they got from the canoe to the inside of the UFO. Both just remembered suddenly

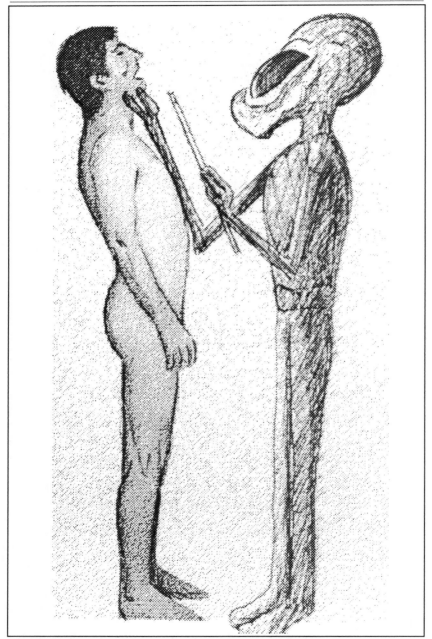

Figure 13. Jack Weiner's drawing of one of his abductors examining him with a penlike instrument.

finding themselves in a strange, hazy room. In any event, after the aliens probe Jack with the unknown instrument, several other creatures arrived on the scene. Two of them took Jack by his arms and began to move him:

JACK:	They're moving me.
TONY:	How are they moving you?
JACK:	They just (pauses) take my arms (pauses) and move me.
TONY:	Do your legs move as they move you?
JACK:	They move...I'm walking but I don't feel like I'm walking.
TONY:	Why don't you?
JACK:	(Breathes heavily.) I'm (pauses) paralyzed. I can't move...I feel like they (his legs) are far away. My feet are so far away. Ohhh! (Pants.) They move me out (pauses) to another spot.
TONY:	Do you see Jim, Jack or Charlie?
JACK:	No.
TONY:	Describe where you are. What do you see as you look around?
JACK:	I see (pause) things—like—machines—like in a hospital. Machines like a hospital...Ohhh!
TONY:	Why like a hospital?
JACK:	They put me in it!
TONY:	Put you in what?
JACK:	In the machine (pauses) and—they—put—something—they put something on me.
TONY:	Where?
JACK:	On my chest.
TONY:	Are you sitting, standing or lying down?
JACK:	I'm lying down—and—I don't know what they're doing.
TONY:	What's on your chest? Describe it.
JACK:	It fits around me.
TONY:	Around your chest?
JACK:	Uh-huh. It's a machine and I know they're going to do something to me.
TONY:	Did they put you on it?
JACK:	Yeah, they made me lie down.
TONY:	Is it a table?
JACK:	No, it is a machine.

RAY:	What does it do? Do you feel anything?
JACK:	No. It makes a buzz. It hums. It's humming.
RAY:	What happens next?
JACK:	They take it off and they make me sit up and they're just there looking at me. Whew! And I don't like the way they're looking at me.
TONY:	Do they ever say anything to you? Do they talk to one another?
JACK:	No. They can't talk. They make motions—motions—with their hands and they nod and they're looking at me and nodding. They're nodding and I don't like it! (Pauses.) They're scary looking. I don't know what they want.
RAY:	What happens next?
JACK:	Ohhh! They (pauses and begins hyperventilating) they're touching me. They're touching my penis!
RAY:	What happens next?
JACK:	They put something on it.
RAY:	What does it look like? Describe it.
JACK:	Like a bell. And it's got a tube. And the tube (pants as he states slowly and methodically) the tube—goes—to—a thing—a bottle. And I can feel it. It's going in. I don't like it! (See Figure 14.)
TONY:	It's going in where, Jack?
JACK:	My—(lowers his voice to a whisper) it's going in my pecker. (Panting, raises his voice.) I don't like it!
TONY:	Where does the tube lead?
JACK:	To a bottle.
TONY:	What's going in the bottle?
JACK:	I'm peeing—peeing into it. I can't stop (pants). I don't like it!
TONY:	Okay, just relax. Relax. What happens next?
JACK:	It's still there. It hurts. It's hurting! It's hurting me! It hurts! Oh-h-h, I want to get off!

Tony had to step in at this point and calm Jack down. The pain, although psychosomatic, was nevertheless real. His face winced with agony. Jack was allowed to relax for several minutes before the questioning continued:

TONY:	Do you remember how long it took them to do this operation?

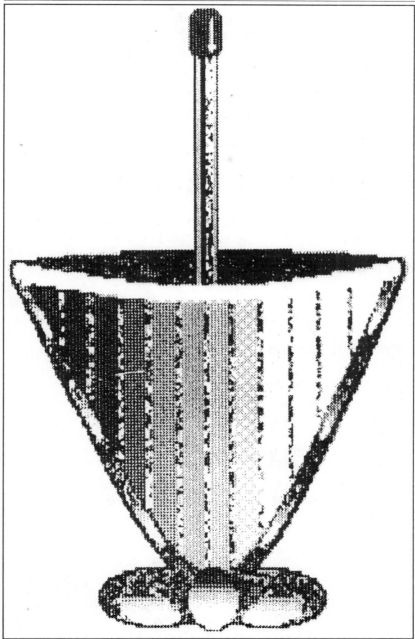

Figure 14. Jack Weiner's drawing of the instrument that was inserted into his penis.

JACK:	(Still breathing heavily.) Too long!
TONY:	Then what happened?
JACK:	Then (pauses) some of them leave. They take the thing, and they leave (pauses) and then they touch me again.
TONY:	Where do they touch you?
JACK:	They take my arms, and they help me off the thing, and I'm cold. I feel cold...and they make me walk again.
TONY:	To where?
JACK:	To (pauses) someplace (pauses) I don't know where they're taking me.

The two aliens escorted Jim through an area where other creatures of the same type appeared to be operating strange-looking machines. He then entered a room and was made to sit on a bench:

RAY:	Okay, what happens next?
JACK:	And—one—leaves and goes—and one stays and it's watching me.
DAVE:	Are you still naked?
JACK:	Yes.
TONY:	How long do you sit on the bench?
JACK:	A long time.
TONY:	And then what happens?
JACK:	(Pause.) Then (pauses) then—and then they make me move.

Jack was moved along by his alien companion into another room where two other aliens awaited. They proceeded to probe his neck, face, mouth and legs:

TONY:	And what happens next?
JACK:	And they're right there. Their faces are right in my face. I don't know why. They're right there, and they're—they want something. I don't know. I don't wanna know. I don't want to know what they want. Oh-h-h! (Starts breathing very heavily.)
TONY:	(Calming Jack down.) Just relax.
JACK:	Oh—they're—they're saying things. They're explaining things.

DAVE:	How are they doing this?
JACK:	With their eyes.
TONY:	Do you hear them?
JACK:	In my head.
TONY:	What are they saying to you?
JACK:	They're saying, "Don't be afraid. Don't be afraid. We won't harm you. We won't harm you now." (Pauses.) They say, "Do what we say. Just do what we say."
TONY:	What do they want?
JACK:	They tell me to spread my legs. "Stand wide," they say.
TONY:	And do you?
JACK:	I try—and I do it—But—I don't feel like I'm doing what they want. And they're saying, "Just do it. Don't be afraid." And then (exhales loudly) and then they're looking. They're looking at me. Ohhh! (Grimaces.) They're putting something in me!
TONY:	How do they put it in you? Where?
JACK:	Up my ass. I'm afraid (pauses and groans).
TONY:	What do they insert? Can you tell me?
JACK:	I don't know what it is. It's—it's—it burns. It's like an enema (pauses). It's uncomfortable—but no—it's not so bad.

Jack had used the expression, "It's not so bad," a number of times when the aliens were examining him. Sometimes, because of the traumatic nature of the exam, I wondered how he could make such a statement. The answer was forthcoming during this particular segment. It was a product of alien mind control:

JACK:	It's them. They're saying, "It's not so bad." And I'm saying, "Okay, it's not so bad."
TONY:	How long do they do this?
JACK:	Not long.
TONY:	Do they withdraw it?
JACK:	Yes.
TONY:	What happens next?
JACK:	One leaves. And they make me sit down.
TONY:	What do you sit on?
JACK:	A bench.

TONY:	Is it like the other one you sat on?
JACK:	Smaller.
TONY:	What do they do next?
JACK:	It tells me, "Don't be afraid."
TONY:	What do you tell him?
JACK:	I'm afraid.

We knew from many past cases that communication between aliens and humans was accomplished by what we would call *mental telepathy*. It was interesting to note that in Jack's present, alien-induced mental state, he, too, was able to communicate by the same means:

TONY:	How did you tell him that you were afraid?
JACK:	With my eyes.
TONY:	Did you use your mouth?
JACK:	No, my mouth doesn't work (temporarily paralyzed).
TONY:	Did he use his mouth?
JACK:	No, they don't have mouths. *They just look at me, and I know.* No mouths—mouths, but not like our mouths.
TONY:	Did you say anything else to him?
JACK:	I say, "Where's Jim?"
TONY:	Does he answer?
JACK:	He says, "Jim is all right. Don't be concerned about Jim." And then he says, "You're almost finished. Just a little while longer." And I'm glad (sounds relieved). I'm really glad!
TONY:	What do you say?
JACK:	I say, "I want my shoes." He says, "When you're done."
TONY:	And then what happens?
JACK:	He's watching me.
TONY:	How long does he stay there?
JACK:	It seems like a while.

Jack sat on the seat with the alien for quite a while and then saw his brother Jim coming into the room with two aliens:

JACK:	I see Jim.
TONY:	How do you see Jim?

JACK:	He's coming towards me.
TONY:	Is someone with him?
JACK:	No. Two of them. Two of them.
TONY:	Describe Jim.
JACK:	He's scared. He's looking at me and he's, he's scared.
DAVE:	Is he dressed?
JACK:	No. He's like me. He's naked.
TONY:	Where did they take him?
JACK:	They move him to where I was. Now (pauses) now he's gone.
TONY:	Did Jim see you?
JACK:	Yes.
TONY:	Then what happened?
JACK:	Then I wait, and I wonder when I'm going to end. When they'll be finished. And...(pauses, breathing heavily).
TONY:	How much longer do you sit there?
JACK:	I don't know. It's funny. Time is funny. Seems like a long time (pauses). And then—I see Chuck—and they have Chuck.
TONY:	How many?
JACK:	Two.
TONY:	Describe Chuck.
JACK:	He's naked.
TONY:	Where are they going?
JACK:	Where they had Jim.
TONY:	Where's Jim?
JACK:	Where they had me.
TONY:	And then what happened?
JACK:	Chuck looks at me.
TONY:	Does he say anything to you?
JACK:	With his eyes.
TONY:	What does he say?
JACK:	Help me! Help me! And then he's gone—to where they took Jim (pauses). And I wait—and I wait—and then Jim comes.
TONY:	Where do they put Jim?
JACK:	Next to me.
TONY:	Is he sitting down?
JACK:	Yes.
TONY:	Do you and Jim say anything?

JACK:	With our eyes.
TONY:	What do you say?
JACK:	Get me out of here! Let's get out of here!
TONY:	And then what happens?
JACK:	And then Charlie—then I see Charlie.
TONY:	Is he alone?
JACK:	No. He's being taken.
TONY:	Where?
JACK:	Where they had me.
TONY:	Describe Charlie.
JACK:	He's naked.
DAVE:	How do you know that they were taking him to where you were?
JACK:	Because it seems like it's the same direction that I came from, and they're taking him there. And so, I think they're taking him there where I was. And then we wait. And we sit. And they're watching us.
DAVE:	And who is sitting on the bench now?
JACK:	Jim and one of them and me. (See Figure 15.)
DAVE:	Go on.
JACK:	And then they bring Chuck, and they bring him where we are.
TONY:	Does he sit on the bench with you?
JACK:	He—no, no, he doesn't sit.
TONY:	What does he do?
JACK:	He stands...he's standing across from us.
TONY:	Is he alone?
JACK:	No, no they're with him.
TONY:	Why doesn't he sit?
JACK:	I don't know. I don't know. And they're watching us. And then—and then they bring Charlie.
TONY:	Where do they bring him?
JACK:	He's with Chuck.
TONY:	Standing?
JACK:	Yes.
TONY:	And then what?
JACK:	And then, they tell us—they say, "Don't be afraid. Don't be afraid." We're almost done. And we're, we're afraid...and then they move us all together. They move us (pauses) back to a place

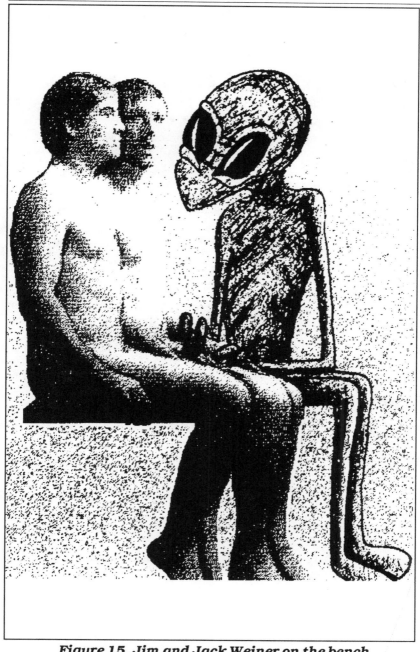

Figure 15. Jim and Jack Weiner on the bench with an abductor.

	(pauses) some room. Some room and my shoes are there. My shoes are there.
TONY:	Are your clothes there, too?
JACK:	Yes.
RAY:	Where is there? Are they hanging up?
JACK:	No. On the floor.
TONY:	And then what happens?
JACK:	"Oh," I think, "Oh, at least they've saved our clothes." And I think, "Oh, I guess it's time to put our clothes on."
TONY:	Do you?
JACK:	And then they help us—they help us put our clothing on. And—I feel weird! "What's going to happen now?"
TONY:	What does happen?
JACK:	They move us, and we don't know—we—we don't know what's going to happen.

Jack had suddenly become very apprehensive, and Tony stepped in to calm him down before continuing to question him:

TONY:	What happens after that?
JACK:	We're done (pauses). They—move us—to—a machine. A big machine.
TONY:	What does the machine do?
JACK:	I don't know.
TONY:	What does it look like?
JACK:	It's—very—simple—A light—A tubelike glass, but not glass. A big tube and—
TONY:	How big is it?
JACK:	I don't know.
RAY:	Can you see through it? Like glass?
JACK:	Yeah.
RAY:	Is it as big as you? How round is it? Square? Whatever?
JACK:	(Pauses.) The tube is big—big as a—big as a Volkswagon.
RAY:	What happens next?
JACK:	They tell us to stand next to it.
RAY:	Next to the tube?
JACK:	Yes.
RAY:	And the tube is in the machine?

JACK:	The tube is the machine and then we're afraid. The tube is scary.
RAY:	Why?
JACK:	Because it starts to—It starts to—move—and it's doing something. It's doing something. It's coming towards us and I don't know what it's going to do! And—It's—Oh-h-h! Oh-h-h! Oh-h-h! (Begins to hyperventilate and there is a long pause.)
RAY:	Does the tube bump into you?
JACK:	No. It makes us come apart. It makes me feel like I'm flying apart. I don't like it! It makes me feel like I'm coming apart! I'm going to be sick. And it's—and it's—happening so fast! And I can't stop it (puffs out air). And I feel funny. I feel real funny. I feel—I feel like—scared (pants).
TONY:	Do you feel like you're coming apart? Do you get the sensation that you're coming together again?
JACK:	Yes.
TONY:	Where are you now?
JACK:	I'm in the canoe.
TONY:	Where is it?
JACK:	In the water.
TONY:	Is there anybody inside it?
JACK:	Jim.
TONY:	Who is sitting in front of you?
JACK:	Charlie.
TONY:	Is there anybody in back of you?
JACK:	Chuck—and *it's* there?
TONY:	What's there?
JACK:	The beam. And we're paddling away from it. And we get to the beach. And we walk out of the canoe and it's there.
TONY:	What's there?
JACK:	The thing (the UFO).
TONY:	How long does it stay there?
JACK:	Minutes.
RAY:	What does it look like?
JACK:	It's big and round. It's spherical and very bright.
RAY:	Did it ever dim its light?
JACK:	The beam goes out—and now it's just floating—floating in front of us.

Jack again relived what had happened when the four reached shore. I was extremely curious about the tubelike machine that Jack had described and decided to try to find out more about it. Apparently, the aliens used whatever it was to transport them back to the canoe. Most likely, it was the instrument that controlled the hollow beam that had originally brought them up to the craft. So, for further questioning on this topic Jack was hypnotically brought back on board the craft to the time that the four stood in front of the tubelike machine:

RAY: When you were beside the machine...the tube—when you felt yourself coming apart—could you see what was happening to Jim and Chuck and Charlie?

JACK: I see their faces, and they're all screaming, and I'm screaming, and this tube is getting closer, and it's bright and it's doing something.

RAY: Okay. Now, when it's doing something, tell me what happens to the three other than yourself. You're watching them! You're watching them!

JACK: I see they're watching the tube and they're—they're getting funny.

RAY: What do you mean...does it change their appearance any?

JACK: Yes.

RAY: How?

JACK: They *disappear into it.*

DAVE: Into what?

JACK: Into a light—the light that comes from the tube.

RAY: Any shape to it or just, just the light?

JACK: No, it's like, it's like (sighs) it's like running through something thick and it sticks, and it makes you come apart, and you can feel it! You can feel it! I can feel it! I can feel it! I can feel it!

RAY: Can you see while you feel it?

JACK: Yes.

RAY: You can? What do you see while you're feeling all of this.

JACK: I see bright, bright, blinding light and images in my mind. I see images in my mind that are funny.

RAY: Like what?

JACK: Like little pieces of things. Like little pieces of things...threads—threads and little pieces of things coming towards me...

RAY:	Can you see yourself?
JACK:	I see myself coming towards myself.
RAY:	Do you see two of yourselves, you mean?
JACK:	No, no I see—like a mirror.
RAY:	Face to face?
JACK:	I can see my face and I—and I'm screaming. And my eyes are open real wide, and my mouth is open real wide, and my tongue is sticking out, and my ears are *coming off* (pants heavily). And, and these things are coming towards me, and I feel like I'm thick! I feel like I'm thick!
RAY:	Do you still see yourself?
JACK:	No. No. It's over now. That was strange.
RAY:	And where are you?
JACK:	In the canoe—paddling the canoe. Oh-h-h! (Pants.) We make it to shore.

The familiar expression, "Beam me up, Scotty!" came to mind, as I visualized what had happened out on Eagle Lake. The device used to transport the Allagash four to and from the hovering craft was strikingly similar to what was envisioned by the science-fiction writers of *Star Trek*!

Jack again described watching the glowing UFO from shore.

At that point, I wondered if any other encounters had occurred on the Allagash, and fired a quick question at him. Luckily, Jack's answer provided another startling bit of new information to this already highly provocative case:

RAY:	When is the next time you see these strange creatures?

His answer was not what I expected, but it did confirm what I had already suspected. This was neither his first nor his last encounter with the alien creatures:

JACK:	(Pauses.) The next time I see them—they're—they're—in my dream. They're in my dream. How did they get there? (Sounds puzzled.)
RAY:	What dream? Can you describe the dream?
JACK:	(Pauses.) They—were at our house.
RAY:	In Vermont?
JACK:	Yes.
RAY:	How did they get there?

JACK:	They came in the door.
RAY:	What happened before that?
JACK:	There was a light.
RAY:	Where?
JACK:	In the window.
RAY:	What color?
JACK:	Blue.
RAY:	What happened next?
JACK:	They watched me.
RAY:	Where was Mary?
JACK:	In bed.
RAY:	Did Mary see them?
JACK:	Mary wakes up but won't look...and they see our dog.

We were so engrossed with this new turn of events that, for a moment, we forgot that Mary, Jack's wife, was with us. Dave waved at me and indicated that we'd better stop Jack's description. Mary was wide-eyed and unbelieving as she stared at her husband. If future interviews with Mary were needed, we didn't want to taint her mind with Jack's description of the mutual experience. Momentarily, we just froze, wondering what to do next. Tony continued:

TONY:	Does your dog do anything?
JACK:	Nothing. And I think, "Stupid dog! What's the matter with him? Why doesn't he do something?" And they ignore him. They come over and take *us*!
RAY:	They take us? Where?
JACK:	Outside.
RAY:	To where?
JACK:	To the light!
RAY:	What happened next?

By this time, Dave was waving frantically at me to signal Tony to stop Jack's talking. I agreed and Tony got my message just as Jack answered my last question:

| JACK: | They say, "Don't be afraid. Don't be afraid." And I say, "I know. I know. You won't hurt us." And, and they say, ah, they say, "Remember, we didn't hurt you before." And, and Mary's scared. |

	She's real scared. And I'm worried. And—then— the blue light—the blue light comes—and— and—I think, "Holy shit! I don't believe it! Not again!" And —(pants heavily)— I don't want it to happen!
TONY:	Just relax, Jack, just relax. Jack, you've done really very, very well....

Upon our instruction, Tony slowly but surely brought Jack out of hypnosis. As he did, he instructed Jack to remember every thing that had happened, so that he could draw what he had seen. Jack began to move his fingers and arms and his eyes blinked open. I left the tape running to record his reaction to what he had just relived under hypnosis. At first, he just stared into space, and then he looked at us in utter amazement:

JACK:	That was really bizarre, you guys!
RAY:	Can you remember what happened?
JACK:	I remember a lot more. I mean it's making me feel really, you know, like I'm going to freak out. Holy mackerel! Holy shit! (breathlessly) Unbelievable! What is this all about?
RAY:	We'd rather not comment, at this point, until we're through with the whole—the whole thing (i.e., our investigation).
JACK:	Is this something that is a dream or is this something that really happened? Am I nuts or what?
RAY:	You aren't nuts.
JACK:	That was pretty bizarre. What's coming back is really strange. How come, ah, how come we couldn't remember that before?
RAY:	Apparently, ah, whatever (i.e., the aliens) used something like hypnosis and said that you couldn't remember.
DAVE:	We can assure you that your, ah, situation's not unique. We've heard this sort of thing before.

All eyes were riveted on Jack. We had temporarily forgotten Mary, who was sitting on a nearby sofa quietly taking all of this in. Our captivation with Jack was shattered when a soft, trembling, incredulous female voice wafted across the room, ending the emotion-draining session with an unintentional touch of levity.

"Are you guys for real?" Mary asked.

CHAPTER **5**

"It's like a Physical"

When Mary asked, "Are you guys for real?" she meant it in all seriousness. Although Jack had briefly described MUFON to her, she was full of questions concerning the organization and our intentions. Both Dave and I gave her a detailed description of MUFON. We explained that a report would be written and that all names would be kept confidential if the witnesses so desired. We promised that everyone would get a copy of the final report generated for MUFON. I suggested that all transcripts of the hypnosis sessions be copyrighted in the witnesses' names to protect them from unwanted publicity. At that time, writing a book about the case was the farthest thing from my mind. My intention was to let Dave Webb take over the case. My schedule was busy enough with running my planetarium, teaching, lecturing and editing my new book, *The Watchers*. Added to this were my personal priorities—home, church and gardening activities.

Mary, of course, was very upset about Jack's dream of their abduction from home. It had only been less than a year since he had the unsettling nightmare. However, she had strange dreams of her own. She related them to us. One concerned watching Jack walk right through a closed door to put their dog out. Another was about deer coming in the house—a strange deer with huge eyes that stared at her. Still another concerned an object hovering over their house. She was visibly shaken by the implications posed by such dreams. I told her that we would examine

Jack's dream later, using hypnosis. We also asked that she consider the prospect of being hypnotized as well. Both were asked not to discuss Jack's dream further. They also agreed to keep the contents of the rest of the session to themselves until the investigation was over. Two very frightened people headed back to Vermont that evening. I did not envy them. This was certainly reflected in the following letter received from Jack and Mary several days after the session:

April 18, 1989

Dear Ray, Tony and Dave:

Greetings friends.... What an afternoon we spent together. Both Mary and myself have been in semi-shock ever since. And we both must confess that our expectations and apprehensions turned out to be minute, compared to what actually transpired. To say that the implications are simultaneously enormously inconceivable and outrageously frightening is sheer understatement. Our fundamental reason for hypnosis was to possibly arrive at some answers to the Allagash incident that would enable us to better understand and accept what happened that fateful night. Instead, we open an enormous can of worms and end up with a quillion more questions that are even more difficult, if not impossible, to find explanations for.

Our impressions of you all were exceedingly positive, yet simultaneously, a little disconcerting. We thought that all of you were very sincere, friendly, understanding, and very professional. We also trust you, no questions asked. But, we could tell that you know a lot more about this "alien-abduction" issue than you dare disclose publicly, and that it is an incredible responsibility that weighs heavily upon you all. We're aware of the vast importance of accumulating data and evidence.... It's obviously an overwhelming and exhausting task. You all have our deepest respect and gratitude.

I was truly amazed because I thought that I'd be too nervous to allow the hypnosis to take effect. There's no doubt, in my mind anyway, that I was in an "altered state," the likes of which I had never experienced before. An extremely relaxed, flowing sensation prevailed, and "in my mind" there was a "movie" of the events that happened. I'm convinced that the hypnosis

took effect, and that there was simply "no faking it."
But, it was the results of the hypnosis that we find so
annoying and worrisome.

Here are our honest thoughts concerning further
investigation into the matter. We are scared....We'll
just have to deal with whatever happens. It is too late
to turn back now.... Mary is a bit frightened about the
prospect of hypnosis. She wants to know, but at the
same time doesn't want the "shit scared out of her.",...
What if she remembers nothing?... And, if she remembers the aliens, what if she doesn't want to live here
anymore? Will she ever feel safe and secure again? I'm
sure you are well aware of all of these feelings and
doubts and realize how difficult this is for most people.
In any case, there you have it. I could go on, but I must
stop here. Please contact us when you want to set up
a date for the next session.

Sincerely,

—Jack Weiner

It was quite apparent that Pandora's box had now been
opened. All of us would pay the piper in one way or another as
the contents of her box were laid bare.

During the weeks following Jack's session, we decided that
a probe of Jack's dream could wait. All of us felt that an initial
investigation of the Allagash incident should be completed first.
Tony, as usual, wrote up an evaluation of the session with Jack
for the record:

April 15, 1989
Dear Ray,

Good to see you and Dave again, and it was good
to finally meet Jack Weiner and his wife, Mary. I wanted to send along my impressions as soon as possible.

I was quite pleased with our session today. Again,
we started out slowly to gain Jack's confidence, to allow him to relax as much as possible, and it certainly
seemed to pay off in a whale of a lot of information.

I was impressed with the ease with which Jack
entered a deep state of relaxation, and with his use of
the present tense—an indication that he was "reliving"
rather than merely remembering what had occurred.

I was also struck by how many details of his story
coincided with Jim's version—the canoe, the "hollow"

light, being naked, being "led" away. Emotionally and factually, the stories seem to correspond....Your returning him to the tube of light and extracting that extraordinary information from him was a stroke of genius. I'm really quite pleased and thrilled (yes, and unsettled!) with today's fascinating session.

—Tony

During the weeks that followed, I continued the tedious task of transcribing the recorded hypnosis sessions for the report that would be prepared for MUFON. It was also important to have them in this form for our own use in planning for and comparing with other sessions. We decided that Charlie Foltz, the canoe bowman on the Allagash trip, would be next to sit in the hypnotist's chair.

Hypnosis Session #1–Charlie Foltz (May 20, 1989)

I reached Tony's home around two o'clock. Tony and Charlie were having a get-acquainted chat when I arrived. Dave had phoned to let me know that his son's soccer game had to take precedence over the meeting. So, it was just the three of us.

Charlie is a midwesterner with a slow, matter-of-fact way of expressing himself. He felt it was his duty to cooperate, and he seemed to take the prospect of being hypnotized in stride. However, just before Tony began the hypnotic process, Charlie warned us that when he got nervous, he smiled. When Tony asked Charlie to close his eyes and relax in the big easy chair, his face broke into a broad grin. We would see that smile quite often during the next few hours. Charlie was nervous!

Tony soon had Charlie in a very light state of hypnosis. When asked questions, he answered very matter-of-factly without any emotion. We could tell that he was recounting the incident from conscious memory. When first asked, he wasn't sure about the twins' seating arrangements in the canoe. However, as he proceeded to describe the UFO experience, his recall of the seating arrangements was correct. We decided to let him tell us what he could remember in this light hypnotic state. Then, as we had done with the others, Tony would deepen the level of hypnosis. We'll pick up his account when the four first noticed the UFO:

CHARLIE: Ah, I remember holding a flashlight—aiming it into the water and looking at the way it dispersed through the water and, ah, vegetation in the water. Ah, it was quiet, the water was as motionless as a mirror would be. It reflected all the stars in the sky. I remember hearing the loons and other sounds that night has up in the woods. And I remember Chuck saying, pretty suddenly like, "What the hell is that?" At which point, I remember turning and looking over my shoulder at, ah, what I at first thought was the moon rising above the trees. And then, no sooner had that thought gone through my mind than I realized that it wasn't the moon but a sphere, a globe of light. It looked like when you would turn on an incandescent lamp or an incandescent light bulb—how you see the brilliance of the white, but at the same time you can see the yellow of the filament glowing as a distinct color... it was bright but it didn't hurt your eyes to look at it. Ah, I remember that we just sat there and stared at it for a few minutes.... And then it began to move along the tree line right at the water's edge about 10 to 15 feet above the tops of the trees.

TONY: Away from you? Towards you? Or...?

Charlie's voice droned on with the precision of an automaton. The smile on his face had long disappeared. He showed no emotion and described the incident as an aloof observer of the past:

CHARLIE: To our right. As we watched it, it moved parallel with the shore. And I remember taking a flashlight, which was a large flashlight with the push-button switch in front of the handle. And I aimed it at the sphere of light and I pushed off an S.O.S.—three quick flashes, three long flashes and three quick flashes at which point it stopped. And when it stopped, I remember it seemed as though it were coming towards us. A solid object that you could see through a transparent object. And a shaft, or beam of light with a bluish cast, but it looked...solid. It came straight down and hit the reeds in the water and started coming out across towards us, at which point, it seemed like a unanimous decision that we could see it just as well from our campsite as we could from where we were. We didn't have any life jackets or anything. I remember Jack or Jim saying something about, you know, "Let's not drown. Let's get out of here,"—or something

like that. But it was like instantaneous, ah, that
we were paddling toward our camp, and then I
remember as we started pulling away, the light
extinguished but the sphere stayed. Ah, then I
remember standing by the canoe, in, ah, in the
water right at the shore. My feet were wet. I
looked at my watch. I had a, a watch that I
bought while I was in the service, a Seiko diver's
watch, ah, large stainless steel watch with orange face. And I remember the time was about
10:10 P.M. And I looked at the sweep hand, and
I looked back at the sphere which was then going along it's original course toward the peninsula or point of land opposite us. When it
reached the point of the peninsula, it ascended
up and away and it, ah, I, I don't know what angle. I would guess a 45 or so degree angle. There
were two small clouds in the sky—long and narrow. Once again, this beam of light came on like
a headlight from a car, and it passed the two
clouds. I noted the sweep hand on the watch
when it started moving away and I watched it,
and it just became a pinpoint of light. Never
made a noise. It was going up and away and becoming smaller and smaller until we lost sight of
it. It was a pinpoint of light with the stars. I
looked at the sweep hand of my watch again,
and it seemed as if only eight or ten seconds had
passed. And then I remember standing, talking
with Jim and Jack and Chuck and speculating
as to what we had just seen. Ah, I knew that it
wasn't an aircraft that I was familiar with. Ah, it
was not a balloon. And, ah, we told the ranger at
our next campsite about it.

Charlie did not remember falling asleep at the table. He
thought they had talked about the object for a few hours before
going to sleep. He did recall that the fire was almost out and
that they were puzzled as to how it burned down so fast. Charlie
also did not remember the beam catching up to the canoe. He
remembered paddling and suddenly being ashore, watching the
object moving away from them. It was at this juncture, that we
felt it was time to place Charlie more deeply into the state of
hypnosis. Tony did this and a dramatic change took place.
Charlie no longer sat upright in the easy chair. He now slumped
deeply into the chair as if he were in a deep sleep. His normal,
matter-of-fact voice became sleepy-sounding and very slow.
Tony brought him back to where the beam from the UFO was
moving toward the canoe. Charlie was smiling again!

TONY:	Do you see that beam of light?
CHARLIE:	Um-hum.
TONY:	Describe the light to us.
CHARLIE:	It—just—looks like a tube of light.
TONY:	How do you know that it looks like a tube of light?
CHARLIE:	Cause it looks like a tube of light.
TONY:	What does it do now?
CHARLIE:	(Voice becomes anxious.) Keeps coming at me!
TONY:	Does it finally reach you?

Charlie would not answer. His face became contorted as if he were in great distress. Finally, after Tony calmed him, Charlie answered the question:

CHARLIE:	I don't know.
TONY:	When do you first realize that it is a tube of light and not just a solid beam?
CHARLIE:	You can see it. It looks like, ah, like a glass—blue glass tube. Solid.
TONY:	How close does that glass tube get to the canoe?
CHARLIE:	I don't know.

It soon became apparent that Charlie's memory block had taken effect just before the beam of light engulfed the canoe. All he could remember was the beam of light blinking out and then being on shore. So, Tony again eased Charlie into a deeper level of hypnosis before probing Charlie's mind on the matter:

TONY:	You're paddling for shore and—when does the blue light go out?
CHARLIE:	I don't know (with a shaky voice). It's out. We're paddling. It's out.
TONY:	How soon after the light goes out do you reach the shore? Seconds? Minutes?
CHARLIE:	I don't know. It seems, ah, time—doesn't—seem—to—be—moving.
TONY:	Just relax. You're doing very well. Go back when that blue light is on. Do you look up?
CHARLIE:	I'm looking at the sphere of light.

Suddenly, the next question broke through the memory block. It unintentionally snapped Charlie's memory to an incident that he experienced while on board the craft:

TONY: Are you on the outside (i.e., of the blue tube) looking at it or are you inside looking out?

CHARLIE: Jeez!!! (Becomes very agitated.)

TONY: Relax, you're doing very well. Does anything surprise you now as you're sitting there thinking about this?

CHARLIE: Yeah! (Breathlessly.)

TONY: That's all right. It's okay. You're doing very well. What is that?

CHARLIE: The canoe!

TONY: The canoe? What about it?

Charlie's voice was trembling as he finally told us what was troubling him:

CHARLIE: It's in the water—it's underneath us!

A chill crept up my spine when Charlie made this revelation to us. I glanced anxiously at Tony with anticipation. Tony, as always, took things in stride and proceeded calmly with Charlie:

TONY: In what way is it underneath you?

CHARLIE: I'm looking at it!

TONY: From what distance?

CHARLIE: I'm above it! (Lets out deep sigh.)

TONY: How many feet above it are you? Just relax. You're doing fine. Just relax.

Charlie did not respond. He was panting so heavily that he could hardly catch his breath. He knew where he was now, and it wasn't in the canoe!

TONY: Just relax. Everything's safe. Where is the canoe now?

CHARLIE: (Still fights for breath.) It's...below me. It seems—it's just—it's sitting there on the water. Oh God! (See Figure 16.)

TONY: How far above it are you?

Figure 16. Charlie Foltz's drawing of looking down at the canoe from 80 to 100 feet in the air.

CHARLIE: I dunno, maybe 100 feet—80 feet.

TONY: What is above you?

CHARLIE: I dunno. I'm not looking up. I'm looking at the canoe.

TONY: How long do you look at it—for one minute?

CHARLIE: I can't take my eyes off it.

TONY: What happens one minute after you find yourself above the canoe?

CHARLIE: (Does not respond.)

TONY: It's perfectly all right. What happens two minutes after you notice the canoe beneath you?

CHARLIE: (Agitated/long pause.) I don't know. I feel like I want to look around but I don't want to look around.

TONY: Did you look around?

CHARLIE: (Does not respond.)

TONY: Look around where? Look around for what?

CHARLIE:	Behind me. Beside me. I just want to look for-ward. I just want to see—see the trees and see the water and see the lake.
TONY:	How long do you continue to see them? Just re-lax. How long do you continue to see them? It's perfectly all right.
CHARLIE:	(Pants heavily; tries to answer, but swallows hard and does not.)
TONY:	Does there come a time when you don't see the trees anymore? Or the lake? Or the canoe?
CHARLIE:	(Pauses.) Yeah. It's like a ceiling. It's gray, white—white. Pearl.
TONY:	What has a ceiling?
CHARLIE:	Whatever I'm looking at.
TONY:	And what—describe it again please. What color is it?
CHARLIE:	Like a pearl. A gray-white (pauses).
TONY:	What do you see in front of you? Just relax. Just relax. It's perfectly all right. You're perfectly safe. Just relax.

It seems as if watching the canoe, lake and trees were like a security blanket for Charlie. He didn't want to see what was around him:

CHARLIE:	I want to see the canoe!
TONY:	But what do you see instead of the canoe?
CHARLIE:	(Sighs deeply.) I dunno.
TONY:	Just relax. Just relax. Look down at your feet (pauses). What do you see?
CHARLIE:	My toes.
TONY:	Your toes? Why don't you see your shoes?
CHARLIE:	(With panic in his voice.) I don't know! I see my toes!
TONY:	What are you standing on?

Tony's question about standing appeared to instigate Charlie's mind to jump to still another traumatic segment of his experience aboard the UFO. When Charlie saw his toes, it was not when he was standing, watching the canoe:

CHARLIE:	I'm not. I'm lying down.
TONY:	You're lying down on what?
CHARLIE:	My back. (See Figure 17.)

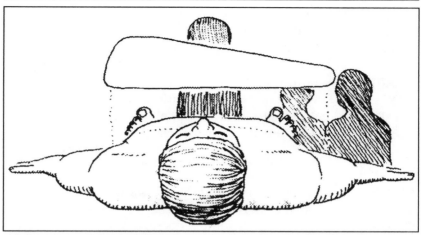

Figure 17. Charlie Foltz's impression of seeing his toes and realizing that he was naked. The panel is on his chest.

TONY: Are you on a floor. Are you on a table? Are you
                on a...

Charlie's violent reaction to this question stopped Tony mid-sentence. He immediately went to his assistance and tried to calm him down:

TONY: Just relax. Keep your eyes closed and just relax.
                Just relax. Why are you lying down?
CHARLIE: I dunno.
TONY: Are your eyes open while you're lying down?
CHARLIE: I don't want to open 'em. I keep 'em closed.
TONY: Why are you scared? What is there to be scared
                of?
CHARLIE: (Pauses.) I'm nervous.
TONY: Why are you nervous?
CHARLIE: 'Cause I'm not in the canoe.
TONY: Who is with you?
CHARLIE: (Does not respond.)
TONY: Can you hear anything?
CHARLIE: My heart. I hear my heart.
TONY: Why is it that you can see your toes?
CHARLIE: 'Cause I lifted my head and looked at my feet.
TONY: Are there any other articles of clothes missing?
CHARLIE: Yeah, I'm not wearing anything.

TONY:	What is the texture of what you're lying on? What does it feel like?
CHARLIE:	It's like—it's like cool leather.
TONY:	How long do you lie there?
CHARLIE:	I dunno.
RAY:	Where are Jim, Jack and Chuck?
CHARLIE:	(In a scared voice.) I don't know! I don't know!
TONY:	Just relax. Just relax. You're doing okay. Every time you exhale, every time you exhale, just relax. (With a demanding voice.) Why are you on that table?
CHARLIE:	(Does not respond; is still somewhat agitated.)
TONY:	Do you know?
CHARLIE:	I'm afraid. It's like a doctor's office. It's colder.
TONY:	Do you see anything that suggests that?
CHARLIE:	(Does not respond.)
TONY:	What happens after you're on the table?
CHARLIE:	Just, just keep thinking I want to be back in the canoe.
TONY:	I understand. Just describe anything that's significant between the time you're on the table and the time you get back in the canoe.
CHARLIE:	Over here is something in the wall that looks like a, like a doctor's (pauses) equipment. It's like it would be a cabinet, but it's in the wall.
TONY:	Glass doors or solid doors?
CHARLIE:	No, they're like white but there's like a (pauses) black (pauses) screen. It's like looking in the oven when the light—when the oven is closed (sighs).
TONY:	Okay. When did you see it—before you were on the table? While you were on the table or after you were on the table?
CHARLIE:	I looked at it when I was lying on the table, and I closed my eyes.
TONY:	What else did you see before you closed your eyes?
CHARLIE:	(Does not respond; suddenly starts gasping for breath.)
TONY:	It's perfectly okay. You're doing very well. It's okay to share with us. What is it you see?
CHARLIE:	I see (gasps as he talks) I see Jim and Chuck and Jack!
TONY:	Where are they?

Figure 18. Charlie Foltz, with the panel on his chest, sees his companions sitting on the bench. By Charlie Foltz.

CHARLIE:	They're sitting on the bench.
TONY:	What bench?
CHARLIE:	Just, ah—outside this room.
TONY:	What are they doing?
CHARLIE:	(Voice trembles.) They're just sitting there and doing nothing. Just looking. Just—they're looking out in front of them. (See Figure 18.)
RAY:	Are they alone?
CHARLIE:	(Breathes heavily.) There's somebody with their back to me in front of them (pants).
RAY:	What does he look like or what does she look like?
CHARLIE:	Just see their back—like a kid.
RAY:	Why?
CHARLIE:	Looks like a (pauses) they're standing there with their back to me.
RAY:	Can you see the back of the head?
CHARLIE:	Yeah.
RAY:	What does that look like?
CHARLIE:	Smooth.
RAY:	Much hair?
CHARLIE:	No hair.
TONY:	Why did you say "They?"

CHARLIE:	'Cause there's somebody standing by my right shoulder and somebody over by my left by my side.
TONY:	You said—"Like a kid"—Why did you say that?
CHARLIE:	'Cause they're as big as a kid.
TONY:	How big is a kid?
CHARLIE:	(Pauses.) Maybe four foot eight? Five foot tall.
TONY:	You said they have no hair?
CHARLIE:	Yeah.
TONY:	Just come down lower—on the head—on the face and tell us what you see.
CHARLIE:	(Does not answer; becomes very agitated.)
TONY:	(Calms Charlie, then continues.) What do you see? Just relax. If you were going to do a sketch—if you were doing a realistic sketch, what would you include?
CHARLIE:	The head is like almond-shaped—like egg-shaped and a long thin neck like a girl—petite, like an Asian girl.
TONY:	What about the facial features?
CHARLIE:	(Pauses for a long time before answering.) They're like Asian (pause). Like large Asian al-mond eyes.
RAY:	Do they have eyelashes?
CHARLIE:	(Pauses.) I don't know.
RAY:	Do they have eyelids?
CHARLIE:	They close their eyes.
RAY:	They do? How do they close? Up and down? Sideways?
CHARLIE:	(Pauses.) Like a bird's. There's a flash or some-thing that goes across the eye when the eye, when the eye closes (pauses). Like a bird.
RAY:	Do they have pupils?
CHARLIE:	I don't know.
RAY:	Continue describing the rest of the face.
CHARLIE:	(Pauses for a long time before answering.) They don't—they don't have like a mouth—like—like if your lips were sealed. But they, the one that had its back to me had something under his chin here.
RAY:	You missed the nose. You talked about eyes, you talked about a mouth—what about a nose?
CHARLIE:	It's like an Asian nose.
TONY:	In what way?

CHARLIE: It's long—doesn't protrude out (pauses) comes down like this.

RAY: Large nostrils or small nostrils?

CHARLIE: Small compared to mine.

RAY: How were the ears compared to yours?

CHARLIE: Smaller.

RAY: Do they stick out like our ears?

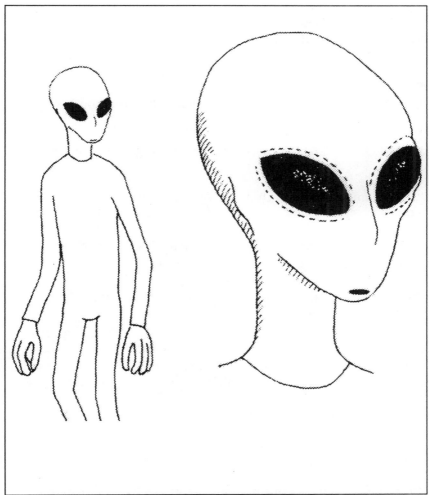

Figure 19. Charlie Foltz's impressions of the alien's physical appearance.

CHARLIE:	They're like the nose and the mouth. But they're ears.
RAY:	How can you tell?
CHARLIE:	That's where they belong.
RAY:	What does the ear look like? Does it protrude out?
CHARLIE:	From the back, it lies close. (See Figure 19.)
TONY:	You said how many were standing by you? By the table?
CHARLIE:	Two.
TONY:	And where are they?
CHARLIE:	One by my right shoulder and the other by my side on the left.
RAY:	What are they wearing?
CHARLIE:	(Pauses.) Clothing—something—smooth—close-fitting but loose. Not baggy but...
RAY:	What color?
CHARLIE:	Like a gray-white. Everything seems to be a gray-white.

It should be noted that the aliens' shiny coveralls reflected and took on the color of their surroundings at any given time:

RAY:	What would you compare it with or to?
CHARLIE:	Sort of like, ah, those aerobic clothes.
RAY:	Do they have gloves?
CHARLIE:	The one by my side, I think, has gloves.
RAY:	Why do you think that?
CHARLIE:	I can see part of his hands.... He's doing something.... He's looking at something.
RAY:	What's the something look like?
CHARLIE:	It's like a tray (sighs) or a panel or something. It's cool.... It's above my chest.
TONY:	When do you sit up?
CHARLIE:	I sit up—I am sitting up now.... The one behind me helped me sit up.
TONY:	What happened to the tray that was over your chest?
CHARLIE:	(Does not respond; starts to hyperventilate.)
TONY:	Just relax. Just relax. What did it feel like when he helped you sit up?
CHARLIE:	Like I was tired.
TONY:	Why were you tired?

CHARLIE:	(Breathes heavily.) Because I wanted to get out. I want to get back to the canoe.
TONY:	Okay, just relax. You're doing very well. You're doing very well. Just relax. Just relax. Tell us why you wanted to get out.
CHARLIE:	(Blows out air and coughs.) We shouldn't be here!
TONY:	How do you know? Why not?
CHARLIE:	(Becomes extremely upset.) We should be in the canoe!
TONY:	After you sit up, what happens next?
CHARLIE:	I sit on the bench.
TONY:	What bench?
CHARLIE:	With the guys.
TONY:	All of them?
CHARLIE:	(Shakes his head "No.")
RAY:	Why not all of them?
CHARLIE:	'Cause, 'cause (pauses) there's only three of us here.
RAY:	Who's missing?
CHARLIE:	Jim.
RAY:	Do you see Jim?
CHARLIE:	He's where I just came from.
RAY:	Where is that?
CHARLIE:	Just in the room. Just on the other side. Just a few feet from where I am.
RAY:	What is he doing?
CHARLIE:	He's going to lie down.
TONY:	What's he wearing?
CHARLIE:	(Pauses a long time before answering.) Nothing. I see his feet. They're bare, too.
TONY:	Can you see the rest of him?
CHARLIE:	(Pauses.) Just about up to his knees (pauses). And his left leg.
RAY:	What happens after he lays down?
CHARLIE:	(Starts breathing heavily again.) One fellow stands at his head like he did with me and the other at his side.
RAY:	What do they do?
CHARLIE:	They have a panel or tray—panel—above his chest.
RAY:	What's holding it there?

CHARLIE:	I can't see.
RAY:	What do they do with the tray?
CHARLIE:	They're doing something. They're taking things from it and putting things back on it.
TONY:	What do they do with the things they take off the tray?
CHARLIE:	They're touching Jim.
RAY:	Where?
CHARLIE:	On his arm and his chest, and, ah...

Charlie stopped mid-sentence and looked reluctant to continue his description of what the aliens were doing to Jim.

CHARLIE:	(Sighs.) I don't want to watch.
RAY:	Do you watch?
CHARLIE:	Um. They're taking (pauses) like skin—scratching—scraping.
RAY:	Where?
CHARLIE:	On his arm and shoulder. His leg (pauses).
RAY:	Yeah, what happens next?
CHARLIE:	I don't want to watch.
RAY:	Do you watch?
CHARLIE:	(Does not respond.)
RAY:	(In a demanding tone.) Do you watch?
CHARLIE:	I just look—look—look at it. Just look out at the sky.
RAY:	Look out at the sky? How can you look out at the sky? You're in a room.
CHARLIE:	Um, where we were watching the canoe. Over there to the left of where we are.

Later on in this session, Charlie described a large port or window, in a wall to the left of the bench. Earlier he had seen the canoe in the lake below through it. Now all he could see was the night sky from this particular vantage point:

RAY:	What happens to Jim?
CHARLIE:	He's back.
RAY:	Back where?
CHARLIE:	On the bench beside me.
RAY:	Who else is on the bench?
CHARLIE:	Just Chuck and Jim and me.

RAY:	Where's Jack?
CHARLIE:	He's next.
RAY:	Next? What do you mean?
CHARLIE:	(With trembling voice.) H-H-He's in there.
RAY:	He's in there? What can you remember seeing?
CHARLIE:	(Rehearses sequence of events.) Person brings Jim out and he sits. And Jack stands—and they lead him in.
RAY:	What does Jack have on?
CHARLIE:	His clothes.
RAY:	Do they stay on?
CHARLIE:	(Shakes head "No.")
RAY:	How do they come off?
CHARLIE:	He took them off.
RAY:	What comes next?
CHARLIE:	Sits down—lies on his back. They stand like they stood before and do what they did before.
RAY:	What do they do?
CHARLIE:	They put the panel over your chest—and they scrape your arms—and your chest—your legs—your thighs. It's like a physical.
RAY:	What else do they do?
CHARLIE:	(Pauses for a long time before answering.) They look at Jim.
RAY:	I thought Jim was on the bench beside you.
CHARLIE:	Um-hum, they just look at him, and they look at Jack.
RAY:	Who looked at Jim—the same people that are looking at Jack?
CHARLIE:	The one standing by his shoulder.
RAY:	Whose shoulder?
CHARLIE:	Jack's shoulder. Looks toward Jim (pauses for a long time). It's like they're interested why they look the same.
RAY:	How do you know that?
CHARLIE:	(Does not respond.)
RAY:	What do they do next to Jack?
CHARLIE:	They bring him back out.
RAY:	What happens next?
CHARLIE:	(Pauses.) They put us back in the canoe.
RAY:	How?
CHARLIE:	I don't know.

RAY:	You're all on the bench. What happens next?
CHARLIE:	I'm looking at the canoe again.
RAY:	Before that. How did you get your clothes back on?
CHARLIE:	I must have put them back on.
RAY:	Do you remember putting them back on? How do Jim and Jack and Chuck get their clothes back on?
CHARLIE:	They had 'em on.
RAY:	They had 'em on? How did they get them on?
CHARLIE:	I guess they put them back on.
RAY:	Did you see them put them back on?
CHARLIE:	Uh-uh, but I can see the canoe again.
RAY:	How can you see it?
CHARLIE:	From the window.
RAY:	What does the window look like? What shape?
CHARLIE:	It's like a picture window, curved.
RAY:	What happens after you look through the window?
CHARLIE:	(Pauses for a long time before answering.) I just want to be back in the canoe.

It had been obvious to us for some time that Charlie was only reliving certain segments of his on-board experience. His mind seemed to jump indiscriminately to particular events. Sometimes this was triggered by a word or phrase used during our questioning. For the time being, we decided to let him continue his description of how the four got back in the canoe. He wanted desperately to do so. This desire was paramount in his mind from the beginning of his on-board memories. It served as an impediment to our goal of obtaining a chronological account of the event:

RAY:	What happens after you look through the window?
CHARLIE:	(Pauses for a long time.) I just want to be back in the canoe.
RAY:	Um-hum, but what happens after you look through the window?
CHARLIE:	They take us away from the window.
RAY:	Where do they take you?
CHARLIE:	It's like in another room. It seems like it's a couple steps down.

RAY:	Um-hum. What's in the other room?
CHARLIE:	There's panels with lights.
RAY:	Okay, you're in the room. You've gone a few steps. You see panels with lights. What happens next?
CHARLIE:	(Pauses a very long time before answering.) We're getting back in the canoe.
RAY:	How did you get there?
CHARLIE:	We're stepping into the canoe.
RAY:	What happened before that? You're in the room with the panels and lights. What happened just after you went in the room with the panels and lights?
CHARLIE:	Well, we're standing there together.
RAY:	Together? And what do you see?
CHARLIE:	We followed the person that brought us in and two others.
RAY:	Okay. What did they do?
CHARLIE:	They just stand over in a corner.
RAY:	Where are you standing? What's right in front of you?
CHARLIE:	This person that brought us in the room.
RAY:	What's to the left of him?
CHARLIE:	Nothing. There's the wall behind him.
RAY:	What's to the right of him?
CHARLIE:	(Pauses.) Like a wall.
RAY:	Like a wall? Is it a wall?
CHARLIE:	It's where we're going out.
RAY:	So, you're heading toward the wall. What happens next?
CHARLIE:	We're getting back in the canoe.
RAY:	Who's with you?
CHARLIE:	The fella [alien] helping us into the canoe.
TONY:	And then what happens?
CHARLIE:	We sit there for a second.
TONY:	And then what?
CHARLIE:	And this thing goes back to the trees.
RAY:	What goes back to the trees?
CHARLIE:	The sphere [UFO].

Charlie did not describe the machine that Jack had mentioned in the same manner. We could assume Jack's round light in the wall and Charlie's panels of light in the wall were different ways of describing the same device. Charlie also described his passage through the wall as being like going through a door. I made a note to check on this later. A joint meeting was planned to be held after all hypnosis sessions were completed. At this time, we planned to go over any questions raised during the sessions. I had hoped that Charlie would mention the beam. I felt certain that it had something to do with transporting them to and from the object. I did not want to ask him about this directly. We did our best not to ask leading questions. But I did inquire about the whereabouts of the mysterious beam:

RAY: Where is the beam?

CHARLIE: It's out.

RAY: When was the last time you saw the beam?

CHARLIE: When it was turned on. When it was going through two small clouds [i.e., during the UFO's departure].

RAY: Did you see the beam when you were in the room before you went into the canoe?

CHARLIE: Yeah.

RAY: Where was it?

CHARLIE: (Matter-of-factly) It moored the canoe.

RAY: It what?

CHARLIE: (Loudly) It moored the canoe!

RAY: Was it touching the canoe?

CHARLIE: Yeah.

RAY: Where was the other end?

CHARLIE: Under our feet somewhere....When we were looking at the canoe. We're like above it.

RAY: Is the beam hollow?

CHARLIE: It looks like it. It's like a tube.

This was extremely interesting. It would appear that the beam stretched from where Charlie stepped through the wall down to the canoe. Charlie stood looking down through the tube at the canoe below. His next impression was stepping down upon something he referred to as a landing and then being helped into the canoe by an alien being. He did not remember the extreme physical discomfort experienced by Jack as he went through the machine in the wall:

RAY: Did all of you step on the landing together?

CHARLIE:	We all did—one at a time.
RAY:	What happened next?
CHARLIE:	We're in the canoe.

Tony and I wondered whether Charlie could remember the abduction at this point. He did not remember. Like the twins, all he remembered was the close encounter with the UFO and paddling away from it. We decided to find out why, before proceeding with other questions:

TONY:	Why didn't any of you discuss what had happened?
CHARLIE:	I never thought anything happened.
TONY:	Why didn't you think something had happened?
CHARLIE:	I never thought anything happened except that we saw the sphere. It came toward us with the light [beam], and then the light went out.
TONY:	Why is that all you remember?
CHARLIE:	'Cause that's all I remember seeing.

Tony then took some time to deepen Charlie's level of hypnosis and then popped the proverbial 64-milion-dollar question:

TONY:	I'm going to ask you a question. You've been doing extremely well—extremely well for us. I'm going to ask you a question, and I want the first answer that comes to your mind. I don't want you to stop and think and analyze my question. Just give me the first answer as quickly as you can that comes to your mind. Did somebody tell you not to remember what happened?
CHARLIE:	Yes!
TONY:	Who told you not to remember?
CHARLIE:	The one that helped us into the canoe.
RAY:	How did he tell you?
CHARLIE:	(Pauses.) It was almost like he said it with his eyes.
RAY:	Did he ever tell you anything else with his eyes?
CHARLIE:	"Don't be afraid. Relax."

Since Charlie was once again mentally back on board the UFO, we decided to try to find out more about what the aliens did to him during the remaining few minutes of the hypnosis session. Thus far, he had been reluctant to describe their physical examination of him:

RAY: Did they hurt you in any way?

CHARLIE: I don't remember being hurt—scratched.

RAY: Did they take anything from you?

CHARLIE: (Pauses.) Sk-skin.

RAY: Anything else?

CHARLIE: S-S-Some samples of fluid.

RAY: Fluid from where?

CHARLIE: From my mouth. Some blood.

RAY: How did they take the blood?

CHARLIE: (Pauses.) The panel. There's something in the panel [i.e., the device they had lowered over his chest].

RAY: The panel did it, or they did it?

CHARLIE: Something they did with the panel.

RAY: Did you ever see the blood?

CHARLIE: (Pauses.) Something they put in the panel. Looks like it's a small pipette [a narrow glass tube in which liquid is drawn up through suction].

RAY: Where did they take the blood from?

CHARLIE: (Pauses.) Seemed like my neck.

RAY: What else did they take from you?

CHARLIE: Some skin scrapings.

RAY: What else?

CHARLIE: (Pauses.) T-T-Took some saliva from my mouth.

RAY: Yeah, what else?

CHARLIE: (Pauses; speaks drowsily.) Urine and feces. Some hair—fingernail clippings—toenail clippings. Um, when I close my eyes, I don't know what they're doing.

RAY: What did it feel like they were doing?

CHARLIE: They're taking scrapings from the insides of my thighs.

RAY: What else do you feel that they were doing [i.e., when he had his eyes closed]?

CHARLIE: Pressing—pushing. They test with other equipment—ah, groin.

RAY: What did they do around the groin area?

CHARLIE: They took sample of urine. They probed my testicles.

RAY: How did they probe your testicles?

CHARLIE: With something in their hand.

RAY: What did it look like?

CHARLIE: (Pauses.) It sort of put me in the mind of—like a hand-held scope. Sort of like a —like a micro-scope type of device.

RAY: Did it just touch? Did it penetrate? Did it rub? What did it do?

CHARLIE: Like gripped—had like—fingers. They put it down and clamped it, and then they looked, and they disconnected it.

RAY: Did they touch your penis?

CHARLIE: Just to examine it. Hooked urethra—took test swab—checked the scrota.

RAY: What did they do with these samples?

CHARLIE: They put them in the cabinet in the wall. But that's when they let me out.... They helped me up and sat me on the bench.

RAY: Where are your clothes?

CHARLIE: I put 'em on. They helped me.

RAY: What happened next?

CHARLIE: (Lets out a big sigh of relief.) They put us in the canoe and said that we were okay, and there was nothing to be afraid of and to go back to our place—not to remember—do not be troubled.

TONY: And what did you understand that to mean?

CHARLIE: Push it out of your mind. Don't worry about it.

I glanced at my watch. It was late and past our allotted time for the hypnosis session. Tony saw me signaling for him to close the session. He proceeded to bring Charlie out of hypnosis. I watched Charlie's body slowly but surely stiffen and come back to life from what appeared to be a deeply relaxed sleep. Like the others, he opened his eyes and just stared into space with a strange look on his face. The tape was left running for a few minutes to record his posthypnotic reaction. Tony broke the chilling silence that filled the room:

TONY: So, how do you feel?

CHARLIE: Feel like I've been sleeping.

TONY: How much time do you feel has elapsed.

CHARLIE: Maybe 15, 20 minutes.

TONY: Ah, closer to two hours.

CHARLIE: Really?

TONY: Yeah.

CHARLIE: (Looks disconcerted.) You know? I didn't remember any of that stuff before this.

RAY: (Laughs.) That sounds like a recording. Neither did the others.... How do you feel about what you remembered?

CHARLIE: Nervous. 'Cause—I don't think I—I would tell anybody anything that I said here at all.

RAY: You don't feel frightened about the incident at all?

CHARLIE: (Sighs.) Anxious. Ah, I feel like I just got off an elevator that just dropped too quickly—that hollow pit in your stomach. That's what I got right now.

RAY: We would be very appreciative if you don't talk to Jim, Jack or Chuck about anything that you remember at all. When this whole thing is over—when we've gone through this whole thing—we'll get together and talk about it then—but not until it is all over. We don't want to contaminate the others' minds with what you remember and vice-versa. It's very important that we just don't talk about it.

CHARLIE: (In his matter-of-fact way.) One thing seems—that strikes me funny—now it's understandable—was Jack's reaction when he came back from his session. He walked in the door and he said, "I have to have a drink!" Well, like I need a drink now!

TONY: (Laughs.) Wait until you get home.

We gave Charlie some time to calm down before he set off for Boston in his car. The distraught expression on his face showed the effect of the vexing memories that now flooded his mind. To Charlie, like the twins, life would never be the same again.

CHAPTER **6**

Through the Portal

During the next several weeks, I pored over the typed transcripts of the hypnotic regression sessions. I felt as if I were working on a gigantic jigsaw puzzle, trying to piece together a coherent, chronological account of the Allagash abductions. Most of the pieces fitted together easily but others did not. These pieces involved memories that were peculiar to each abductee's vantage point. In addition, Charlie had resisted remembering certain traumatic events on board the craft. Of the three, his testimony was the hardest to extract. Tony highlighted this difficulty in his evaluation, written just a day after the session.

May 21, 1989

Dear Ray,

Yesterday was another enlightening experience.... Charlie Foltz presented the greatest challenge to me, as a hypnotist, thus far, out of the three we've worked with.

During the pre-induction talk, his literal answers to common metaphorical comments and questions suggested a personality whom it would be difficult to hypnotize.... Perhaps even more disconcerting, while serving as further evidence of his inability to relax, was his constant smiling during the induction and subsequent deepening. When Charlie was asked to relate what happened, he again smiled frequently and related those events in the past tense while he was in the canoe...("we were rowing...we sat up and discussed"). Approximately one hour into the induction, a change came over Charlie. His narrative was less and less interrupted with smiles; his head drooped; his body and demeanor assumed what we generally expect from a hypnotized subject; his voice slowed; his breathing became more shallow; and he began to speak in the present tense ("One is standing by my side...the others are sitting on the bench..."). Also, if you will recall, he clutched his hands together, tight—loose, intermittently, an indication to me that he was agitated about what he was remembering/reliving.

If anything, Charlie's initial nervousness made me believe more readily that what he recalled was what he experienced. While I can't estimate what percentage of information from these three individuals coincides, it seems to me to be very consistent. What will be especially enlightening is that future get-together when all can speak—give and take—so we can establish a more precise chronology of what happened to whom, etc.

Good to see you and work with you again, Ray. Keep in touch.

—Tony

I also looked forward to the joint meeting that Tony alluded to in his report. I hoped it would answer a number of questions that had arisen during the initial sessions. But such thoughts were premature. Such a meeting would not take place in the near future. A number of totally unexpected revelations would prevent this. In the meantime, we had the last of the Allagash four to deal with—Chuck Rak.

Hypnosis Sessions #1, #2—Chuck Rak (June 10 / October 3, 1989)

Dave's schedule again prohibited him from attending the hypnosis session. Poor Tony had a terrible cold that had suddenly blossomed overnight, however he was in attendance along with Chuck Rak, Mary Weiner and myself. Mary came along to keep Chuck company on the long drive from Vermont. Chuck's wife, Kim, could not make it that day.

It didn't take long to discover that Chuck was as different from his companions as night is from day. He came across as tough, self-reliant and fearless. As I looked him over and listened to him talk, I could easily picture him living in that tree hut of past years. Chuck had instigated the Allagash camping trip and had directed his fellow campers like a drill sergeant. He was strictly a no-nonsense man, and was ready to get down to the business of hypnosis at once. Clearly, he wanted to know what had occurred during the missing hours on the Allagash. However, Tony and I sensed behind this show of brashness, a bit of apprehension on Chuck's part concerning hypnosis.

Tony, between sniffles and blowing his nose, placed Chuck in a light state of hypnosis. Chuck, like the others, rehearsed the events that had led up to the encounter. When he mentioned the building of the bonfire, Tony queried him regarding its size. At that time, the fire was the only physical clue we had that indicated a period of missing time!

TONY: Was it a big fire?

CHUCK: Yeah, it was a big fire—as big as we dared to make it. We cleared all the way around it. And Jack was worried that it was going to get out of control. And we told him, "Don't worry, it will be okay."

Then Chuck was allowed to continue the now familiar narrative up until the time the UFO appeared in the sky:

CHUCK: Well, we went fishing when we got to the spot (pauses). And we caught another chub...we got discouraged and started paddling back towards the fire. And I was in the back...paddling and steering. And I had a sensation of (pauses) something looking at me. And I turned over my right shoulder, and there was this ball of light hanging in the sky. Noiseless...quite stark against the night sky. And I said to everyone else in the canoe, "That's a hell of a case of swamp gas!" It kept on changing color from red to green to white. And it [the colors] had a way of moving around the polar and equatorial...seemed to be energy impulses that helped to initiate a fluid color change. It was a heavy, dense fluid like plasma.

Chuck then reiterated how Charlie flashed off an S.O.S. signal at it with his flashlight, which caused the object to react:

CHUCK: At that point, the thing sent down a cone-shaped beam of light. It was not as bright as the actual object. It was kind of a dull bluish-gray. It formed an ellipse on the surface of the water and it started moving towards us.

Chuck showed absolutely no emotion as he described what should have made most people frightened out of their wits. The cool, analytical manner in which he depicted the unfolding event was also reflected in his actual personal reaction to it:

CHUCK: And I remember being very interested. My curiosity was at the highest point it has ever been in my life. And I felt that we were going to make some contact with something very unusual. And then, one of the twins mentioned that we had to get out of the water. And I thought, "Why? We're all right staying here." And then a panic ensued. And they [twins] dipped their hands into the water [i.e. to paddle—only Chuck and Charlie had paddles]. I kept staring at the object, never taking my eyes off it, thinking—"It's too bad about their [the twins] parochial school upbringing and that they believe in witches and demons. We're perfectly all right where we are. No need to go to shore." And I felt very disappointed.

RAY: And then what happened?

CHUCK: (With a puzzled expression) And then we got back to shore. We're at the shore! I don't even remember how we found ourselves at shore. Seemed like we were sleepy and ready for bed. Sat around at the table for awhile...and we all went to bed. The fire was out.

It was apparent that Chuck was retelling, not reliving, the Allagash experience, and with little or no emotion. Tony decided to deepen the hypnosis and bring Chuck back in time to where the beam approached the canoe. At present, he had no recollection of the beam ever reaching the canoe. His next remembrance was suddenly being on shore watching the UFO whisk away into the night.

Try as he may, Tony could not get Chuck to remember the beam actually reaching the canoe. Over and over again, like the repetition of a taped message on a recorder, Chuck recounted the same thing. In desperation, Tony again deepened Chuck's hypnotic state and tried again. Finally, there was a breakthrough. Chuck even exhibited a little emotion—but not much:

TONY:	Okay, how close is it now?
CHUCK:	It seems to be right near us.
TONY:	And then what happens?
CHUCK:	It's right (pauses)—it's right (pauses) over—it's over!
TONY:	Over what?
CHUCK:	Over us.
TONY:	Look up and tell us what you see.
CHUCK:	It's like a tunnel.
TONY:	And then what happens? Just relax. It's so good to relax. I know. And then what happens?
CHUCK:	(Does not answer and starts to breath heavily.)
TONY:	Just relax. It's like watching a slow-motion film. What happens?
CHUCK:	(Sounds frustrated.) I'm trying to remember.
TONY:	I know. You're doing very, very well. Just relax. Just relax. Ah, this beam of light is over the canoe, and you said it looks like a tunnel. And then what happens?

During a follow-up hypnosis session, Session #2, Chuck told us that at this same point he "felt separated" and that his companion's voices were getting dimmer until he heard them no more. It was apparent that he was being lifted from the canoe through the beam and into the glowing craft. This was borne out as he continued his testimony during this session:

CHUCK:	Something's at the end of the tunnel.
TONY:	What do you see at the end of the tunnel?
CHUCK:	It's almost like a barrier...seems solid.
TONY:	Okay, and then what happens?
CHUCK:	Getting drawn towards it.
TONY:	And then what happens?
CHUCK:	(Swallows hard, clears throat but does not answer.)
TONY:	And then what happens?

At this point, Chuck paused for a long time before answering. When he did finally respond, he sounded surprised:

| CHUCK: | Um, I—passing through a barrier! |

TONY:	Okay, you pass through the barrier—and—tell us what you see.
CHUCK:	(Groans; does not answer.)
TONY:	Just relax, just relax.
CHUCK:	A room.
TONY:	What kind of a room?
CHUCK:	Circular.
TONY:	What colors do you see?
CHUCK:	Um, sort of a yellowish-silver-blue.
TONY:	Look down at your feet and tell us what you see.
CHUCK:	It's bright, bright, but not overly so.
TONY:	And you're standing on it [i.e. this bright area]?
CHUCK:	Yeah.
TONY:	Now, look to your left and tell us what you see.
CHUCK:	(Starts breathing heavily again; does not answer.)
TONY:	You're doing very well. It's so pleasant to sit quietly. Just relax.
CHUCK:	Seems like a rib structure of some kind.
TONY:	Okay, look to your right and tell us what do you see?
CHUCK:	(Breathes heavily.) It's a continuation of an ellipse.
TONY:	And look overhead. As you raise your head up—what do you see?
CHUCK:	A brighter area. Seems to be encircled with (pauses) dark—a dark circle.
TONY:	Can you draw all of this for us later?
CHUCK:	Yeah.

For several minutes, Chuck began reliving the experience and actually showed some emotion. This seemed to be the result of suddenly finding himself in strange surroundings and not being in the canoe. Then his disposition again became calm, cool and collected, as he became accustomed to his new environment. In its own way, Chuck's uncanny temperament was just as disconcerting to us as Charlie's illogical smile had been:

TONY:	Good, can you move as you stand there?
CHUCK:	(Pauses.) Not really (pauses). I—moving isn't the issue.
TONY:	What is the issue?

CHUCK:	Just wanting to know.
TONY:	Know what?
CHUCK:	Just wanting to know where I am!
TONY:	Is there anyone there with you?
CHUCK:	(Pauses.) Ah, I can't—I don't have a clear memory.
TONY:	Can you look behind you?
CHUCK:	No.
TONY:	Why not?
CHUCK:	Don't desire to.
TONY:	Why not?
CHUCK:	'Cause I want to go forward.
TONY:	Where do you go?
CHUCK:	Forward and a little bit to the right.
TONY:	Describe the area, Chuck?
CHUCK:	(Pauses.) Oh, look's like the vet's office.
TONY:	What is there that's similar to a vet's office?
CHUCK:	A silvery table…. Um, I keep thinking I'm seeing figures…. Ah, they're—don't have a very clear image of them—they're not the same—not the same frequency. It's like a radio station—can't get it in clear.

From the time Chuck stepped off the bright area and moved forward, he seemed to be in a somnambulistic-like state. It was as if he were moving in a trance and not under his own volition. In fact, in a later hypnosis session, [Session # 2] he exclaimed, "It's like, it's like I have no control over myself. No voluntary control."

Tony continued his questioning:

TONY:	Is it possible for you to sketch what you see?
CHUCK:	In a vague way.
TONY:	Okay, and then what happens?
CHUCK:	They're ushering me to the table.
TONY:	How many?
CHUCK:	Three or four figures, but they're not all the same distance from me.
TONY:	When they usher you—do they touch you?
CHUCK:	(Pauses.) Gently…they put me on the table (pauses) a little bit cool (groans) they put me on the table.
TONY:	Do you notice anything about yourself?

CHUCK:	Almost like I'm drugged.
TONY:	Let your eyes turn on your body, and what do you see?
CHUCK:	I see my midsection...they're examining me...they're rolling down my pants.
TONY:	And then what happens?
CHUCK:	(Sighs.) They just seem very interested in that part of my body...they're looking at it intensely...they put more light on it...they (swallows hard)—something—it's almost like something fluttering—like a butterfly—it's coming, it's coming down on me.
TONY:	What area of you?
CHUCK:	It's my penis.
TONY:	And then what happens?
CHUCK:	(Pauses for a long time.) Something black and—black—then I can't remember.
TONY:	And then what happens?
CHUCK:	(Breathes heavily; appears to be in great distress.)
TONY:	Just relax. Just relax.
CHUCK:	Something oozing.
TONY:	Oozing from where?
CHUCK:	Ah, from my penis.
TONY:	Did they cause that?
CHUCK:	Yeah.
TONY:	And then what happened?
CHUCK:	They (pauses) take it [the sperm sample] away.
RAY:	In what?
CHUCK:	Black—this thing they—they used to—they're taking it away—it seems to have joints to it.
RAY:	How big is it?
CHUCK:	It's bigger than my folding lamp. It's, it's like they use in a dentist's office...something with a long end, and it's got joints and it can fold and move.
TONY:	And then what happened?
CHUCK:	(Takes big breath and exhales loudly.) I'm moving.
TONY:	Where are you moving?
CHUCK:	To my right, it seems.
TONY:	What is there?
CHUCK:	Another couple of figures.

Figure 20. Chuck Rak's illustration of one of his abductors.

TONY:	Are they any more distinct than the other figures you saw?
CHUCK:	Slightly.
TONY:	Can you draw them later?
CHUCK:	Yeah. (See Figure 20.)
TONY:	Okay, and then what happens?
CHUCK:	They're leading me to a bench.
TONY:	And then what happened?
CHUCK:	I'm waiting.
TONY:	What are you waiting for?
CHUCK:	For my friends.
TONY:	Where are they?
CHUCK:	They're coming in.
TONY:	Tell us exactly what you see.
CHUCK:	Some more detail's apparent. They're, they're coming into the—the room. They're being led in.
TONY:	How many?
CHUCK:	Three.
TONY:	Give us their names.
CHUCK:	Jack, Jim and Charlie.
TONY:	And then what happens?
CHUCK:	There's—both of them are coming over to join me—on the bench.
TONY:	Who is?
CHUCK:	Jim and Charlie.
TONY:	And where is Jack?
CHUCK:	Jack is in some kind of harness, it looks like.
TONY:	What does it encircle?
CHUCK:	His shoulders. His upper rib cage.
TONY:	And then what happens?
CHUCK:	They're taking him over to an area—in the room there—telling him to raise his arms.
TONY:	You can hear them say that?
CHUCK:	No.
TONY:	Well, how do you know they're saying it?
CHUCK:	'Cause he does it—he raises his arms (pauses). It's like they're frisking him almost.
TONY:	In what way?
CHUCK:	They're touching his rib cage.
TONY:	Using what?
CHUCK:	Their hands.

TONY:	How many fingers do they have?
CHUCK:	At least three.
TONY:	And then what happens?

At this point, Chuck sighed, took a deep breath and became agitated again, but did not answer. Tony had to calm him down:

TONY:	Just relax, just relax.... Then what happens?
CHUCK:	They've got his one arm up. Seem to be probing him.
TONY:	What are they using?
CHUCK:	(Pauses for a long time.) Um, looks like something tubular.... Looks like his right arm.... They seem to be probing his upper rib cage near his armpit.
TONY:	What is Jack doing?
CHUCK:	He's looking at us.
TONY:	Does he say anything?
CHUCK:	Just with his eyes, "Get me out of here?"
TONY:	Just relax, just relax. And then what happens? What happens to Jack?
CHUCK:	Puts his arm down. They're leading him—over—to our right—they put him on a table. There seems to be moving with the—movement with the—something like hydraulic machinery. It's almost like a telescope, the way it collapses on itself. Something, ah, reflective and shiny. It's like they're moving him on this thing with it.
TONY:	Moving him where?
CHUCK:	Adjusting his body.
TONY:	Is he standing on this or is he lying on it?
CHUCK:	He's lying on it.
TONY:	And then what happens?
CHUCK:	They're probing him around the belly button.
TONY:	And then what happens?
CHUCK:	Looks like they're doing the same thing with him as they did to me.
TONY:	In the area of the penis. Is that what you mean?
CHUCK:	Yeah.
TONY:	Okay, is there anything about this probing that is different from your probing, or is there anything about it that is the same?

CHUCK:	Um, it's pretty much the same except I can see the table that's, he's on, and it seems like machinery underneath.
TONY:	The contraption that they are using to probe him with—can you describe it?
CHUCK:	Tubular.
TONY:	Similar to what was used on yours or different from what used on yours?
CHUCK:	Seems like it's thicker. (Pauses.) Seems like it's a solid conduit—solid tube—where as mine seemed to have joints. His seems to be collapsing.
TONY:	Then what happens?
CHUCK:	They're moving it away.
TONY:	How many are there?
CHUCK:	There's at least four or five figures in the room. They seem to be in different locations. A couple of them are around Jack.
TONY:	Can you see them any more distinctly than before?
CHUCK:	Well, they're sort of whitish. They—they're sort of—looks like an embryonic chicken head, almost.
TONY:	Describe it from the top.
CHUCK:	Cranium almost looks like a duck—oblongated from front to back.
TONY:	Come down a bit lower and what do you see?
CHUCK:	(Pauses.) Oh—dark eyes...absence of color. They're black.
TONY:	What shape are they?
CHUCK:	Elliptical.
TONY:	Describe the eyelids?
CHUCK:	(Pauses.) Um, seem to be like a frog. Like a membrane.
TONY:	Come down a little bit lower and what do you see?
CHUCK:	(Pauses.) They seem to have a long oblongated face from up to down.
TONY:	What is right under the eyes? Do you see anything?
CHUCK:	Ah, it's almost like embryonic folds.
RAY:	How big is the mouth?
CHUCK:	Like chicken lips [Chuck's drawing shows small slit for a mouth].

Chuck went on to describe the aliens as best he could. Things were hazy, and he felt drugged. He stated that their heads were bald and covered with smooth translucent-like skin. He described their necks as being like a "turkey gizzard." His impression was that their coverall suits took on the color of the surroundings. Unlike the others, he felt that when he saw them, they were dark in appearance. It was difficult for him to count the number of fingers on the aliens. He guessed that they had "at least three" and maybe another which he termed a "vestige." After getting him to describe his captors, we returned him to the bench to see what happened next:

CHUCK: I think Jack is standing in front of me. Seems to be some movement.

TONY: How did he get in front of you?

CHUCK: They moved him, and then they sat him next to me. Must have taken Jim out.

RAY: Where's Charlie?

CHUCK: He's on the other end of the bench. There's some commotion.

TONY: And then what happens?

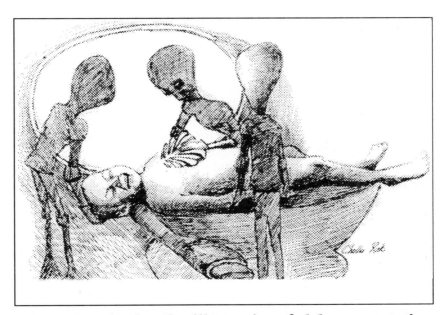

Figure 21. Chuck Rak's illustration of abductors entering Charlie Foltz's rib cage with a tubular instrument.

CHUCK:	(Pauses.) They lead him over. They lead him over to...the table.
TONY:	And then what happens?
CHUCK:	(Pauses.) Seem to be probing his side.
TONY:	With what?
CHUCK:	Some kind of a tubular instrument....They scoop him. (See Figure 21.)
TONY:	What do you mean—"They scoop him"?
CHUCK:	They enter him. They invade his rib cage with it. Maybe it's his rib cage. Maybe it's a little further.
RAY:	Lying down or standing up?
CHUCK:	He's on his side lying down.
RAY:	On what?
CHUCK:	Table.
TONY:	And then what happens?
CHUCK:	(Takes deep breath.) They take it out. Almost dragging it across his back. Almost like peeling a potato.
TONY:	While it's still inserted?
CHUCK:	Seems to be.
RAY:	Does it leave a wound?
CHUCK:	Doesn't seem to be a big one.
TONY:	How much bleeding is there?
CHUCK:	None.
TONY:	And then what happens?
CHUCK:	(Takes deep breath.) They put him on his back.
TONY:	And then what happens?
CHUCK:	He's looking at the ceiling. They seem to be grabbing his arms...seem to be helping him off the table.
TONY:	And then what do they do?
CHUCK:	They're walking towards us.... They put him on the bench.
TONY:	Where's Charlie?
RAY:	All four of you are on the bench?
CHUCK:	No, they're—seems to be—I don't know what they're doing. They're—they've got something slender around Charlie now...seems almost like a bandoleer around his shoulder and around his side.
TONY:	And then what happens?
CHUCK:	(Takes a deep breath and sighs; pauses for a long time.) They're (pauses) see some sort of a

	device on him...looks like a silvery—looks like that thing in Sydney, Australia—that opera house (Pauses.) It looks like the—like it's got curves on it. It's almost like—like it sucks something.
RAY:	Where is it placed?
CHUCK:	Right under his pectorals—on his midsection.
RAY:	And he's still sitting on the bench?
CHUCK:	I can't tell where he is—pretty close to us.... He's prone (swallows hard). He's got his head tipped way back...(sighs). It's almost like he's in pain.
TONY:	How can you tell?
CHUCK:	It seems like a pain reaction. This thing on his chest—whatever they're doing.
.RAY:	Why don't you help him?
CHUCK:	It doesn't occur to us—we can't...we're—we can't help him. We're just—all we can do is just watch him.
RAY:	Can you move?
CHUCK:	No.
TONY:	And then what happens?
CHUCK:	(Takes big breath and blows it out; appears agitated.) I can't remember!
TONY:	(Calms Chuck, then continues.) When do they take that contraption off Charlie?
CHUCK:	It's on for a long time.
TONY:	And then what happens?
CHUCK:	They take it away.... Charlie sits up.... He's pretty low. It's almost like we're looking down on him.
TONY:	And then what happens?
CHUCK:	They help him off...this thing. It's almost like a—it's like a—body-forming bench almost....They take him out.
TONY:	Where do they take him?
CHUCK:	To my—to my right.
TONY:	What's on your right?
CHUCK:	Charlie (pauses). Seems to be some straight, very thin tubular shapes. Parallel. Four or five of them going straight up and down.
TONY:	How wide?
CHUCK:	Um, six inches maybe.
TONY:	And then what happens?

CHUCK:	They have Charlie stand in front of them....They—looking at his wrists—turn his hands over so his hands are facing outward—looking at his wrists.
TONY:	And then?

Once again, Chuck did not answer, but blew out air and seemed agitated. Tony took some time to calm him and continued questioning him about Charlie. Chuck told us that the aliens were bending Charlie's elbow, raising his left arm and examining the upper part of his chest. Finally, Charlie was led back to the bench:

TONY:	Are you still on the bench?
CHUCK:	Yeah.
TONY:	What happens next?
CHUCK:	Pushing over for Charlie to sit down....There's a figure on our left.
RAY:	Do they ever talk to you?
CHUCK:	(Pauses.) Um, not really.
RAY:	How do you know what they want?
CHUCK:	Seems like it's obvious.... It's like they're directing us.... We don't have any control.
RAY:	What happens next?
CHUCK:	The figure on the left just turns away from us and toward the...interior wall. It seems to be moving away from us while looking at the wall.
TONY:	Okay, and then what happens?
CHUCK:	We're following him.
TONY:	Did someone tell you to get up or did you just know to get up?
CHUCK:	We just know. We just know to do all these things. We just know.
TONY:	And then what happens?
CHUCK:	(Pauses.) It's almost like he spreads his hand over something above him...like he waves his hand above on the wall. It's one of these, ah, seems to be rib-like structures.
TONY:	Okay, and then what happens?
CHUCK:	And then we're out!
TONY:	What do you mean, you're out? Where do you see yourself?
CHUCK:	We're into—we're going into the portal. It's like a portal.

TONY:	And then what happens?
CHUCK:	(Pauses.) It's like we're going down.
TONY:	Down where?
CHUCK:	To the canoe.
TONY:	Describe step by step. Use the technique of a one-frame camera. How do you get down into the canoe?
CHUCK:	(Becomes very agitated; does not answer.)
TONY:	Just relax. Just relax and your unconscious will tell you. How did you get into that canoe? You're into the portal and then what happens?
CHUCK:	(Pauses.) I don't really know how they do it.
TONY:	Do what?
CHUCK:	How we're into the canoe. It doesn't seem to be very important. We're just there.
RAY:	What do you mean by portal?
CHUCK:	It's almost like a place in the wall where something happens. And it's like we're penetrating a membrane.
TONY:	When you're in the portal, do you hear anything, or do you see anything before you permeate?

Tony had good reason to ask this question. Thus far, only Jack had described an excruciating experience at this juncture. He had recalled passing through the wall via a machine that looked like the lighted end of a round tube. It felt as if his body were being pulled apart. We wondered why the others could not remember this aspect of passing through the portal:

CHUCK:	Can't really see anything. Just darkness.
TONY:	What is the first thing you can see after this darkness?
CHUCK:	The lake.
TONY:	The lake? Where are you in relationship to the lake?
CHUCK:	(Pauses.) Sixty feet maybe.... It's right there. Right below us.
TONY:	How do you get from 60 feet into your canoe?
CHUCK:	Seems to be a floating motion—floating—very gentle.
RAY:	Are you floating in the open air?
CHUCK:	Seems to be. It's dark.

RAY:	Before you entered the portal, did you see any-thing else in the room where the portal was?
CHUCK:	These long tubular things.
RAY:	What color were they?
CHUCK:	Blue-gray, I think.

I continued to probe Chuck's mind regarding these tubes because Jack had used similar language in describing the machine. Charlie added a piece to the puzzle when he described "panels of light" in this area of the UFO. However, since Jim had a complete mental block regarding how they got back into the canoe, we hoped that Chuck would remember this part of the aliens' transportation system:

RAY:	Did you go away from these blue-gray tubes or toward them?
CHUCK:	The portal seemed to be amongst them.
RAY:	As you approach the blue tubes with your friends—what happens to your friends?
CHUCK:	They're out ahead of me.
RAY:	Okay. Describe what happens, step by step. When you enter, what happens?

Again, as before, when Chuck reached this crucial point, he became very upset. He groaned, as if in pain, let out a deep breath and did not answer. His extreme (out-of-character) agitation and cryptic comment that "something's happening" were intriguing. Something extraordinary was obviously happening to him. But he either would not, or could not, describe it. We wondered if he were seeing and feeling what Jack did at this same juncture. Perhaps the event was too traumatic for his conscious mind to accept. The session continued:

RAY:	Does anything happen even before you reach the portal—describe exactly what happens?...Who's ahead of you?
CHUCK:	Jack and Jim.
RAY:	Okay, now what happened to Jack and Jim?
CHUCK:	They're heading down towards the canoe.
RAY:	Before that.
CHUCK:	They go towards the portal.
RAY:	The portal is part of the blue tube?
CHUCK:	The blue—the, the tubes are—they're very small in diameter....They seem to stretch horizontally

all around the room—at about eye level—maybe a little bit higher...they're a series of four or five, maybe five tubes—parallel—one on top of another—circular—following the room—at about eye level.

RAY: And where is the portal in relation to the blue tubes?

CHUCK: Just below them.

RAY: Okay, what happens after that?

CHUCK: The figure's (alien is) doing something with his hand.

RAY: To what?

CHUCK: The area above the tubes.

RAY: What does he do?

CHUCK: He's raising his arm. His, his, his fingers—he seems to be manipulating some kind of instruments.

RAY: What happens next?

CHUCK: The portal opens.

RAY: A door?

CHUCK: It's not like a door...it's like a membrane.

RAY: What happens next?

CHUCK: We're (pauses) we go out. We go out through the portal.

RAY: Walking?

CHUCK: At first.

RAY: What happens after—what do you mean, "At first?"

CHUCK: We walk to the edge. We walk as far as we can.

RAY: Then what happens?

CHUCK: It's almost like we're in a some, somewhat of a sitting pose.... Almost like we're being lifted down.

RAY: By whom?

CHUCK: By this figure [alien]—almost like a ski-tow operator.

RAY: He's actually physically lifting you?

CHUCK: No, he's operating the ski tow, and we're going backwards down the mountain instead of up.

RAY: What are you sitting on?

CHUCK: Can't tell [Charlie had told us it felt like a bench or a "landing"].

TONY: And then what happens?

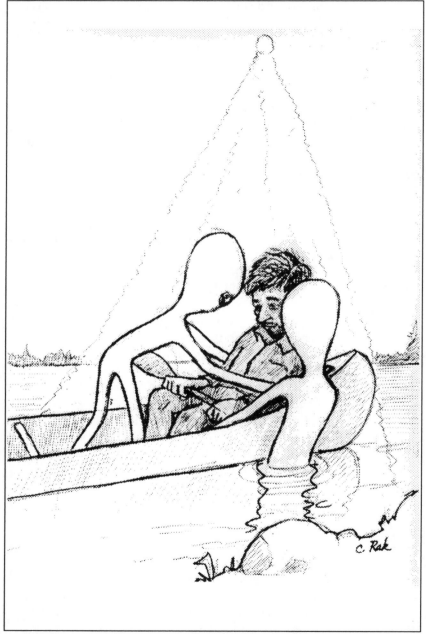

Figure 22. Chuck Rak's drawing of the two aliens replacing him in the canoe after the abduction.

CHUCK:	We seem to be near the shore—right at the shore!
TONY:	When were you put into the canoe—where was the canoe?
CHUCK:	Near shore.
TONY:	And how did you get to shore?
CHUCK:	Inertia.
TONY:	In what way? Did you apply it?
CHUCK:	Not me.

Chuck explained that, when they were taken from the canoe, it had been about 1,000 feet from shore. When placed back into the canoe, it was only 30 feet from shore. It was moving much faster than they could paddle it. The bow was actually out of the water! Chuck did not paddle. Charlie had the only other paddle. Yet the canoe was somehow guided directly to their camp landing!

Again, we brought Chuck back to the point where the four were descending toward the canoe. We wanted to know how they got back into it:

| RAY: | How did you get into the canoe? |
| CHUCK: | We were placed...one of them [an alien] is...arranging our seating positions (See Figure 22.) |

Chuck described how the two aliens stood waist deep in water beside the canoe. One arranged the seating positions by the light from the glowing sphere, which silently hovered behind them. After they were properly seated, the aliens left them. Chuck assumed that they waded or swam back to the hovering object, but did not see them do this. He then described the departure of the object from the area, as the others had done. It was already past time for the session to end. On an impulse, I quickly asked Chuck an important question, prompted by my studies of other abductees:

RAY:	Um, these figures—these entities?
CHUCK:	Yeah.
RAY:	Had you ever seen them prior to this?
CHUCK:	(Pauses.) Um, yeah.
RAY:	Where?
CHUCK:	In my bedroom, when I was little.

Tony and I exchanged knowing looks as Chuck continued to describe the typical bedroom visitation scenario characteristic of so many other abduction experiences. (This topic will be discussed later in the book.) Tony then brought the session to a close. Again, I left the tape running to record Chuck's impressions when he awakened from hypnosis. Chuck's eyes slowly opened and blinked several times, as he looked at Tony and then glanced over at Mary and me. A puzzled look crept over his face. He said nothing. I was the first to break the stony silence.

RAY:	Can you remember?
CHUCK:	(Frowns.) Yeah.
RAY:	What do you think about all this?
CHUCK:	Well (pauses) I don't know. I don't know what to think about it. Ah, I've got an open mind. But, ah, I don't know really what to think about it. I think it will, ah, again I need some time to think about it.
RAY:	Does it, ah, cause any fear or worry or...?
CHUCK:	No. None at all. I don't feel like I've, ah, had a traumatic experience at all. I'm a bit concerned.... I read, ah, Budd Hopkins' *Intruders* and ah...Strieber's book. So, I'm not sure what to think, if this really happened, or these are just a conglomeration of ideas.
RAY:	Do you feel that it really happened?
CHUCK:	Well, I know that the, ah, I know we saw the thing in Maine. I know that happened for sure.
RAY:	But the other part, the on-board experience. Where would those memories have come from if they hadn't happened?
CHUCK:	I don't know. It seemed to be like I was being led through a series of events. I don't know how it got there in my head.

It was getting late. We continued to chat as I began to pick up my belongings and unhook the tape recorder. Mary, who had been sitting quietly, suddenly came to life. Chuck's description of bedtime visitations had jolted her memory about something. She volunteered some provocative information about the twins. They had once frightened her with stories about a poltergeist in their childhood home. I quickly switched the recorder back on and asked her to elaborate:

RAY:	I'll get that on tape. Go ahead.

MARY:	Well, it's 19 years ago now. They told me all about this, which scared me at the time. Um, they had what they called poltergeists—what they referred to as poltergeists in their home.
RAY:	As youngsters?
MARY:	Yeah, as they, they—from the time they were little until like, I said, we [i.e., she and Jack] met when, when we were 18 and it hadn't—I never experienced it in their house.... They said they saw things in their rooms, heard things calling them. Their mother saw things.
RAY:	Is their mother living now?
MARY:	Yeah.
RAY:	Where does she live now?
MARY:	In Allentown, Pennsylvania.
RAY:	And what is the father's name?
MARY:	The father's dead. He died in '80, I think.
RAY:	So, the telephone number would be under her name?
MARY:	I don't—are you going to contact her?—Do you mind if I tell Jack that?

I assured Mary that I would not call Jack's mother about this unless Jack gave me permission. However, I hoped that he would grant it. The implications of this new tidbit of information were staggering. Did the twins also have alien bedtime visitations? Time would tell. And time finally sent each of us on our way from Tony's house.

Chuck had certainly reacted differently from the others to the Allagash abduction. Relatively speaking, he showed little emotion or fear during his recounting of the obviously fearful experience. Also, he did not seem to reach the same deep level of hypnosis that caused the others to actually relive their encounter except in a few instances.

These facts were not lost on either Tony or Chuck. I soon received letters in the mail from each of them. Tony was confused with Chuck's reactions. He wrote:

> As you recall, when we began with Chuck in a
> light state, he spoke in the past. After about 1/2 hour
> of this light state, I deepened his relaxation and he
> spoke in the present tense, even to the point where he
> answered a question with, "Just now...." I'm not sure
> what to make of Chuck's account of the Allagash inci-
> dent.... I'm trying to "characterize" Chuck, yet I can't
> really come to any conclusions. He was never an-

gry...never said or indicated that he felt violated—never indignant at being "kidnapped"—never indignant that his genitals were being examined....While the other three individuals (during the initial sighting) voiced concern and the need to "get out of there," Chuck perceived the incident as an opportunity to learn.... He referred to his companions' fright as "parochial Sunday-school upbringing."

I had less of a problem characterizing Chuck. Whether in or out of hypnosis, he appeared to have a unique personality. I privately nicknamed him "Macho-Man." Nothing seemed to bother him, and he made no bones about letting people know it!

Then Chuck's letter arrived. He was bitterly disappointed by his failure to completely relive what had happened. He had hoped to experience the event with vivid imagery: "I thought I was about to relive the Allagash incident through all five senses."

Chuck was also very introspective and analytical in his letter. He wondered if he had been influenced by UFO books or the twins' dreams. He feared that these might have contaminated his testimony. I appreciated his concern and his attempt to be as objective as possible. Nonetheless, I could not help wondering if some of this reaction was caused by an underlying desire to deny the reality of his experience.

Unfortunately for Chuck, our guidelines prevented him from listening and comparing the hypnotic sessions at this time. Had he had such access, I believe he would have agreed that his session was far from being a failure.

Several months later, Tony again hypnotized Chuck. His reaction to hypnosis was no different. Nothing new was added to his testimony other than what has been mentioned.

Regardless of unfulfilled expectations on his part, Chuck's hypnotically-recalled memories were a vital link in a chain of verification. The four complementary accounts provided compelling circumstantial evidence for the physical reality of their incredible experience. But, the Allagash abductions would prove to be just the tip of the proverbial iceberg. Pandora's box was far from empty!

CHAPTER 7

"Not Again!"

Jack and Mary live in a small Vermont town that is tucked within a valley surrounded by the forested hills of rural Vermont's Green Mountain range. Even before I met Jack and Mary, this town held special significance for me. It had played host to a mysterious event during the month of December, 1974. The strange details underlying this incident trickled through my mind as I began to probe the possible abduction of Jack and Mary from their country home. Little did I know, the two events would be linked by a synchronism of utmost improbability.

Such synchronisms have plagued me during 30 years of UFO investigation. This one is worth mentioning and will set the scene for the rest of this amazing chapter. The 1974 event is aptly described in my book entitled *Casebook of a UFO Investigator*.[1] On December 14, 1974, at about 7:30 A.M., Mr. and Mrs. Herbert Lower, of this same town, discovered a strange, circular impression in the snow on their property. During the night, their 14-year-old daughter Colleen awoke when a pinkish glow shone through her window; however she did not get up to investigate. At 4:00 A.M., Mrs. Lower woke up. The dogs were barking, and she too saw a pink glow coming through her window. Too tired to get up, she dismissed the glow as the probable sunrise and assumed the dogs were barking at deer.

1. Fowler, Raymond E., *Casebook of a UFO Investigator* (Englewood Cliffs, N.J.: Prentice-Hall, Inc., 1981).

In the morning, the Lower family discovered a melted circle in the field adjoining their home. They realized something very strange had taken place the night before. At about 8:00 A.M., they phoned the local newspaper, the *Brattleboro Reformer*, about it. The local reporter interviewed the family, photographed the circular trace and filed the data for the following week's edition.

An acquaintance of Mrs. Lower, who was interested in UFOs, suggested that the circle in the field might merit further investigation. He referred her to MUFON investigator, Bob Jackson. Bob called me about the event and I phoned the Lowers for firsthand information and assigned the case to MUFON investigator John Meloney.

John arrived at the Lower home at 2:30 P.M. He photographed the area, secured soil samples, and took temperature readings at various soil depths. Later a radiological check was made, with negative results. At that point, Mr. Lower dropped a bombshell.

Mr. Lower casually told John that he had put up a "keep out" sign, as instructed by the man on the telephone. John asked, "What man?" Mr. Lower said that several minutes after I had talked with him, the phone rang again. An authoritarian male voice identified himself as representing a government agency in Washington. He claimed that the incident had been reported to them and questioned him about it. The man asked if it would be permissible—and possible—to land a small helicopter on his property. Assuming that I had notified this agency, Mr. Lower granted permission without questioning the man further. However, since it was still snowing, it was agreed that the helicopter would be sent on the following day.

At about noon on the following day, Mr. Lower and his son were emptying rubbish not far from their house. Suddenly, a whirring sound made them glance up. An unmarked helicopter was descending over the field where the circular trace lay. It hovered for awhile and then flew off.

Numerous questions flooded our minds. Who was this man? How did he know about the incident? How did he obtain Mr. Lower's unlisted telephone number? What agency flew in an unmarked helicopter the next day to check out the site? Many witnesses saw it. After thoroughly checking military and commercial bases, I was still unable to ascertain the origin of the helicopter. No one who knew about the Lower incident had reported it to a government agency—or to anyone else, for that matter. The answers to our questions would remain a mystery. The synchronism involving the Lowers and the Allagash four became less of a mystery as that December day in 1974 wore on.

It was about 4:00 P.M. when John Meloney bade the Lower family good-bye. However, falling sleet and snow turned the unplowed back roads into curving paths of ice and kept him from getting too far. As John cautiously made his way down a hill, his car went out of control and hit a tree. The car was completely destroyed.

Bleeding and in shock, John stumbled down the country road, looking for help. It seemed like an eternity before a pickup truck slid to a halt beside him. The driver helped John into the passenger's seat and took him to the local hospital. There, John stayed for weeks for treatment of multiple fractures. During this time, he received visits from the fellow who had picked him up and driven him to safety.

Sixteen years later, during my investigation of the Allagash case, I sat chatting with Jim, Jack, Chuck and Charlie. During the course of our conversation, Chuck casually remarked that I was the second UFO investigator that he had met in his lifetime. Curious, I asked him who the first one was. Chuck told me that back in the mid-seventies he was driving along a back road during a snowstorm and came across a bleeding man staggering along a road. Chuck lived in a neighboring town and was on his way home at the time. Chuck Rak, one of the Allagash four, was the Good Samaritan who rescued my investigator. Despite this uncanny coincidence, it is still not as incredible as the revelations yet to unfold in what was turning out to be a classic case of its kind.

To delve further into this case, it is essential to learn more about Jack and Mary Weiner. In 1974, Jack Weiner was still attending Mansfield State College, in Pennsylvania, as a psychology major. After graduating, he moved to Boston with his brother, Jim. There he met and fell in love with Mary Donlan. They were married in 1976. Jack told me:

> By 1979, Mary and I were getting a little "itchy" in
> Boston. We decided to buy some land in Vermont and
> build our house up on a high mountain, in the middle
> of the woods, where nobody could see us or bother us.
> That's what we wanted, a little isolation away from the
> crime of the city, a place where, on a crystal clear
> night, one could look up into the sea of stars.

Jack and Mary followed through on their dream and built an isolated homestead in southern Vermont. It lies off a steep mountain thoroughfare. The first glimpse of their red, corrugated metal roof poking through the trees comes about two miles up the partially paved road.

Their dirt driveway is entered on the right, and it curves uphill for about 500 feet before it egresses onto a clearing on the side of the mountain. The Weiner's simple Cape Cod-style home lies at an elevation of almost 2,000 feet with neighboring houses thousands of feet away and out of sight. The sides of the house are oriented to the four magnetic compass points: the front door faces southward to the whole western range of the Green Mountains, the northern rear of the house backs onto a thick pine forest, the western side of the house faces the driveway and the eastern side faces a huge field, which measures about 500 by 1,000 feet. It was in this large, open, grassy tract that they would receive unexpected visitors in the night. Jack and Mary had indeed built a home where, "nobody could see us or bother us"—except aliens.

Hypnosis Session #2—Jack Weiner (July 22, 1989)

My mind was full of anticipation as I drove to Tony's home to meet with him and Jack Weiner. Again, Dave could not be present because of family commitments. Our last session with Jack had left us hanging in suspense. If you will recall, I had asked Jack a provocative question as the session was coming to a close:

RAY: When is the next time you see those strange creatures?

JACK: (Pauses.) The next time I see them—they're—in my dream. They're in my dream. How did they get there?

How they got there was the subject matter for Jack's second hypnotic session. Jack had continued to describe what seemed to be a real-life abduction experience.

JACK: And Mary's scared. She's real scared. And I'm worried. And—then—the blue light—the blue light comes—and—and—I think, "Holy shit! I don't believe it—not again!"

If you will recall, I had moved quickly to cut Jack off at this point, since Mary was present at the session. We did not want to contaminate any future testimony that she might give us.

Jack and Tony were waiting for me when I arrived. As usual, Jack was excited and talking a blue streak. I again wondered how such a person could respond to the hypnotic process so well. Both Jack and Jim were excellent subjects and were able to be placed in a very deep level of hypnosis.

We continued to talk for a while in an attempt to calm Jack. Then Tony eased him into a hypnotic trance. The questioning began:

TONY:	Let's go back to a night that you had mentioned on your last visit here. I believe you were asleep...in Vermont...Mary was beside you.... I believe you say something to the effect—"The dog wants to go out." I believe that you rise from bed and let the dog out.... You can correct... slight deviations if I am incorrect.... You may start speaking now from that point when you awakened to let the dog out. So please continue.
JACK:	The dog jumps out of bed. He does that normally. Normally the dog gets up and he jumps down off that bed, and he goes over to the door and he scratches at the door. And I'm in bed thinking— "Oh boy! I gotta get up and take the dog out now." So I get up. I don't really mind. And I look for my pants, and I find my pants, and I put them on. And he's at the door scratching. And I'm walking towards the door. And I notice that there is light coming through the window. The kitchen window to my left.
TONY:	What color is that?
JACK:	It's blue. A blue light. And I think, "That's funny. That's not like the moon." And then I go to the window and I look out the window, and what I see is amazing. I see a bright light. A big, bright light. And it's right over the truck, in the field outside the house. And I'm thinking, "Oh my God! I can't believe that!" And so I say, "Mary get up. Get up and look!" And I run to the door, and I go out the door, and I'm running towards the light up in the field. And I can't believe it. It's just amazing. And I'm yelling for Mary and then— then I see the dog down there in the field. And he's running alongside of me. And I think, "Oh, he's going to get lost." And so I reach down and pick up the dog. And I'm thinking, "I've got to get him inside. I've got to get the dog inside." And so, I know that the light's there, but I'm thinking, "I've got to save the dog." So I pick him up and I run back to the house, and when I get to the house, I know that the light is still there. And it's moving. It's moving towards the back. And then, I put the dog back in bed and I'm thinking, "I

don't want to do this. I don't want to do this
now."

TONY: You don't want to do what Jack?

JACK: I don't want to look at the light. I don't want to
know what the light is. I don't feel safe. So, I'm
going back to bed. And so I go back to bed and
I'm thinking, "I don't want to deal with this now.
Why are they here now?" And I'm scared. And I
don't want to look at them. And so, I pull the covers over my head. And I'm lying in bed under the
covers with the dog. And Mary's next to me. And
then I know, I know that something's in the
house. I just know that they're there and I'm under the covers and I think, "Oh boy! Why are
they here now? I don't want this to happen. I
don't want to look at them." I'm scared. And
then, I know. I know they're right there. And I
am freaking. I think, "Oh God, oh God, why are
they here now?" (Gasps.) And then the covers
move and I feel something on the cover and I'm
thinking, "Oh no! Oh no! No—I don't want this to
happen!" And that doesn't make any difference.
It doesn't make any difference. And then—the
covers are down. And I'm looking there, and I
was right. They're right there! Oh God! Oh,
they're right there!

TONY: How many do you see?

JACK: I see one, and it's right there! Right next to my
bed!

TONY: Beside it?

JACK: Right beside my bed.

TONY: Describe what you see.

JACK: (Answers with a trembling voice.) I see a dark figure that has a strange face. Not like our face.

TONY: How do they differ?

JACK: It has big eyes. Big eyes. Two big eyes and a big
head, and it's darkish and there's light behind it,
coming in the door. And it's just taking the covers away and I don't want to look at it. And I look
at it and I'm thinking, "Holy mackerel! Holy—I
don't want to do this." And I look at Mary because I want to scream or, or something—
scream or warn Mary, and then it's even worse.
It's even worse because (pauses) now I know
there's another one there and it's next to Mary.
And I'm thinking, "Oh my God! Oh my God! I
don't believe it." And it's taking the covers down
and I wish, I wish I could do something. I wish I

	could do something, but I can't. I have to do what they want. And the light is out there, and they want me to go out there. And they (pauses) they touch me on my arm. They're lifting me. It wants me to get out of bed—ha! Oh boy!
TONY:	Are you walking?
JACK:	I'm standing—and I'm looking—and Mary's standing—and they're making us move towards the light. And I don't know why, but the dog—the dog is watching. And the dog isn't doing anything. And they're making us move, and I don't want to go. And now, the door—we're through the door—and it's right back there.
TONY:	What is?
JACK:	This light. I can't believe it. It's right back there. And they want us to move towards the light.
TONY:	Do you?
JACK:	Yes.
TONY:	Both of you?
JACK:	Yes. We walk up the lawn and I feel like I'm floating there. I can't help myself. I'm just going there with them—and they're holding me—and they're holding Mary.
TONY:	How are they holding you?
JACK:	By our arms. They just have a hold of our arms.
TONY:	Are your feet on the ground?
JACK:	Our feet are on the ground but it feels funny, because my feet are not doing what I want them to. I want my feet not to go, but they are anyway and that feels funny, because I'm not doing what I want to do, but I'm doing what they want.
RAY:	What happens next?
JACK:	We're walking towards a light.
RAY:	How big is the light?
JACK:	It's big!
RAY:	Compared to a house.
JACK:	Oh, it's bigger than our house.
RAY:	What shape is it?
JACK:	It's round but it changes—it changes the way it looks.
TONY:	In what way does it change? In color or shape?
JACK:	By the shape and the color. It's weird the way it moves and it's not like anything—
TONY:	How does the shape change?

JACK:	It changes from—like a ball to a different shape—like a thing that has edges. But it's not like anything that I have seen. It's funny. It changes that way. And then it goes back to being round, and it pulsates.
RAY:	What color?
JACK:	It's—changes from bright, bright white, yellow, and then it changes—it changes color to a deeper orange and purple and white—and that's weird.
RAY:	What happened to the blue light?
JACK:	The blue light is underneath it—and it's sitting, sitting on the blue light. And that is weird. It flickers, and it moves and—
RAY:	Does it make noise?
JACK:	It makes no noise.
RAY:	Do you smell anything unusual?
JACK:	(Sniffs.) I smell the grass, and I smell (sniffs) like—something weird.
RAY:	Can you compare it with something that you know?
JACK:	It smells like (pauses) like a freezer. Maybe like a freezer.
RAY:	How does a freezer smell?
JACK:	Like when, when you open one of those freezers with a lid and it smells (pauses) tangy—sour (pauses)—uhhh, like cold or chemical. It's weird. A weird smell.
RAY:	What happens next?
JACK:	We walk toward the blue light and they want us to walk to the light.
RAY:	Do you?
TONY:	What happens next?
JACK:	We stop right by the light and I'm looking at Mary—and she just seems like she's not there— like she's scared but like she's not there.
TONY:	Are her eyes open?
JACK:	Yes. She's looking around and—but I feel that she is not there and—I wish that it wasn't there. And I think that we have to do what they want.
RAY:	What do they want?
JACK:	They want us to go with them.
RAY:	Do you?
JACK:	Yes.

RAY:	Describe that.
JACK:	They just turn and make us walk with them into the blue light, and the light is right over and I feel that I'm done. I can't resist anymore.
RAY:	Describe what happens.
JACK:	And we're in the light and it seems that everything changes. And I'm looking at Mary and I see her face and I'm thinking that, "It's changing." And, "Something's happening—something's happening now." And I don't know what is going to happen next, but I feel that something is going to happen.
RAY:	How does Mary change?
JACK:	She just gets hazy looking, and she seems like she's going away—like we're going away—And I think, "She's being taken away (almost cries) and I don't want them—I don't want them to take her away."
TONY:	Just relax, just relax.

Jack was visibly upset and on the verge of tears. Tony stepped in and calmed him. He decided to help Jack through by having him visualize what was happening on an imaginary TV screen.

TONY:	What happens next?
JACK:	Somehow we're in a room and everything is different now (speaks in a puzzled voice). And we're not in the house and I know that (sounds alarmed) that I am there and I know that I'm on that thing!
TONY:	What thing?
JACK:	In that light, and I know that something's going to happen now.
TONY:	Describe what you see as you look around. What do you see?
JACK:	I see a large space that is confusing, because it seems to go on forever, and I'm looking and I don't see where it ends.
TONY:	Look to your left, and what do you see then?
JACK:	I'm looking—and it's the same bright, bright light and hazy light.
TONY:	Look to your right and what do you see?
JACK:	I'm looking (pauses) all over, and I see something—and I know it's one of them because it's

standing close by me and it seems to be watching me and I think, "What does it want?—What
does it want?" And then I look—and then I remember Mary, but I don't see Mary. I just see it
there, and I'm looking up.

TONY: What do you see?

JACK: I don't see anything there, and I don't know
           what's going on—I can't move! I can't walk!

TONY: Can you see your feet?

JACK: I can see parts of me. I see my hands, and I look
           and I think, "Am I all here?" And I say, "Yep, I'm
           all here." And I look, and it's watching—but I
           don't see Mary.

RAY: What happens next?

JACK: I'm just (pauses) now I know that it's coming to-
           wards me. And I think, "I know it won't hurt me
           if I don't do anything to it." [Did Jack receive a
           telepathic warning from the alien?] And it comes
           up to me, and I look at it. (Whispers.) Oh, God.

TONY: Had you ever seen it before?

JACK: I've seen it somewhere. It looks familiar to me. I
           think that it looks familiar (voice rises in alarm).
           And I think, "Oh God! It must be—it must be
           them!"

TONY: Who is them?

JACK: The ones we saw before, in Maine.

RAY: Do they look the same?

JACK: They have eyes—their eyes are like them, and
           their heads—their heads are like them, and they
           have hands.

RAY: How many fingers?

JACK: Their fingers are not like mine.

RAY: How many fingers?

JACK: (Pauses, as if counting.) Four.

RAY: Any thumb?

JACK: No.

RAY: What happens next?

JACK: It's coming towards me, and now it's come right
           to me!

   I thought to myself—"This is our chance." We had gotten a
rough description of the aliens during the previous sessions
that dealt with the Allagash abduction. This was a great oppor-

tunity to get a more detailed description of these strange denizens of the night:

RAY: Now he's right beside you? What is he or she wearing, starting with the head and going right down to the feet?

JACK: The head looks like—it's not wearing anything on the head.

RAY: Any hair?

JACK: No.

RAY: Okay, continue right down from the head.

JACK: It's got big eyes—

RAY: Um-hum.

JACK: —that shine like the light—the light around us [i.e., reflective]. And they look wet—like they have wet eyes. And its face? It's not like our face.

RAY: Why?

JACK: Because it doesn't have a nose, and it doesn't have a mouth but it's smooth [i.e., not like ours].

RAY: Ears?

JACK: No ears [i.e., not like ours].

RAY: What is it wearing, starting from the neck down? It has a neck?

JACK: It has a neck. It has something on that looks like something smooth and (pauses) not shiny but like—smooth.

RAY: What would you compare it with?

JACK: I think that it looks like a skier—racing—in a suit.

RAY: What color is it?

JACK: It's the same color as the head—brown (pauses) it doesn't wrinkle. I don't know how it does that.

RAY: Does it have a belt or buttons? Suspenders?

JACK: No buttons. No wrinkles. No seams. A thing near the middle but (pauses) what is that?

RAY: What does it look like?

JACK: It looks like (pauses)—some kind of (pauses) oval, oval-shaped, ah, what—like—I don't know.

RAY: Where is it located?

JACK: On the front—lower than its chest.

RAY: How is it attached?

JACK: (Pauses.) It (pauses) it's just a piece of the suit.

RAY: Same color?

JACK:	It's a different color. Like lighter, lighter than brown and (pauses) brighter—like light on it.
RAY:	Does this suit...cover the whole body?
JACK:	Yes.
RAY:	Including the hands?
JACK:	(Pauses.) No.
RAY:	The hands are bare?
JACK:	The hands are different. The hands don't look the same [as ours].
RAY:	Are they covered?
JACK:	No, I don't think so.
RAY:	Do they have fingernails?
JACK:	No, no.
RAY:	How many fingers?
JACK:	Four.
RAY:	What do they have on their feet?
JACK:	Their feet—they don't have shoes—their feet are covered with the same material as the suit.
RAY:	Can you see any digits on the foot? Toes?
JACK:	I see parts.
RAY:	Parts?
JACK:	Two parts with a spacing between.
RAY:	What happens next?
JACK:	The thing is in front of me now. And it's doing something to the side—like it's getting something. And now it has something that (pauses) is going to do something. What is it?
RAY:	What does it look like?
JACK:	It brings it to my face, and it seems like something that they're going to touch my face with. And it's looking at me—looking at my face.
RAY:	What's looking at your face?
JACK:	The thing looks at me...the, the instrument is being used to look at me. That's what it's doing.
RAY:	What part of you does it look at?
JACK:	It's looking at my eyes very closely.
RAY:	What does it [the instrument] look like when it's looking in your eyes?
JACK:	It's a plain-looking surface that's bright and not like metal. And it's got this part that seems to be doing something that—I don't know what it's doing!
RAY:	Do you feel anything?

JACK:	(Pauses.) I feel a feeling that it's looking at me through that thing—and I feel like it's using it to look at me in some way.
RAY:	What happens next?
JACK:	Next—it lowers it, and I see its face over the top of the thing like it's looking at me again. And now the thing is being lowered to my throat— and it seems to be something that's looking at me or something. It feels, it feels like it's doing something.
RAY:	Does it touch you?
JACK:	No.
RAY:	How does it feel?
JACK:	It feels like something is—like thrumming— humming—thrumming.
RAY:	Where?
JACK:	In my chest and in my throat and in my shoulders. And I feel a thrumming, but it doesn't touch me.
RAY:	What happens next?
JACK:	It's still there—the thing—and it's still holding the thing, and it seems to be just lowering it some more. And it seems to be interested in looking at my body with it.
RAY:	What part of the body?
JACK:	My chest and my stomach and my groin. And it makes me feel thrummy when it's there. Wherever it is, that's where I feel thrummy.
RAY:	Does it stop at your groin? Does it continue?
JACK:	It stops.
RAY:	What happens next?
JACK:	It raises the thing to its face and it is looking at it and moving its fingers on it, and then—and now it's finished.
RAY:	What does he do with the instrument?
JACK:	He does something with, with its hands.
RAY:	With its? His [alien's] hands or its [instrument's] hands? What hands are you talking about?
JACK:	The thing's [alien's] hands do something to the thing [instrument] and then he's reaching over and handing it to another.
RAY:	Like him?
JACK:	Just like him.
RAY:	What happens next?

JACK:	It takes it and it looks at the thing [instrument], and it's doing something with its head—like it's moving funny—and then it turns and walks away.
RAY:	What is the room that you are in made of? What does it look like it's made of?
JACK:	The room looks like the whole thing is made of some kind of thick, fuzzy light.
RAY:	What shape is the room?
JACK:	The shape—don't, can't tell what shape it is.
RAY:	Okay, what happens next, after the instrument is taken away?
JACK:	The thing is just there and it's reaching out to-wards me, and it's touching my face and my eye—touching my eyes and making them open.
RAY:	With his fingers?
JACK:	Yes.
RAY:	What does that feel like?
JACK:	Oh! It feels awful. It feels like it's got squishy fin-gers.
RAY:	How could he open your eyes if they were already open?
JACK:	They made them go open more—like it reached out and it wanted to see more of my eyes. And now it stops, and it's looking up my nose—it's made my head go back and its fingers are mak-ing my nose [nostrils] get big, and it just seems to be looking there—like it's looking for some-thing—but I don't know what it would be looking for.
RAY:	What happens next?
JACK:	Now it's opening my mouth, and it's looking in my mouth. And now it has something in its hand.
RAY:	Describe it—size—shape—what it's made of.
JACK:	It looks like a kind of rod—a rod of some kind.
RAY:	What does it look like?
JACK:	Looks like it's made of something that sparkles like crystals or, or like water, but hard water.
RAY:	How long is it?
JACK:	It not too short—probably more than a foot, more than a foot and a half—maybe twenty, twenty inches long.
RAY:	How, ah, what's the diameter?
JACK:	Not large. Very thin.

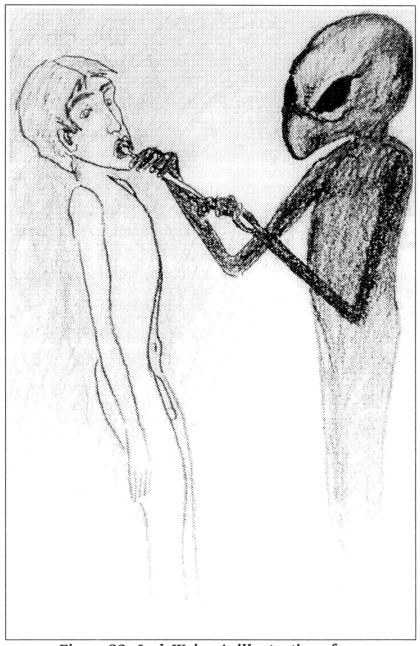

Figure 23. Jack Weiner's illustration of an alien examining Jack's mouth with a lighted rodlike instrument.

RAY:	Compared to a pencil—is it smaller? What would you compare it to?
JACK:	Thinner, thinner than a pencil.
RAY:	Does it glow by itself or does it reflect the light?
JACK:	It has a light. There's a light on the end of it—some kind of bright bulb-looking substance that is bright.
RAY:	What does he do with it?
JACK:	He puts it in my mouth (See Figure 23.)
RAY:	Does it touch the inside of your mouth? What does it feel like?
JACK:	(Pauses.) Oh! It makes me think of when I chew tinfoil and how that makes my filling feel like. Cause when it touches my teeth, it hurts.
RAY:	What happens next?
JACK:	It's touching my mouth and it's very close, and it's looking in there and then it's finished—I think it's finished.
RAY:	Why?
JACK:	Because it seems to have hesitated like it's not finished. And then—something touches my throat way, way back, and I don't like the feeling of that. And that makes me feel funny.
RAY:	Is your mouth open?
JACK:	My mouth is open, and I don't like that!
RAY:	And what touches your throat?
JACK:	Something on the end—something on the end of that [rod] is touching my throat.
RAY:	How far down?
JACK:	Way far, cause I feel like I'm going to gag or choke, and that's weird cause I don't like that and oh, I wish I could stop that! (Long pause)
RAY:	And then what happens?
JACK:	And then—and then it's gone!
RAY:	What's gone, Jack?
JACK:	The pain, the pain is gone. Whew! Oh boy! Now I think, "I'm glad that's over." And it's going away.
RAY:	What's going away?
JACK:	The, the being is going away now.
RAY:	Are you alone?
JACK:	I look—and I'm looking for Mary—and I'm looking but I don't see Mary.
RAY:	Are you alone?

JACK:	(Pauses.) No.
RAY:	Who's with you?
JACK:	There are more—there's still one of those [aliens] and it's far away.
RAY:	What happens next?
JACK:	I'm watching the thing that's far away.
RAY:	Then what happens—after you watch it?
JACK:	Then I see that its face is watching—and it's moving—and then I feel like I'm moving towards it, and it's getting bigger, but I don't know how I'm doing this.
RAY:	Are you walking?
JACK:	I'm not walking.
RAY:	Are you on the floor?
JACK:	No.
RAY:	Are you above the floor?
JACK:	I'm on something that moves—I'm not moving.
RAY:	What happens next?
JACK:	The thing that was far away is getting closer, and I see another room or something in front of me. I'm being moved, moved somewhere—yeah, yup.
RAY:	What's in that room?
JACK:	It's a different color of light that is very powerful—color—very thick orange—orange color that's different.
RAY:	Can you see the dimensions of the room—the sides, floor, ceiling?
JACK:	I see a ceiling that seems to be not very high.
RAY:	How high?
JACK:	Taller than me but not twice as tall.
RAY:	Can you see the sides of the room?
JACK:	Yes.
RAY:	What shape is the room?
JACK:	The room is shaped like a "U," and in the ends—it has two ends. And, in the middle, there's a smooth-looking wall or something that sticks out. And there are others, other things [aliens] there. And they're looking at something...funny-looking—that connects to the wall. And now I'm going in this room and I look to one side, and I see that end of it. And I look the other way, and I see that end to it. And now they're moving me towards the funny part. (Pauses.) And it [the funny part] moves out towards me—uh-uh, it's

something that they want me to sit in, and so I have to get very low, like I'm sitting on the floor.

RAY: What does this funny-looking thing look like, if you were to describe it?

JACK: It looks like—it starts out like a one-piece kind of cabinet that, that's not a cabinet. It's something that moves, and it's changing its shape. And it separates and changes into some kind of thing that they want me to sit on. And it's smooth, and it's doing something that—I don't know how it's doing that.

RAY: Doing what?

JACK: It changes. It changes its shape, and it changes the way it looks, and it's like it's alive or something that's alive because it can't do that!

RAY: It changes from what to what?

JACK: It changes from a smooth, rounded-shaped kind of cabinet or something—and it comes towards me, and it's low—and, as it comes towards me, it flattens with round things at the edges—and it's like it's alive.

TONY: And then what happens?

JACK: And then it gets under me, and I feel like I'm on the floor of something. And the chair is still changing right under me—like it's changing right around me. And it moves with me in it. And I feel like I'm an egg.

RAY: Does it surround you completely, like an eggshell?

JACK: (Pauses.) It looks like—it goes up past my shoulders, but it's funny because I can see through the top.

RAY: What happens next?

JACK: (Pauses.) I feel very strange like I'm (pauses) numb. And everything—is—happening—very—slowly. And I feel thick, and I feel like an egg, and I want to just stop and do what they want.

RAY: What do they want?

JACK: They want me to do nothing and to just be still and not move.

RAY: And then what happens?

JACK: (Pauses.) The thing [enclosing instrument] feels funny, like it's doing something—and my body feels like something's being done to it, but I don't know what.

TONY: What does it feel like?

JACK: Like I'm getting thicker and thicker and thicker—like I'm turning solid and thick—and I can barely see past the top.

TONY: And what happens next?

JACK: And then the things [aliens] are watching me. And I can see them looking at me—looking down. And I think, "What are they going to do? They're up to something." But I can't feel it—I can't feel what they're doing. And it seems like I get more opened at the top, and I think, "Something's happening now," because I feel that the top is coming off and I can see more. And now I feel that I'm lying down—and they're around me—and I feel better [now] that I'm out of that [instrument]!

RAY: Then what happens?

JACK: And then I look, and I move my head around. I'm looking, and I think, "Oh boy, oh man, am I glad that's over! Oh, oh, I'm glad that's over."

RAY: What event happens next?

JACK: I'm lying (down) and I feel movement like the thing [instrument] is still moving underneath me—like I'm on the back of something moving—and I notice that everything is changing—and I seem to be spinning or rotating in a different way now—and everything seems to have changed its place—and it's different—and they're [the aliens are] still there—and they're touching something on a surface of the wall—to my left (points to his left) is a wall that has what looks like—(pauses) clear glass round tanks—but, I don't know what that is—but it looks like something with water in it, or something like water.

RAY: What shape are the tanks?

JACK: Their shapes are round, like spheres.

RAY: Have they openings?

JACK: They're in openings of the wall.

RAY: Are they filled with water? Half-filled with water? Three quarters full of water, or liquid?

JACK: There are one, two, three, four on top—four—the same on the bottom—And they are full of something.

RAY: Clear liquid?

JACK: I don't know. They look like something that is like a light behind it. And I don't know what color the stuff is—or is it the light that makes it look like that?

RAY:	What happens next?
JACK:	The things are reaching up to the wall with their fingers, and they are doing something to the wall that looks like they're holding in one hand—something up. (Pauses.) They're touching... something—with one hand, and in their other hand, they have a round tube that is held like a—(pauses) something and...it has a top that changes colors and stripes. And they're watching this device. And, at the same time, they're touching the wall; they seem to be deeply involved in waiting and watching for something to happen or something that (pauses) that's strange. I'm thinking, "They're thinking! They're thinking things." And I am amused by the look on their faces and thinking that, "They're curious and they think." And then I feel better about it all, because I feel like they're kind of like me in that way, and that they like their work.
RAY:	What happens next?
JACK:	And then I'm lying there, thinking these thoughts and feeling that, this is really something—I can't believe this is happening!
RAY:	Go through the events from that particular time to the time that you returned to the house, in summary fashion.
JACK:	Okay. I'm watching them and I feel, I'm feeling as if I know them somehow. And then the next thing I know, they are doing more things. The thing [instrument] that I am on keeps changing, and it makes me move different ways. And now it's growing or something on the way so that I am on my side, and I'm being put—they're doing something to my back and the back of me. And I can't see what they're doing, but I feel it. And it feels really strange. Like a sponge—like a big sponge is on me—all over the back of me. I feel like a big sponge. And they just seem to be going about their business—and I'm thinking that it's like the hospital—they're just doing their job.
RAY:	What happens next?
JACK:	And then I feel this spongy, this spongy feeling on my back. And Oh! It feels really funny like it's being glued to me. And then it stops, and I think, "What was that?" And then their thing [instrument] changes, and it's moving around me and—that is so weird—the way that just, it just moved.
RAY:	What is it made out of?

JACK:	It's made out of some kind of stuff that is like clay—or like clay—but not wet or slimy like clay—but it moves like clay.
RAY:	By itself?
JACK:	All by itself.
RAY:	What happens next?
JACK:	I'm sitting partially upright.
RAY:	What have you got on?
JACK:	Not a thing.
RAY:	When did they take your clothes?
JACK:	When did they take my clothes? (Sounds puzzled.) I don't remember.
RAY:	Okay, and then what happens?
JACK:	Then I'm watching something in front of me on the wall, and I'm thinking, "What is that?" And I'm looking, and the beings are there, and they seem to be involved. Their hands are moving up and down on the wall—and they're watching me—and I know that something is supposed to happen, 'cause I can tell they're moving and watching me.
RAY:	What does happen?
JACK:	I am leaning back, and I'm being told to relax and stay calm and not to be afraid.
RAY:	How do they tell you that?
JACK:	I see the words in my head. It's like—it's weird! It's like I see the words and hear them in my head.
RAY:	I see. What do they do next?
JACK:	And they're telling me not to move. And everything is changing again around me—and then they seem to be getting further away and further away and—now I'm outside the room again, where I was before I was in the room!
TONY:	Outside where, Jack?
JACK:	Outside the room with the funny chair. And I'm being moved back someplace, someplace else that I don't know where. It just seems to be a big, empty room.
RAY:	What happens next?
JACK:	I am still unable to move, and I don't know where I am. I'm like there, but I don't know how I'm there.

Something had moved Jack, such as a moving floor or conveyer device, in the same manner in which he was moved into the room. If a conveyor device was not used, perhaps he was floating above the floor. Our questioning continued:

RAY: Do you still have your clothes off?

JACK: Ah, I still have my clothes off.

RAY: Then what happens?

JACK: Now the beings are walking—one on each side—and I am moving somewhere, but I don't know how I am moving.

RAY: Where do they take you?

JACK: I'm in a room of similar appearance to where I was before and—the beings are going over my body with some kind of other thing that—I don't know what it is but they're all the way down to my feet, and they're all over my body.

RAY: One being has this instrument or more than one?

JACK: More than one.

RAY: Are they all the same-looking instruments or different instruments?

JACK: One has something that is not big in one hand, and it seems to be rubbing me with like soap but not soap—rubbing me with it. And they both are doing that.

RAY: And then what happens?

JACK: They are rubbing with this [soaplike substance], and I don't know why.

RAY: What happens after they finish rubbing you?

JACK: I remember that they stand up again, and they're looking right at me. Right in my face, and they're saying, "Okay, he's ready. He's ready. He's ready. Get him ready," I think. They're saying, "Get him ready."

RAY: Then what happens?

JACK: I think, "Wow! Oh man! I don't know what they're getting me ready for, but I want to get out of here." And then they move me back—I'm going backwards—and backwards—and they're like pushing me. And I feel like I'm stumbling—and I have no control—and I feel like—this is weird, kind of like when I was little, and some bully pushed me, and I didn't like it and I didn't know why. I felt like they were pushing me.

RAY: Where do they push you to?

JACK:	I stop because something touches my back, but I can't tell what it is.
RAY:	And what does it do?
JACK:	It stops me from moving, and then—now it feels like it's kind of—feels kind of good like—(sighs) that's strange, like, like something caught me, and it's taking my body very softly and very tenderly —and it's conforming to my body. And now I feel better, and now I feel like they're doing something to me. They're touching me—and it's confusing. I, I'm being touched from my feet and my arms, and they're making me move forward. And I think that I've felt this before like when I was little and my mother dressed me to go in the snow.
RAY:	Are they dressing you?
JACK:	I, I don't know.
RAY:	Do you have clothes on?
JACK:	I, I just feel that, that must be what they're doing. And then they stop, and they let me lean back—and they're telling me to relax and be calm and not to worry about Mary—and then I feel like I can believe them and I feel good.
RAY:	What happens next?
JACK:	And then, (pauses) the next thing I feel like (pauses) it's starting all over at the thing where I feel like—ah, there's a light, and I look up and I remember seeing that [when he first entered the UFO]. And I look over and I see Mary—and—it's just like when we went [i.e. to the UFO]. And I see the grass—and I see the house—and I think, "I wonder if the dog is still there?" And I think, "Wow—I don't believe it!" And then I feel like I should do what I'm told, and that I have to just go back and go to bed and do what I'm told. And so—
TONY:	In addition to, "Go home and go to bed," did they tell you anything else?
JACK:	They told me to go home now and go to bed, and not to tell anyone, because it would hurt me if I told.
RAY:	How would it hurt you?
JACK:	They didn't explain.
RAY:	How did you get back to the house?
JACK:	They—whew!—it was like a story—like a happy ending. They just opened their arms and said, "Go back to bed now!"—and we just floated in.

RAY:	Floated in?
JACK:	Floated.
RAY:	From where to where?
JACK:	From the light to the bed.
RAY:	Did you go through the door?
JACK:	Right through the door.
RAY:	Was the door open?
JACK:	I don't know how it could be, but it doesn't seem to be open. We just floated to bed.

I wondered if Jack were describing what is known as an OBE, an Out-of-the-Body Experience. Some UFO abductees have experienced OBE's during their encounter. However, this did not seem to be the case with Jack and Mary, based on Jack's response to my next question.

RAY:	What was in the bed when you approached the bed?

(I wondered if their physical bodies were still in bed.)

JACK:	The dog.
RAY:	Nothing else?
JACK:	Nothing.
RAY:	Then what happened?
JACK:	Then I remember pulling the cover over my head and thinking, "I don't want this to happen now. I wish they'd go away and leave me alone." And then I felt safe and peaceful and sleepy, and I could go to sleep.
RAY:	Did you go to sleep?
JACK:	Yes.

Incredibly, at this juncture, Jack again was back to square one. He had no remembrance of the abduction. The period of missing time was blocked out from his conscious memory. He thought he had been dreaming.

RAY:	How much did you remember the next morning?
JACK:	(Pauses.) I remember a dream of going to the door and seeing a light outside.
RAY:	Did you ask Mary if she had a dream or tell Mary about the dream?

JACK:	Yes. She said I was weird. And she said it must have been a dream.
RAY:	Were you ever told by the beings not to remember this? Or did they just warn you that it would be better not to tell anybody?
JACK:	(Speaks slowly and deliberately.) They said, "Not—to—tell." Just like that, "Not—to—tell."
RAY:	What would happen if you did?
JACK:	They said, "It would be harmful."
RAY:	In what way?
JACK:	They didn't say. They just said, "It would be harmful if you tell."

Tony motioned to me that it was time to quit, since it was getting late. As he started to bring Jack out of hypnosis, I thought of something that I had not asked him.

RAY:	Can I ask him one more question?
TONY:	Sure, what's that?
RAY:	(To Jack) Did you ever see those beings and/or the ship again since that incident?
JACK:	(Pauses for a long time.) No.

When Jack came around, I recorded his first impressions of what he had just relived under deep hypnosis.

TONY:	How do you feel?
JACK:	Whew! Ah, I feel strange (laughs nervously). Very strange.
RAY:	Can you remember what happened?
JACK:	I, I, do remember—a lot of it—I hope I remember. How long was I under there [i.e., under hypnosis]?
RAY:	A long time.
TONY:	Two and one half hours.
JACK:	Whew! Two and one half hours? Doesn't seem that long. It seems like 15 or 20 minutes.
TONY:	The funny thing is that your voice—you were almost hypnotizing me (laughs)!
RAY:	Yeah, I almost fell asleep (laughs).

Jack had been in a very deep level of hypnosis. He had spoken in a very slow, deliberate—almost mechanical—manner. It was as if someone had slowed his normal voice down by recording it and then playing it back at a slower speed. Additionally, he seemed to have actually relived his experience in real time:

TONY:	You see, different people have different responses.... Some people don't see anything—they hear. Some people don't hear, they sense, they feel. You're very good because you tend to use your hands as you're sitting there [i.e. to point out things that he was seeing].
JACK:	Well, I feel like I'm there!
RAY:	You were actually in the present.
TONY:	That's why you're such a good subject.
RAY:	What you've done in two and one half hours is go through a very, very logical chronology. It doesn't seem like a dream.
JACK:	Well see, Ray, it didn't happen like a dream.... It happened...as if I were awake. I mean, I remember the dog getting up—going to the door—that happens all the time. There's nothing strange about that or getting out of bed or swearing at the dog, you know? And looking out the window and running out. Everything seemed to happen with a logical sequence. I remember saying to Mary, "You know, it just, it just really, ah affected me because it didn't seem like a dream."
RAY:	When you told Mary about your dream—did you remember all this detail?
JACK:	No, all I could remember the next day was, um getting up and seeing the light and running outside and picking the dog off the ground and then taking him back to the house and then thinking that, that—one minute I was running towards this thing, and then suddenly I didn't want to have anything to do with it and went to bed. And I didn't know why I wanted to do that. It was stupid. I don't know how to explain it, but I was running out there. I was screaming, "Mary, Mary look at this thing! Look at this thing!" And then, the next thing I knew, I'm crawling back into bed saying, "The heck with it. I don't want to deal with it." And then I pulled over the covers. But, the covers had come off my head, and I was forced to look, and I saw this thing standing at the bed—standing there looking at me. And then, that's all I remembered from the dream. The rest I didn't remember.

RAY:	If you think of the things you dream about, they seem to be extremely logical when you dream them. But, when you wake up...you really think the whole thing over. It's very illogical.... I think last time, we discussed the date and the time, but you might think about that again.
JACK:	Well, I remember the dream occurred in May. It was a Friday night in May. For some reason, the 22nd sticks in my mind. I know it was the latter part of May, and that it was a Friday night...last year...in '88. I remember that I was teaching at the time, at Leland-Gray High School.
RAY:	Did you notice any clock—the time it happened?
JACK:	No.
RAY:	Was it cloudy? Did you see stars?
JACK:	It was clear, and it was warm because I remember having on a pair of shorts...to take the dog out. It was warm and the grass was green and tall.
RAY:	You mentioned the moon. You thought (at first) that the blue light was the moon. Was the moon out that night?
JACK:	No, it wasn't.... I thought it was the moon, so I went over to look.... I thought it was peculiar the way this light came in the window. I thought, "It's the moon." And that's what made me go look, and when I saw this thing out there, I started out screaming, and I ran outside to get a better look at it.

The tape ran out at this juncture, which was just as well, as we had run overtime and the hour was late. However, prior to leaving, arrangements were made to interview Mary under hypnosis.

Several days after the session, Tony's evaluation arrived in the mail. He was very impressed with Jack's testimony and reactions under hypnosis.

July 23, 1989
Hi Ray,

Good to see you and Jack Weiner yesterday, as we continued our "look-see" at the Allagash four.

Again I was impressed with Jack's session and with his openness, integrity and spontaneity. He was in a deep state of relaxation, as evidenced by his general physical and facial demeanor. He spoke in the present tense; his voice was "inflected"—emotions were commensurate with what he was describing, as were his facial expressions, such as his eyes and mouth. Frequently, he would look in the direction of a description and/or slightly raise a hand in response to a memory. His sighs of relief and his expressions of distaste all indicate a true regression, rather than merely remembering it. I am impressed with, for want of a better expression, his "childlike innocence" regarding this experience he shared with us. Recall his interjections, such as, "Oh boy!" Again, Jack comes across as a decent, honest, perplexed, but curious individual who has experienced something extraordinary and who wants to understand as much of it as he can....

—Tony

During the period between sessions, I established the date of Jack's "dream" and compared what he had described with knowledge gleaned from other UFO case studies. Jack's dream had occurred on a Friday night in May of 1988. He knew that it had taken place on a Friday night. The date, May 22, had stuck in his mind. But, Friday was on May 20. He also stated that he saw no moon in the sky. A check with astronomical records showed that the moon was five days old and in its waxing crescent phase on May 20, 1988. It had set shortly after midnight. Thus, Jack's dream must have taken place on the night of the 20th, but after midnight, which would place it in the early morning hours of Saturday, May 21, 1988.

In my estimation, what Jack related under hypnosis was much too complex to have been a dream. He appeared to relive the event in the real length of time and in the first person with corresponding emotions. Such a "dream" is a typical component of abduction phenomena. Memory of the abduction is usually buried in the subconscious mind by alien induction. Nonetheless, many times it surfaces via memory flashbacks and vivid lifelike dreams. When abductees experience conscious recall of all or part of an abduction experience, they dismiss the memory as an extraordinary nightmare. For some, to acknowledge the reality of such inexplicable memories would be tantamount to doubting their sanity.

Jack's description of the aliens was interesting. He appeared to recognize them as being the same types of creatures encountered on the Allagash, but dressed in different apparel.

I was especially struck by Jack's description of the object and the smell that emanated from it. The blue glow emitted from the bottom of the object was reminiscent of the cone-shaped, blue beam witnessed on the Allagash. In both cases, entering the beam or glow resulted in being transported aboard the UFO.

The pulsating glow around the UFO is also representative of other close encounters. Sometimes it dims to reveal a structured object behind it. Jack himself had noticed this phenomenon when staring at the glowing UFO on the Allagash. It had dimmed momentarily to reveal the shape of the solid craft. He had described it as looking like two hemispheres, one inverted upon the other, surrounded by a pink, glowing ring. UFO researchers refer to this typical configuration as being Saturn-shaped.

In the case of the southern Vermont UFO, it had also temporarily dimmed to reveal solid edges. Such multicolored glows around UFOs are theorized to be plasma or ionized gas caused by electromagnetic fields emanating from the object. Its reaction to the immediate air surrounding the object would result in the pungent smell that Jack detected. He could have been smelling ozone, a blue, gaseous form of oxygen created by the silent discharge of electricity in the air. It too has a peculiar, sharp odor, and is often smelled by witnesses who have close encounters with UFOs.

Jack's vivid descriptions smacked of reality—not a dream. However, A 64-million-dollar question still remained. Would Mary remember her part in the abduction when under hypnosis? We would have to wait another month to find out.

CHAPTER 8

"Mary-You"

We were all a bit concerned about how Mary would react to hypnosis. She had accepted our invitation, but she had done so reluctantly. A part of her wanted to know if Jack's dream represented memories of a dual abduction, but another part was afraid to recall something that might frighten her for the rest of her life.

Tony was also worried about Mary being alone with us during the hypnosis session. Prior to the meeting, he expressed his concern to me in a letter from which I quote:

> I have one suggestion concerning our session with Mary. August 12 is ideal for me. As you realize, during these sessions, the subject must sometimes reveal information that is sometimes personal/intimate ("He placed a cap over my penis," etc.) Do you feel it would be a good idea to invite Mary to bring a girlfriend, sister, aunt, etc., with her, so she would not feel too uncomfortable if she had to share a similar personal experience? I feel a bit uneasy (and think she will too) having her sit in a room with two or three men with the possibility of that type of information being revealed. Perhaps you could mention it to Jack and get his opinion.

I followed up on Tony's suggestion. Mary agreed wholeheartedly with the idea. She made arrangements to bring Chuck Rak's wife, Kim, along with her.

Hypnosis Session #1—Mary Weiner
(August 12, 1989)

When I arrived at Tony's house, Mary and Kim were sitting on the sofa, talking to him about hypnosis. As I was introducing myself to Kim, Jack suddenly strode into the living room from the bathroom. He had brought Mary and Kim down from Vermont and was on his way out to visit Jim in Boston. As he said good-bye to Mary, he admonished her not to be nervous. However, it was like the pot calling the kettle black. Jack seemed beside himself with nervousness.

I felt sympathy for the petite woman who sat warily in the large easy chair that Tony employed for hypnosis. She was not only nervous about hypnosis, but terribly frightened about what might result from it. She knew Jack was worried that she might relive things that were contrary to what he had experienced. Neither wanted him to appear dishonest. She was also concerned about coping with the scary memories that might surface while she was under hypnosis. Tony tried to assure Mary that he would help her to remember only what she wanted to remember after the session, but Mary did not look convinced about this. (See Figure 24.)

Figure 24. From left to right: Jack and Mary Weiner,
Jim Weiner.

Finally, Tony went through a similar routine that he had successfully used on the others. First, he attempted to place Mary in a light state of hypnosis. Mary, however, responded differently. She fidgeted in the chair. Her eyes fluttered open and closed. It was quite apparent that she was continually slipping in and out of the hypnotic state. The following are excerpts representative of Mary's reaction to being hypnotized:

TONY: I'm going to ask you to recount whatever you recall occurred on the night of Friday, May 20, 1988. Whatever you recall after Jack got up to let the dog out. You may begin speaking whenever you are ready.

MARY: (Long pause.) I don't really recall anything.

TONY: Do you recall Jack saying anything to you?

MARY: (Pauses.) I, I feel like I want to open my eyes.

TONY: Just keep them closed for just a few moments.

Tony proceeded to talk to Mary very softly and gently. He sought to overcome Mary's resistance to the hypnotic effect by deepening her state of relaxation.

TONY: Please do keep your eyes closed. Why don't you explain to us why you want to open them?

MARY: I, I don't feel like I'm really relaxed.

Mary was not responding. Tony then attempted to find out those things that Mary felt were relaxing to her:

TONY: What would make you feel that you were relaxed?

MARY: I don't know. I just (laughs) don't know.

Undaunted, Tony suggested that Mary envision situations that would relax her. Mary continued to flutter her eyes:

TONY: Don't try to keep your eyes closed. Just allow them to stay closed.

Over and over again, Tony attempted to place Mary in a state of hypnosis. Kim and I watched, entranced at the mental duel that was taking place before our eyes:

TONY:	Do you remember getting into bed that night?
MARY:	(Pauses.) No.
TONY:	Do you remember getting out of bed?
MARY:	(Pauses for a long time.) I, I still feel as if I could just could open my eyes right now (laughs). I, I don't know if I'm—I'm, I'm not trying to fight you or anything I just—
TONY:	Just relax, just relax.

To make a long story short, Tony tried in a variety of ways to place Mary under hypnosis. The following comment by Mary sums up the results of his first hypnosis session with Mary Weiner.

MARY:	I feel like I'm—I, I,—this is awful. Nothing's happening, Tony.

Finally, I signaled Tony to stop the session. It was quite apparent that Mary either could not, or would not, be hypnotized. As usual, I left my recorder running to catch Mary's first words after the session:

TONY:	So, whenever you feel that you are ready, just open your eyes.

Mary nonchalantly opened her eyes and glanced around the room shyly.

MARY:	(Laughs softly.) It didn't work...I never felt like I got—like I was (pauses).
TONY:	Hypnotized?
MARY:	Yeah (laughs).
TONY:	Had you been hypnotized, what would you have expected to feel or experience?
MARY:	Relaxation. I, I never—I was real tense. And I was thinking like, after you, when you first asked, "What happened on May 20th." And then you started bringing me back again, it was—I kept thinking in my head, May 20th, May 20th, so I couldn't concentrate. I knew that you were going to start asking me again about May 20th.
TONY:	And that made you kind of uptight?
MARY:	Yeah.

TONY:	So you were uptight about the date to begin with?
MARY:	(Speaks softly.) Yeah.
TONY:	I sense resistance from what you said before and from some of the things I see, as you sit there. I think you are afraid of remembering, and then, as you say, "I don't like to be afraid." So, when you get home and you're alone and you're going to remember this—if anything happened—you're going to be afraid. And you didn't care for that.
MARY:	Umm.

After the session, I drove Mary and Kim to the local station to catch a train to Boston, where they would be met by Jack. On the way, I tried to assure her that she had neither failed us nor Jack—that she couldn't help her nervousness. It was a normal reaction to the circumstances at hand, especially for a person who feared remembering something that would be frightening. Tony had suggested a second attempt at hypnosis, if she were willing. She promised to think it over. A few days after our meeting, I received Tony's evaluation.

> August 12, 1989
> Hi Ray,
>
> Sorry that the session did not turn out as successful as previous sessions.... I thought it was natural for Mary to be "nervous" anticipating this session.... I did become concerned when Mary said she was frightened—and that she was afraid of being frightened when she got home because of what she might remember. I took a bit more time trying to assuage her fears. But, I think that while she accepted my comments intellectually, she was still frightened emotionally.
>
> ...an increase in Mary's self-confidence, might result in a more successful hypnotic induction, if she chooses to try again. About all we can do is wait and see.
>
> —Tony

We did wait and see. Mary did agree to another session. She felt she had failed both Jack and our team. I had tried to dissuade her not to feel this way but to no avail. Yet, on the plus side, that was what motivated her once again to make the long trip down from Vermont to Tony's house for another try.

Hypnosis Session #2—Mary Weiner
(September 16, 1989)

I was surprised to find Mary sitting alone with Tony when I arrived. Kim was not able to accompany her, and Mary did not want to expose herself to anyone else in this situation. I could not help but admire her spunk for going it alone. Dave soon arrived, and the formal session began.

Tony again tried his best to hypnotize a very nervous Mary Weiner. He used a number of time-proven procedures during his attempt. At times, it seemed that he had succeeded placing her in a light state. However, in this state, Mary could remember nothing about the night of May 20, 1988, let alone a UFO experience.

It became apparent that our probe into Mary's mind was futile. Tony glanced at me with a defeated look on his face and pretended to slit his throat with his finger. This was his usual way of signaling the end of sessions. I nodded affirmatively and passed him a note, asking him to give Mary a posthypnotic suggestion to forget his name. We used this ploy to test the level of the hypnotic state. Mary failed the test, which indicated that she had only been in a light state of hypnosis. She pronounced Tony Constantino perfectly! Then, after collecting herself, she commented:

MARY: I, I felt like I was relaxing better but I still don't feel like I was gone.

TONY: Yeah, um, even people who are very deeply hypnotized will say the same thing: "because I heard everything and I was aware of everything, I don't really feel that I was hypnotized."

Tony then went on to explain how differently people react to hypnosis. He told us that 20 percent of a given population can attain what is called the "light state." He felt that Mary had reached this level. However, something had prevented Mary from going deeper. We sought to find the reason why and questioned her about this. Her comment was significant:

MARY: I noticed, um, while you were asking me questions, I felt very relaxed for any questions you asked, until you started asking about that night or about the UFOs. Then I got—could feel myself getting tense and my eyes started flickering and I got nervous.

Thus, it would seem that Mary had no problem with hypnosis, as long as crucial questions were not asked. But, as soon as they were, something inside of her resisted. Was this because the conscious mind refused to accept what might have happened? Was it because she was programmed by the aliens to forget? Was it because nothing happened to her that night? These questions haunted us as the session came to a disappointing end.

During the weeks that followed, I reviewed what we knew about Mary Weiner. First, she had only been privy to what Jack had started to describe about his dream during his first hypnosis session. We had quickly cut him off to avoid contaminating her memory. Moreover, Mary had no conscious memory of what little Jack had related about the abduction in her presence. Based on past experience with alien-induced memory blocks, I looked for other indicators that Mary may have been abducted with Jack. Such indicators usually occurred in the form of mental flashbacks or dreams.

The first clue had come during the first hypnosis session with her husband's brother, Jim, who was relating to us how his brother, Jack, recently had begun to have nightmares about strange alien faces. But, he also alluded to some dreams that Mary had experienced:

RAY:	When did Jack tell you this?
JIM:	Oh, last year [1988] when he started having dreams.
RAY:	Does he remember dreaming the faces, or does he remember seeing faces—actual faces—in real time?
JIM:	He told me that he remembered in dreams. He has similar dreams, him and his wife.
RAY:	His wife, too?
JIM:	Yes.
RAY:	I see. Has she ever seen a UFO?
JIM:	Not that I know of, but she keeps saying that she dreams of deer that come into their house at night with big eyes.

Jim's statement was intriguing. I made it a point to ask Jack and Mary for further details about her dreams. Our conversation was recorded.

RAY: (To Mary) Do you have any remembrance or dreams or flashbacks that may be related to a UFO experience?

MARY: The only dream that I remember is Jack getting up to take the dog for a walk—and um, walking through our door. Not opening the door, just walking through and me going to the door, opening the door, and yelling out, "Jack! Jack!"—You know? "Where are you?" (Pauses.) Well, I had a dream about deer one time.

RAY: With big eyes?

MARY: Yeah, and we have—I just thought because we have so many deer in our backyard that—I don't really remember the dream well.

RAY: Were the deer in the house or outside the house?

MARY: I don't remember that they were in the house.

JACK: You told me they were in the house.

MARY: Jack told me that.

RAY: Jack, do you remember anything else about the dream?

JACK: No, nothing, other than, ah, the next morning she told me. She was visibly upset about the dream. She told me that she dreamt that deer had come in the house and that they were standing next to the bed, staring at her with big eyes. And I said, "Deer?" And she said, "Yeah, they were deer but they had big eyes.... I remember her telling me that.

As I listened to Jack and Mary, several things immediately came to mind. First, unknown to Mary, Jack had described himself and her passing through their closed door when they were floating back to their house from the glowing craft. Second, Mary's dream about the deer had been traumatic. She was extremely upset when telling Jack about it on the following morning. Why couldn't she remember the deer being beside her bed in the dream? All she remembered were deer with big eyes. Third, UFO researcher Budd Hopkins has cases on record where aliens have used animal images as posthypnotic covers to their operations.

One case in particular included a deer! The abductee's name is Virginia. Her experience is chronicled in Budd's book, *Missing Time*.[1] Virginia had contacted Budd through a psychiatrist who had demonstrated the use of hypnosis with abduct-

---

1. Budd Hopkins, *Missing Time* (New York: Richard Marek Publishers, 1981).

ees on an NBC-TV segment about UFOs. She told Budd that she had two inexplicable periods of missing time in her life. Both had occurred when she was a child, and she felt that there was a connection between the two. The first event took place when she was six years old. Ever since then, she had been thinking, "There's something odd about this, and when I grow up I'm going to understand it."[2] Under hypnosis, Virginia relived a typical childhood abduction at age six, in the summer of 1950.

As a child, Virginia had lived on a farm. One day she sauntered off to the barn to collect eggs from the hen coop. Then something inexplicable occurred:

> All of a sudden, I was in the yard and I didn't remember going from the barn into the yard towards the house. I had an itch on my leg, and I reached down to scratch it. I pulled up my blue jeans and when I scratched my leg, I realized it was wet. I was covered with blood, from a cut on the back of my calf. It was a large and clean cut...no dirt or anything. It must have been at least a half-inch deep and an inch long.
>
> It was bleeding but there was no pain.[3]

Under hypnosis, Virginia relived being somehow lifted into a room filled with pearly light and an "ozone smell." There she was put on a soft couch-like table by strange manlike creatures. They had large, dark eyes, bald heads, diminutive facial features, perhaps four fingers and were dressed in tight-fitting coverall clothing. While she was on the couch, an instrument automatically cut a tissue sample from her leg.

The second missing-time event was ten years later, in 1960. It took place in France when Virginia was 16 years old. She was on a family picnic and decided to explore the woods. When she emerged from the woods, she had blood on her blouse. Her family had been searching about an hour for her. All she could remember was being with a deer. What she didn't dare tell her parents was that she and the deer communicated with each other. Under light hypnosis she related to Budd:

> The deer. That pretty deer that I was so fond of....
> It was a person. It was a friend.... How I found him and how the communication happened, I can't remember.
> There's a blockout.[4]

2. Hopkins, *Missing Time*, p. 128
3. Hopkins, *Missing Time*, p. 129.
4. Hopkins, *Missing Time*, p. 199.

However, under deep hypnosis, the truth about the deer burst forth from the hidden depths of Virginia's subconscious mind.

> I'm walking through the woods. There's a bright light. There's a ship just like they have in the movies. It's round. It's top-shaped roughly, but I can't tell exactly.... There's so much light you can't really see clearly.... There was some pink in it, and blue. Bright light. And then I hear almost like a whisper, "Virginia...Virginia," and I think it was in my head that they were calling me.

Virginia walked, mesmerized, toward the hovering, glowing craft. She found herself entering a column of light that it beamed to the ground. Then it happened:

> It was like a conveyor ramp. I stood on it and it lifted.

When on board, the aliens again examined her. The blood found later on her blouse was caused by a probe that was inserted into her left nostril. The deer with hypnotic-like eyes was all that she could remember when she was returned to the woods. In reality, her amnesia and the deer image were mercifully imposed upon her by the aliens.

The glowing object, the bright blue light, the column or beam of light that lifted her into the craft, the typical aliens, the couch that automatically probed her and the missing time are all reminiscent of the Allagash incident. In Jack's dream, he described aliens with big eyes taking Mary and him from their bed. Mary dreamed of deer coming to her bedside and staring at her with big eyes. Could it be that those eyes belonged to the aliens Jack described in his dream? Is it possible that these same eyes provided a hypnotic cover for the abduction of Mary?

Yet another clue hinted that this very well may be the case. It occurred as our first session with Mary was drawing to an end. Just before we broke up, Tony introduced Mary to a procedure sometimes employed by law enforcement agencies: the use of a pendulum to probe her subconscious. The technique involves holding a pendulum perfectly still with one hand. The subject is then told that if asked 'yes' and 'no' questions, the pendulum would respond in a certain way. It would react to a 'yes' answer by swinging up and down. A 'no' answer would be indicated by it swinging sideways left to right. A 'maybe' answer would be denoted when the pendulum swung around in a clockwise motion. An 'I don't know' answer would be expressed by the pendulum swinging around in a counterclockwise motion.

When this technique is used, the pendulum appears to move by itself when responding to questions. In reality, the person holding it is moving it by micro-muscular reactions fed by the subconscious. Mary proved to be an excellent subject. She addressed her subconscious as Mary-you:

MARY: Mary-you, I want to ask you if anything happened on the night of May 20th, after Jack and I went to bed that I should be aware of?

Mary stared in amazement as the pendulum began, at first slowly and then faster, to move up and down:

MARY: (Laughs nervously.) That's a yes.
TONY: Okay, stop it with your other hand.
MARY: Mary-you, is this something that is going to scare me? Is, is this going to scare me, Mary-you?

All of us watched intently as the pendulum again swung up and down, denoting a "yes" answer. Mary uttered a very pensive "thank you" and continued. Her questions and answers are as follows:

MARY: Mary-you, is this something that I should know about?...(Yes)

Mary-you, was I told by somebody to forget what happened to me on May 20th?...(Yes)

Mary-you, I was told to forget?...(Yes)

Mary-you, will it be possible for me to remember whatever happened on that night?...(Yes)... That's weird!

Mary-you, have I ever seen anything that would be considered a UFO?...(Yes)

Mary-you, (speaks nervously) did I see anything that night that would be considered a UFO?... (Yes)

Mary-you, did I see anyone that night from the UFO?...(Yes)

Mary-you, did they do anything to me and Jack?...(Yes)

Mary was visibly upset at the answers she was obtaining from her subconscious (Mary-you) via the pendulum. She decided to ask it some more questions that were not related to UFOs, to see what it would do:

MARY: Is my maiden name Dugan?...(No)
               Is my maiden name Donlan?...(Yes)

Tony told Mary that the answers she was getting need not be true, but that the method usually was indicative of truth. Other questions asked are as follows:

MARY: Mary-you, that night on May 20th—was I exam-
               ined by anyone from the UFO that I saw?...(Yes)

TONY: You might ask, and I'm curious, if the examina-
               tion took a long time.

MARY: Mary-you, did this examination take a long time
               for them to do?...(Yes)

MARY: Was it more than an hour?...(Yes)

TONY: Did the examination take more than two hours
               is a good question.

MARY: Mary-you, did the examination take more than
               two hours?...(Yes)

MARY: Mary-you, did the examination take more than
               three hours?...(Yes)

MARY: Mary-you, did the examination take more than
               four hours?...(No)

The session ended with Mary's tantalizing performance with the pendulum. If accurate in its answers, Mary's subconscious was telling us that she indeed had shared the experience with Jack, and was programmed by the aliens to forget.

Was the abduction a catalyst for Mary's dreams? Were the big-eyed deer staring at Mary at the foot of her bed in reality a distorted memory of the aliens? Was watching Jack passing through their closed front door a real memory from an abduction? I strongly suspect that this is the case. But, only "Mary-you" knows for sure.

CHAPTER **9**

Harry the Ghost

Our investigation to date indicated that the Allagash abductions had the potential of being one of the great classics in UFO abduction history. The fourfold complementary testimony, twins factor and apparent ongoing alien abductions during our investigation formed a combined uniqueness. However, all along, there had been hints that we had only scratched the surface of this remarkable case. One of these clues was "Harry the Ghost." It is widely known among UFO researchers who study CEIV experiences that adult victims have a potential history of multiple abductions reaching back into their childhood. Leading UFO abduction researcher Budd Hopkins and other researchers find that UFO abductions begin in childhood, often as early as the age of three or four. From that time on the abductee is treated as a marked specimen, picked up again and again over the abductee's lifetime as part of an ongoing genetic experiment. The memory of these events is buried in the subconscious. Evidence indicates that this amnesia may be artificially imposed upon the abductee by the alien entities.

The adult abductee usually recalls such childhood encounters in terrifying nightmares of monsters or ghosts. My own experience was of a pale, Asian-looking being with slanted eyes, who periodically took me from my bedroom at night. Mary Weiner's casual mention of the twins' childhood ghost excited my curiosity. It fit the pattern and needed to be checked out.

My first step was to find out how much was consciously re-membered about Harry. I started by telephoning the twins' mother, Jeanne Weiner. She not only confirmed the twins' re-ports, but told me how she and her husband were confronted by it one night.

Harry appeared to the twins' parents as a white-glowing robed, bearded figure at the foot of their bed. I found this inter-esting, since research has shown tall robed humanlike entities have often been seen with the smaller alien-appearing human-oids. The following is a transcript of my conversation with Jeanne Weiner:

JEANNE:	He looked all white.
RAY:	Did you notice any coloring on his eyes, or his face at all, or was that all white as well?
JEANNE:	I don't, I don't remember. I was, I was so scared.
RAY:	What would you say he was wearing?
JEANNE:	It looked like he—to me, he looked like he was wearing a white robe or something long and white.
RAY:	Was he standing or floating?
JEANNE:	Standing. He—my husband kept saying, "What do you want?" Ah, he kept saying, ah, "How did you get in here?" And, ah, then finally I said to him, [her husband], "Go get him!"
RAY:	Yeah.
JEANNE:	It seemed like we were kind of, ah, you know stunned, like we couldn't move or something, you know? We just—I said, "Go get him!"
RAY:	Now, the reason that you could see this in the dark was because it was light enough in the room? Or, was there light coming from the fig-ure?
JEANNE:	There wasn't light. It seemed like he was all white [glowing], to me.
RAY:	Did it ever move while you were watching it?
JEANNE:	He went out of the room. He, he seemed to go out towards the door.
RAY:	So he turned around?
JEANNE:	No, I don't remember if he did or not.
RAY:	Did he move like he was walking on legs or...?
JEANNE:	No, I don't know how he got out of the room, but my husband, he, he got up, and he put his pants on and he went to go after him. And he didn't have very far to go, because we lived in a ranch-

type home, and the bedrooms were at one end of the house and the living room and kitchen ànd, and the garage and everything were at the other side. And, he, my husband was a big man, and he didn't waste any time and ah, he got—he [Harry] was gone!

RAY: Uh-huh. Did it go out the door?

JEANNE: We didn't hear the door.

RAY: Was the door closed?

JEANNE: The door was closed.

RAY: What years were you in that house?

JEANNE: We were there from 1951...until 1986.

RAY: So, this, ah, incident that happened with you would have happened approximately what year do you think?

JEANNE: In the late '50's.

I also phoned Jeanne's other son, Tom. He remembered the so-called ghost but strangely enough, never saw it himself. In addition, neither he nor his mother had ever seen what could be called a UFO. Since the twins had borne the brunt of the strange manifestations, I asked them to tell me everything they could remember of "Harry."

Jim Weiner's Recollection

When we were young, I remember that I would hear voices at night. Not every night, but now and then. Ah, we would go to bed and I would hear this music, which for the longest time...I used to think was a television show coming from our neighbor's house.... It was almost like a drum sound...like a boom—boom, ah, slow booming drum sound.... For some reason, it disturbed me when I was young—hearing that sound. It seemed like whenever I would hear that, I would also hear somebody calling my name. A low male voice that would, ah, call my name. It would sound like this. It would go, "Jim, Jim, Jim, Jim"—and it would sound just like that, repeat "Jim" three or four times. And it would scare the living shit out of me. You know, we grew up Catholics and...when I was a little kid, I always thought it was God calling me or something for some reason, either because I did something bad, or maybe He wanted to take me away from this life. So it used to terrify me, and I'd always wind up...going straight to the bottom of my bed, under the covers, and staying there until the next morning.

There was one incident I still remember, ah, one night. It started out as this deep, male voice calling "Jim," and then there were other voices involved—high-pitched, female voices. There was some kind of background noise that they were making. It was a wailing noise or a whistling noise or something, and I remembered it just really terrified me. Also when we were young, we used to hear knocking sounds in our room. We used to attribute these things to our, to ah, a ghost that we called Harry the Ghost. All these things, weird things, used to go on in our house, and my mother and father would say, "Oh, that's just Harry the Ghost. Don't worry about it. He won't hurt you." I remember, ah, Jack used to claim that he would see these creatures in our room—that they would come into the room and try to pull the covers off his bed and try to take him out of his bed.... Or we would go to bed at night, and we'd wake up with this sound of somebody banging or knocking on the walls with their knuckles...and I would get so terrified. We'd start screaming for my father, and he'd come in the room and say we were having a nightmare.

Listening to Jim describe these paranormal activities struck a number of familiar notes for me. I had heard or read of such things many times in the course of my research activities. It fired my curiosity even more to hear what Jack would say about Harry. I did not have long to wait. Jack responded soon to my request.

Jack Weiner's Recollection

The following is my best recollection of Harry the Ghost:

My first memory of Harry goes back to when I was about four or five years old. It was after we had moved into the new house that my father had built. Our house was the first one built in the middle of a fairly remote area that consisted of vast expanses of cornfields interspersed with undeveloped wood.

Jim and I shared a bedroom at the far end of the house. One night I was aroused from my sleep by a presence in our bedroom. I awoke to find a horrible-looking monster standing next to my bed. I remember that I could see it very plainly, because there was a

night light turned on in our room. It was like nothing
I had ever seen before and seemed to float back and
forth next to my bed. It had large eyes and a big head
and didn't make any sounds. It just seemed to stare at
me for a short time and then began to remove the covers from the bed. At that point, I became extremely
afraid and tried not to look at it. I wanted to scream
out but couldn't. My mouth and my voice wouldn't
work! The next thing I remembered was the covers being drawn up over me and seeing the monster looking
at me again. Then it seemed to just disappear into the
thin air and was gone. That's when I jumped out of bed
and ran into my parents' room so they could save me
from the monster. My parents said that I had a bad
dream, but I knew that I was awake and not dreaming.
I told them that it really was there in our room, and
that I didn't want to go back into my bed again because I was afraid that it would come back to get me.

After that initial encounter with Harry the Ghost,
the frequency of the comings and goings of Harry were
very regular and obvious to the rest of my family members. Both Jim and I were visited often, mostly at
night, and the phenomenon manifested itself as: voices that would call out our names loudly—loud rapping
on the walls of our bedroom—footsteps—an invisible
entity sitting on our beds or pulling the covers off—or
grabbing my feet and trying to pull me out of my bed.
Sometimes Harry would wander into my parents' room
and awaken my parents. My mother even claims to
have seen Harry standing next to her bed.... My older
brother, Tom, also was aware that there was something in the house that was definitely out of the ordinary. I don't remember if Tom ever saw Harry.

There were many instances when doors would
open and close themselves, often locking and unlock-
ing themselves. Also, sometimes, in the middle of the
night or day, the radio or the television would turn itself on, change channels and shut itself off again. Objects would move by themselves, and sometimes there
was an overwhelming sensation that there was some
strange presence in the house.

These occurrences continued throughout our
childhoods until Jim and Tom and I were in our teens.
The last real scare that I can vividly remember occurred when I was about 15 years old. I remember that
I was standing in the kitchen, talking to a girlfriend on

the telephone, when I noticed a bright, yellowish ball
of light, about the size of a beach ball, hovering outside
the kitchen window located directly over the sink. I
was completely alone in the house at the time and was
somewhat frightened by it, because I didn't know what
it was. At first, I thought it was a fire outside the
house. Then, to my complete astonishment, the ball of
light passed right through the kitchen window and
into the kitchen. I stood in the corner of the kitchen in
total horror, as the light traversed around the kitchen
once, then floated into the living room and down the
hall toward our bedroom. It entered our bedroom, hovered in the middle of our room for several minutes and
then floated through the bedroom window and was
gone! It didn't make any noise at all. There were no
fireworks or anything like that. It just floated through
the house and then left. I was left in a state of panic
and then remembered that I had left my girlfriend dan-
gling on the telephone. So, I went back to the kitchen
and grabbed the phone again. My girlfriend was still
on the line, and I excitedly told her what had just happened. That was the last time I remember anything
that strange happening in our house.

So there you have it, Ray. All during those years,
we never thought Harry had anything to do with extraterrestrials. We always thought that it was some kind
of poltergeist or something just unexplainable. But
there definitely was something in our house. I am not
making any of this up. Whatever it was though, it
seemed to be centered around Jim and me. We were
the two who were targeted by Harry the most. Anyway,
I hope that this somehow helps your research into this
case.

The data gleaned from the twins and their mother certainly
did help our research into this case. As mentioned, an abductee's remembrance of childhood bedroom visitations by strange
entities is a benchmark of the abduction phenomenon. It added
strong circumstantial evidence for the physical reality of the Allagash abductions. Jack's response to his bedroom visitation
by a frightening entity had brought to mind my own childhood
encounters. I recently relived my experiences under hypnosis
and felt the same sensation of raw terror. A peculiar feeling of
a presence would awaken me. I would sit up in bed and see a
figure standing at my bedroom door. It would be outlined by a
night light in the hallway behind it. When I tried to scream,
nothing would come out of my mouth. A strange electric-like

feeling pulsed through my body. I could not move as the figure approached my bed. Later, I had flashbacks of leaving my bed with a cloaked entity with a pale face and slanting eyes. Many of the things that the Allagash four described struck a familiar chord within me, thus it was easy to empathize with them.

Also common within abduction reports is the ball-of-light visitation. They have been dubbed "bedroom lights" by UFO researchers. Sometimes the glowing ball will dissipate and disgorge an alien entity. At other times, the alien entity will dissipate and become a luminous ball. Again, with the feeling of déjà vu, I too had an encounter with a small light hovering before my bed when I was a child.

Another significant revelation made by Jim during our interview about Harry the Ghost had to do with a childhood missing time experience:

My father and everyone else in the family seems to relate the story that I went out into this snowstorm and got lost and somehow fell into a open hole at a construction site...and almost froze to death. I have lots of recollections of going out to play in snowstorms when I was a child. But, [of] that specific recollection, I have none—none whatsoever. No matter how hard I try to remember that event, it seems as if everyone else in my family remembers it but me.

There was another incident when I was young. We used to go sledding down this hill on a nearby road that was about a mile away from our house. A farm road. I remember going sledding on this road one afternoon. And, ah, it was getting towards late afternoon, maybe 3:30, 4:00...because the sun was starting to go down. And I thought, "Well, I better get home or I'm going to be late for supper." We always ate at 5:00. I remembered thinking, "Well, if I take the long way on that, I'm not going to make it home in time, so I'll take the short cut...across the fields...And, ah, I remembered going down off the road into the fields. And then, I don't remember anything after that, except being home again, and my parents were really pissed off at me because I was really late.... And they kept saying, "Where were you? Where did you go?" And I kept saying, "I just went sledding down at the road and, ah, I cut across the field to take a short cut to come home.... I, I, ah, remembered just taking a shortcut." That's another thing in my childhood that I've never been able to figure out.... I've always wondered, ah, what happened? Where did that time go when I was coming home from sledding that evening?

Where did that time go? Jim had left the sledding road in plenty of time to get home for supper. This was just one of many intriguing questions that would accumulate during our on-going investigation. Later on, we called upon Tony's services to probe these questions under hypnosis. The following are excerpts from the segment of the session that deal with Jim's missing time as a child. Other provocative items probed during this session will be covered later.

Hypnosis Session #3A—Jim Weiner (March 10, 1990)

Dave Webb and I watched silently as Tony placed Jim Weiner into an initial state of light hypnosis in preparation for our querying. As usual, Jim responded easily and the questions began:

TONY: Just allow your mind, your unconscious, to go back to the late '50's.—to the early '60's. You were sledding on a hill, apparently in a snow-storm, about a mile from home. You decided to take a short cut so that you would not be late for supper. Do you remember that, Jim?

JIM: Um-hum.

TONY: Okay, will you explain to us everything you recall about that incident?

JIM: I remember like it happened yesterday. There was a road, a road with a hill on it that we used to sled down when we were kids. I'm trying to remember the name of [the] road.... Oh, oh, I can see it, and there is a family that lived in a farmhouse there. Their son went to school with—he was one of my brother's buddies...we named it after them. The hill was named after them. But I remember that it was the afternoon. We used to go there and sled. It was a great place. And, and I had gone sledding one afternoon after school. And, ah, we always ate at, ah, 5:00. It was dinner time. So we always had to be home then. And I stayed a little bit longer, and I remember it was starting—it was getting dark. So it must have been sometime in December or so, because it was getting dark already. It was starting to—the sun was starting to go down. And I thought, "Oh rats, I'm going to be in for it now. I better get home." And um, Ruth's, that was it—Ruth's Hill.

That was the name of it. And, um, off to the left of Ruth's Hill, if you're looking east and going east, down the hill, going towards my house—it was all woods then, and corn fields. There was this fairly large woods down at the bottom of the hill. Our house was on the top of this hill and at the bottom of this hill was this woods, which kind of went up another grade. And, on the far side of this woods was Ruth's Hill. And, um, ah, in order to get to my house, you'd have to go all the way east down Ruth's road, and then go all the way up the other side of the hill and then make a left-hand turn down another side road, which was the long way. I decided I'd make a short cut by cutting down left, off the road along the side of the woods, and I'd come up through the bottom and pick up a road at the bottom of the hill, and, and, make a short cut. For some reason, I thought that would be shorter, and I'd get home faster. And so, I cut down in the snow. But, I realized that the snow was getting deeper and deeper and deeper and it was really hard moving. And I remember this snow would be up past my knees and pulling this sled. And I kept thinking..."This is taking me forever. I'm never going to get home in time." Ah, I kept making for the side of the woods and, ah, I finally got to the side of the woods and...it was just starting to get dark. And, ah, then the next thing I remember is getting home, and it was dark already! My Mom and Dad were really—they made like they were really pissed off—but I could tell, you know, that they were really worried and just happy that I made it home. And it seemed like it, it was a couple of hours that had gone by from the time I left Ruth's Hill.

TONY: Can you attribute that to the deep snow? Can you attribute that to the new route home that you took?

JIM: Well, you know, I always, I always did. All my life I've always attributed it to the deep snow, but (pauses) I don't think that's what it was.

DAVE: What time was it when you got home?

JIM: Oh, it must have been after 6:00.

DAVE: Can you look around and see if you can see a clock?

JIM: There's a clock right on the kitchen table, and I know it was dark. It had to be dark already. So it must have been sometime after six.

DAVE:	But do you remember seeing the clock?
JIM:	No, I was too scared. I thought my dad would give me a licking. But you know, there's something strange about that, which, um, makes me doubt, makes me doubt that now [i.e., that the snow and new route made him late getting home]. It involves a dream that I had, ah, this past year. And it was a really corny dream. But, part of the dream brought me back to that time when I was walking with the sled home. And, ah, that's why I, ah, feel confused now, when I think back to that point because there's—part of this dream which was completely out of character with the rest of what was going on. It seemed so real.
TONY:	When did you have this dream?
JIM:	Sometime this past year or last year. Not since 1990, but sometime last year. And, um, I think I may have written it down on a calendar, but I can't remember what day it was now. But the dreams involved—this was the dream part—we were in Allentown, Pennsylvania, and Jack was in the dream. And we were just kids and we were playing, we were playing out in our front yard in the grass, and it was summertime. I remember the grass was green and my mother had these yellow bushes.... They're yellow in the spring. And we were playing out in front, and all of a sudden it was winter again. And, and I was with this sled in front of the woods. And I looked up, and there was this gigantic, round sphere coming out of the sky. It was the oddest thing, because I saw it from real far away. It was, it was up there.... I remember looking up and seeing this thing get closer and closer and closer and closer and closer.
TONY:	This is in your dream now?
JIM:	Yeah, but the dream switched. At first, we were on the lawn in the springtime. And then, all of a sudden I was in the wintertime again, and I was walking home at that time from Ruth's Hill with my sled—looking up. And I remember this thing coming down. It was huge and, ah, that's all I remembered. I don't remember, remember anything after that. I don't. And then the dream switched. And there were these little potato-head aliens that came and got Jack and I. They, they looked like potato heads and, um, I remember in my dream thinking, "This is really ridiculous." You know? "These guys are potato heads,

and how could these potato-head beings have a ship like this?"

Jim had already mentioned this dream to me. It had just added fuel to the fire of my suspicions that the period of missing time and his childhood memories of Harry the Ghost were intimately related. It appeared that our hypnotic probe of Jim's subconscious memories of the Allagash experience had dislodged other hidden memories, which surfaced in this dream. Tony realized this too, and immediately homed in on this likelihood.

TONY:	How old are you in the dream?
JIM:	Oh, must be around nine or ten.
TONY:	How old were you in 1950 or so, when you got home from that sledding incident?
JIM:	It, it wasn't '50. We were born in '51 so it was '60 or so. Yeah, it was around '63.
TONY:	How old were you then?
JIM:	Well, nine or ten.
TONY:	I want to go back to that incident when you were nine or ten. But before I do that, I want you to relax a bit....

Tony took time to place Jack into a deeper level of hypnosis and then resumed questioning him:

TONY: I'm just going to ask that you bring yourself back to that time when you were nine or ten years old and you were sledding. You know that it's getting late, and it's getting dark, and you know that your mother and father want you home by five. I'm going to ask that you pretend—that's all—pretend that someone has filmed—has videotaped—you trekking through that deep snow—trying to get home in time—to avoid being grounded or being yelled at or whatever. And, I'm going to ask you to slow that tape down, so that we can account for what seems to be an unusual amount of time to get home, in spite of the deep snow. After all, it was a short cut. And I'm going to ask that you just recreate—because I'm going to stop talking for a few seconds—I'm going to ask that you recreate that scene. Are you feeling the snow? Feeling it beneath your feet? And even snow has a very distinctive fragrance.

JIM: Yeah, I can smell it. Cold.

TONY: That's it, and while you're doing that, if you will allow me to lift your right hand off your thigh (prepares to further deepen Jim's hypnotic state). May I do that?

JIM: Um-hum.

TONY: And when I lift it up, I want it to be relaxed. I want it to be really limp, so I have to do the lifting. You will not do the lifting. Is that okay?

JIM: Um-hum.

TONY: Okay, I'll just take it like this (lifts Jim's arm). That's it, just like that. That's excellent. Just like that. That's excellent. Now, I'm just going to ask that you hold it there, so that when I let go, it will stay there. I'm going to let it go, and it will stay there. The amazing thing is that when I push down on it, it's going to bounce back to its position. I'm going to push down, and it will just bounce back to where it is. Just like that (pushes down; it bounces back).

JIM: Um-hum.

TONY: The point is that the lower it goes, the more deeply you will relax.... Do you understand?

As Jim's hand slowly descended, his body and facial expressions became more and more relaxed. He slumped further and further into the easy chair. Jim was in a very deep level of hypnosis when the questioning resumed.

TONY: I'm going to ask you to stay at that point of relaxation and that you recreate that scene when you were nine or ten. And, as you know, a cold winter's night has a unique taste—a unique fragrance—just recreate that. The taste of it. The fragrance of it. The resistance of the snow against your knees. And actually see if you can't put yourself back. Now, you've been walking—pushing—through the snow. And, I'm again going to ask your unconscious, not you, but your unconscious to recall anything—to create anything unusual that would have caused you to be late. So, just relax and allow your unconscious to withdraw—to withdraw from those memories anything that might have caused you to have been unusually late. You may speak whenever you feel that you are ready.

JIM:	(Speaks with a shaky voice.) I remember looking up and seeing that big sphere.
TONY:	Now, we're talking about the actual incident, not the dream.
JIM:	So am I. It's there!
TONY:	You look up, and you see a sphere?
JIM:	Yeah, there's pheasants in the trees and something made them fly and that's what made me look up.
TONY:	What do you see when you look up?
JIM:	This big sphere up in the sky.
TONY:	Describe it.
JIM:	It's big. It's real high up in the sky. And it's kind of a bluish-gray with this brown texture. It seems like a texture at first but as it got closer there—there's something protruding from the surface—there's, ah, panels.
TONY:	What does this object do?
JIM:	It keeps getting closer.
TONY:	And how close does it get to you?
JIM:	I don't know. I, the last thing I remember is being totally consumed by looking at this thing.
TONY:	What do you mean by consumed?
JIM:	That's all I can look at—as if nothing else existed except this thing coming out of the sky.
TONY:	It keeps coming closer and closer?
JIM:	Yeah.
TONY:	You can slow time down. You can slow it down. So, slow it down. Let's pretend it would be on a videotape or a movie. Just slow it down. It comes closer in the next frame. It's closer still in the next frame. It's even closer. And then what happens?
JIM:	I don't know. I don't really remember anything after that except (pauses) this feeling of ah, something happening. The air seemed, ah, not heavy, but, ah, pressure—like there's a pressure all around me. And it's getting—it's increasing. It's getting real—it's growing very quickly. Almost like an upwelling sensation. And, ah, I'm just locked in on this thing! And I feel like I'm going to explode!
TONY:	And then what happens?
JIM:	I don't know. That's the last thing I remember.

TONY:	What do you remember after that? What is the first thing you remember after that?
JIM:	I remember being at the road—at the head of the woods—where the road starts.
TONY:	Is this closer to your home?
JIM:	A little bit closer, yeah, but not a whole lot.
TONY:	And then what do you do?
JIM:	I just walk home on the road with my sled.
TONY:	Okay, let's go back. Let's go back in time and this huge object is coming down, closer and closer.
JIM:	Yeah, I can see it really well. And this feeling of pressure.
TONY:	Okay, you're feeling the pressure welling up.
JIM:	Yeah, real fast.
TONY:	At what point do you see the object going away from you?
JIM:	I don't remember seeing it going away from me—just coming towards me, and feeling this sudden upwelling of pressure, as if everything around me is going to explode.
TONY:	Do you hear anything?
JIM:	No. Nothing. Everything—it's just real still. Everything is still [the so-called "Oz-factor" reported in many cases]. I don't hear anything.
DAVE:	Is it dark out?
JIM:	Not yet. There's still light in the sky because I can see the, the light reflecting off the sides of this thing.
RAY:	Are there any lights on the object?
JIM:	(Pauses.) I don't know, it's hard to say.... There must have been lights coming from it in order to see the detail so well on the darker panels. I think the panels, these brownish panels, had light coming from behind them or in between them.
RAY:	Did the lighted panels have any pattern on this thing?
JIM:	There were hundreds of these things.
RAY:	How are they arranged on the sphere?
JIM:	In concentric rows. But they weren't even. They weren't as if they were in squares. It was like uneven patches where it would be, ah, a row on the top that would be so, so long. And the next row would be a little shorter, but, but it wasn't even.

It wasn't like a—it was almost like, ah, ah, like if you look at a map of the globe and you see the uneven borders—the uneven coastlines of the continents—that kind of pattern of these brown things. There didn't seem to be any kind of a symmetry to them.

RAY: Were they all around the object? Or, just on one side? Or two sides?

JIM: They were all around it, but in patches.

RAY: What part of the object were they around?

JIM: Towards, there was, ah (pauses) a patch towards the northern pole on my left. There was a patch up over there. Then there was like a bare area around the equator and more of these things towards the, the bottom, the southern pole. Only they seemed to be—to go more around it in totality except just being a patch.

DAVE: Was the object rotating or fixed?

JIM: No, it was fixed.

RAY: What was around the equator?

JIM: This bluish-grayish metal. What seemed to be some kind of a metal. This thing was gigantic....

RAY: Are there any openings on the object?

JIM: Nothing I can make out. I don't see anything.

DAVE: Do you hear anything?

JIM: Just this pressure.

RAY: Was the pressure pushing you down or pulling you up or pulling you sideways?

JIM: It felt like it was going to make me explode. Like it was not just around me, but inside of me.

TONY: Did any odor change from the usual snow fragrance? Any change in smell?

JIM: Yeah, no smell.

TONY: Is it possible to draw—give us an example of the panels...and the configuration that you described?

JIM: Oh sure. The colors are real vivid on the browns. It wasn't all one color brown.

DAVE: What happened next?

JIM: I don't remember a thing. All I remember is that everything around me—this sudden upwelling of pressure.

RAY: Are you supposed to remember what happened?

JIM: I, I don't get a feeling that I'm not supposed to re-
                  member or that I should remember. I, I, I have a
                  feeling that I want to remember.

DAVE: Then why don't you remember?

JIM: I don't know. It's just like a blank. A total, abso-
                  lute blank, as if that's the last thing I remember
                  and then the next thing I remember—it's like
                  blinking my eyes and then being on, at the road.

TONY: I'm going to ask you to relax a little now.

Now that a UFO was involved, we were determined to get to
the bottom of the missing-time mystery. Tony decided to push
Jim even deeper into hypnosis. He employed what is known as
the "divided TV screen ploy" to probe the memories of Jim's
subconscious mind. To do this, Jim was made to imagine seeing a TV screen. He was told that the right side would light up
to answer yes and the left side would light up to answer no.

TONY: The right is "yes," the left is "no"...it's just the
                  unconscious mind that has all these memories.
                  The unconscious never forgets.... I'm not asking
                  you to remember Jim, I'm asking your uncon-
                  scious to remember.

Tony suddenly fired the $64 million question at Jim, hop-
ing to catch his subconscious mind off guard:

TONY: Do you remember what it [the sphere] did to
                  Jim? Right or left?

JIM: It says, "Yes."

This crack in Jim's blocked memory was what we had all
been waiting for. Tony quickly took advantage of the situation,
and we all waited the results with bated breath:

TONY: Did it leave Jim standing in the snow?

JIM: No (pauses). It took me somewhere!

TONY: Just relax. How did it take you?

JIM: I think it pulled me somehow.

TONY: Did it pull you to the left or to the right?

JIM: No, it's just a feeling of a—suddenly exploding.
                  Like it was pulling me apart and then I was in-
                  side something!

TONY: What were you inside of?

JIM:	This room.
TONY:	Look around and describe it.
JIM:	(Does not answer; begins to breath heavily.)
TONY:	Just relax. Just describe anything that you happen to see.
JIM:	(Does not answer.)
TONY:	Where is your sled?
JIM:	The sled's not there. Just me. Sled's gone.
RAY:	Anybody else with you?
JIM:	I seem to have a vague image of some things—people-type shapes—some kind of beings in a far—in the far corner—far—not a corner, but a far place in this room.
TONY:	Do they stay there?
JIM:	Yeah, they're staying there, and they're watching me.
TONY:	What are you doing?
JIM:	I'm scared!
DAVE:	What do they look like?
JIM:	It's hard to see. I can't—they're, they're in the darkness.
RAY:	When do they get close?
JIM:	I don't know.
RAY:	Do they ever touch you? Do they ever talk to you?
JIM:	I'm just in this place, in some kind of shock or something because I, I'm just looking around.
TONY:	Why are you there?
JIM:	I don't know.
DAVE:	Are you standing or sitting or what?
JIM:	I'm sitting on the floor, and there's, ah, it's dark over here on both sides, but ahead of me, there's a light on the far side. I'm in a room that's—oh, it seems huge! Well, it must be because I'm just a little kid.
RAY:	What do these, ah, persons do?
JIM:	They just stand there, watching me. Like a long time.

It was obvious that Jim was reliving these scenes in real time and that we had to wait until whatever happened played itself out. In the meantime, we kept probing.

RAY:	What do they do after they stand there watching you?
JIM:	(Sighs.) I don't know. I have a feeling that they came and did something, but I don't like it. I don't like this situation.
DAVE:	How many are there?
JIM:	Two—right next to one another.
DAVE:	Can you describe what they're wearing?
JIM:	I can see the light coming from behind them. There's a light behind them and, ah—this is weird! But they have like cloaks on them.
TONY:	What color are the cloaks?
JIM:	Ah, dark.
TONY:	What color are the, ah, the rest that they are wearing?
JIM:	I can't see because they're, ah, what's the term, ah—silhouetted—so they seem dark, but there's a light behind them.
DAVE:	What color is the light?
JIM:	A yellowish—a yellowish light.
RAY:	What do these cloaked figures do?
JIM:	They're just standing there, watching me.

We kept asking Jim questions and waited for what would happen next. Finally, it happened. Jim literally jumped up in the chair, pushed the chair backwards and started to hyperventilate.

| JIM: | Woah-h-h! |
| TONY: | Just relax. Just relax. |

Tony had to spend some time calming Jim down. Apparently something had terrified him. Jim was asked what happened:

JIM:	One of those things! God! All of a sudden, it was right in front of me!
TONY:	What was right in front of you?
JIM:	One of those things [entities]—it just—seemed like it rushed at me!
DAVE:	One of the two that you saw before?
JIM:	Yeah, it just—and it came so fast. It—I jumped. It made me jump.

TONY:	And then what happened?
JIM:	It's just right there in front of me! This thing is looking down at me.
DAVE:	Can you describe it?
JIM:	It's got a, a loose, kind of cloakish, what do you call it—tunic? Or, a, a, no, no, no, tunic, um, a cloak, you know—loose—it's loose—hangs over the body.

Shivers coursed up and down my spine as I listened to Jim's description of the entity looking down at him. One of the entities that I encountered as a child also wore a black cloak.

DAVE:	How about the head?
JIM:	Head? It's those same things [Allagash entities] except, ah, they seemed bigger to me. Like big! But it must be because of my size, and I'm on the floor, and they're just towering over me.
RAY:	What do they have on their heads?
JIM:	Nothing.
RAY:	What happens next?
JIM:	They're grabbing me.
RAY:	What do they do?
JIM:	They're taking me with them somewhere.
DAVE:	Did the other one come? You mentioned the one?
JIM:	The one rushes up, and that really startled me, because I never saw anything move that fast—I never saw a thing, a person move that fast.
RAY:	Did he walk or—
JIM:	It was almost like it rushed at me, but I couldn't see its legs. It was just suddenly—
RAY:	Um-hum, where did it take you?
JIM:	In towards that light.
RAY:	What do they do?
JIM:	They're, they're, they're (pauses) they're putting me on a table. I'm sitting.
RAY:	Um-hum. What do you have on?
JIM:	I got my clothes on.
RAY:	What do they do next?
JIM:	(Pauses.) I don't know, but the next thing I see— the next thing I remember is being—lying down. I'm lying down on this thing—this slab.

RAY:	What do they do?
JIM:	They're looking at me.
RAY:	Where are they looking at you?
JIM:	At my upper body.
DAVE:	What's the slab like?
JIM:	It's just hard.
RAY:	How are they looking at your upper body? Are they looking at your clothes?
JIM:	No, my shirt's (pauses) I think my clothes are off now cause I, I'm looking (pauses) they're right next to me.
RAY:	Okay, what did they do?
JIM:	They, they're turning me over.
RAY:	On your back?
JIM:	On my stomach. I'm lying on my stomach and they're, they're touching my back (pauses) with ah (pauses) something that's cold. It feels cold to the touch—smooth and cold. And, ah—it hurts! There's a pressure, ah a knot of pressure inside my chest.
RAY:	When they touch your back?
JIM:	Yes. And I'm, I'm freaking out. I'm really scared. I don't understand what's going on.
RAY:	Why don't you just get off the table and run?
JIM:	I'm too scared.
TONY:	Do they say anything to you?
JIM:	No.
RAY:	Can you move?
JIM:	Yeah, cause when they turn me over, I'm, it's not like they're doing anything. I'm moving with them.
RAY:	Do you ever see their eyes?
JIM:	It's those same eyes. [I.e. as those entities encountered on the Allagash].
RAY:	What do the eyes say?
JIM:	I, I can't make it out but there's a noise. I hear a noise.
RAY:	What kind of a noise?
JIM:	Ah-wah-wah-wah-wah [the same whispering sound that Jim has heard during other encounters].
RAY:	Where is the noise coming from?

JIM:	It's coming from my left. I'm, I'm lying on the table, and it's coming from over here. Right next to my head. It's going ah-wah-wah-wah-wah [a whispering sound].
RAY:	Is this noise there when they're doing something to your back, or after?
JIM:	While they're doing it. And it, it's...as if somebody's talking to you, but you can't really make it out. You can't quite make out what they're saying. But, you think if you listen a little harder, you'll be able to understand, because there's a pattern to it...like speech. This is just what it sounds like (whispers softly) ah-wah-wah-wah-wah—like that.
RAY:	What happens next?
JIM:	They're, they're doing this thing to my chest, and it hurts like hell!
RAY:	Okay, they're doing it to your back, but it's hurting your chest?
JIM:	Yeah, it's hurting my chest. It makes my chest feel like it's going to explode—like something is inside of me.
RAY:	How long does that last?
JIM:	It seems to last for about five or ten minutes.
RAY:	What happens after that?
JIM:	Then it goes away. The pain goes away.
RAY:	What do they do next?
JIM:	They're turning me over on my back, and they're looking at my stomach (pauses). There's something around my navel (pauses). They're, they're, ah, just touching my navel, but it, it's real sensitive there.
RAY:	Do they touch you with their fingers, or something else?
JIM:	No, it's, ah, a probe of some, some sort.
RAY:	Um-hum. What does it look like?
JIM:	It's about seven inches, six to seven inches long. The thickness of my finger at the base—tapers towards the edge.
RAY:	Like a needle?
JIM:	No, it's not sharp like a needle, because when they poke me it doesn't—it's not sharp like a needle.
RAY:	Is it like a needle with a blunt end?
JIM:	Yeah.

DAVE: Is this object attached to anything?

JIM: Nope. They're just holding it....

RAY: Is that what they were using on your back, or were they just using their fingers, or something else?

JIM: It didn't feel like that's what they were using on my back. It wasn't—this thing wasn't cold. Whatever they used on my back was cold.

RAY: Okay, what happened after they probed your navel?

JIM: They, ah, they're doing something on the side again.

RAY: Not to you, but just doing something?

JIM: Yeah, there is something going on over here. It's like, ah, oh it's that same kind of tunnel vision I had in Maine. I can see things right in front of me, but everything in the peripheral is blurry.

RAY: What happens after whatever they're doing?

JIM: They're—they were doing something over to the left of me and then, um, ah, they stuck—they stuck something in me! Right in my side—like a real—it feels hot.

RAY: How long does that stay in there?

JIM: I don't know. But it went in real far—all the way in—and it hurts! It's hot, and it hurts.

DAVE: If these things hurt, do you cry out or anything?

JIM: I want to cry out, but I can't.

DAVE: Why? Why can't you?

JIM: I, I don't know. It's like I can't open my mouth.

RAY: Okay, when they pull that out again—what happens?

JIM: (Sighs.) They, ah (pauses) they're moving around. I can hear them. They're moving around this way. They're—

DAVE: You can hear them?

JIM: Yeah. I can hear movement like clothing rustling.

RAY: What happens after that?

JIM: They're—they come over to this side now, and they're looking at my, my wrist and my arm.

DAVE: Are they both on the same side?

JIM: Yeah.

RAY: What do they do after they look at your wrist and your arm?

JIM:	(Pauses.) I think from there—they're going down to my genitals.
RAY:	What do they do there?
JIM:	I don't know. I'm, I'm, I'm (pauses) they're feeling down here. This time with their hands. And, um—
DAVE:	Do they hurt you?
JIM:	No, it doesn't hurt. It's like they're just—
RAY:	What do their hands feel like when they do that?
JIM:	They're warm.
RAY:	Okay, what happens next?
JIM:	They're just looking at my genitals. They look at the inside of my legs (pauses) they're, ah, they're looking at the knees. It seems like they're going down. They're just looking down. But, it—I'm getting the impression that they're looking for something (pauses).
RAY:	Keep on going. Tell us what happens.
JIM:	And, ah, they go all the way down. They're checking my toes (pauses).
RAY:	This is all with their hands?
JIM:	Yeah. And then they're coming—they're back—someone is back up around my head again.
RAY:	Not the two, but someone else?
JIM:	Someone else. And, ah, one of them is down at my ankles and, (sounds as if he is in pain) ah! They're doing something to my head!
RAY:	What?
JIM:	It's like they're sticking something in my head.
RAY:	What does it feel like?
JIM:	Sharp! Like a needle and it hurts like crazy! It's going right in the back of my head. And they're, Ah! God, that hurts!
RAY:	How long does that last?
JIM:	They're still sticking that in there!
RAY:	How does it hurt?
JIM:	It's like a burning pressure.
RAY:	Just in that portion or in another portion?
JIM:	In the back of my head.
RAY:	Okay, what happens after that?
JIM:	And, ah—I don't remember anything now.

It was as if the insertion and withdrawal of the needle caused amnesia. Tony stepped in to ease Jim's discomfort:

TONY:	Just relax, just relax….
RAY:	Okay, so they put that thing in the back of your head—right?
JIM:	Yeah.
RAY:	When they pull it out, what do they do next?
JIM:	I don't remember. All I remember next is being on the street in the snow. God, did that hurt! I can still feel the pain.
RAY:	Tony will take care of that for you.

Our inquiry into the phenomenon of Harry the Ghost ended with yet another startling revelation from Jim. It concerned his other childhood period of amnesia. If you will recall, he had fallen into a hole on a snowy day and was finally rescued. Prior to hypnosis, Jim had no memory of the incident, except what his family had told him. These are his first words as he came out of hypnosis:

JIM:	You know? (Sounds surprised.) I remember more. I remember something else when I was a kid.
RAY:	What was that?
JIM:	When I was little, I got lost in a snowstorm one day and, ah, I fell into ah, a ditch. And, ah, it wasn't a ditch. It was a septic tank hole. My grandfather was a builder.
DAVE:	How old?
JIM:	I was really young, like five or six. And, ah, when I was remembering coming back from the sledding incident, that's when I remembered. I remembered…my brother Tom and somebody found me. But, I, when I was remembering the, ah, the walk back from the sledding incident, I remembered something else about that. Cause, there was (pauses) those things [aliens] were there!
TONY:	Where?
JIM:	They were looking at me in the hole.
TONY:	You were five or six when that happened and about nine or ten when the sledding incident occurred?

JIM:	At least...I remember seeing these things [aliens] up in the snow, 'cause it was really coming down and thinking—"Why aren't they going to take me out of here?"
DAVE:	How many?
JIM:	Two.
RAY:	Did they put you there?
JIM:	No, I think I tripped. What happened was that the snow was coming down so heavy, it closed my eyelids...and I stumbled into this...septic tank hole.
RAY:	That's interesting. They showed up afterwards.
JIM:	It was like, seven, eight feet deep. But I remembered, I remembered looking after a while, because I finally got that snow off my eyelids and looking up and seeing these two figures up there. And thinking, well, you know, "Help me." And they just stood there—just stood there looking at me. And, ah, then later Tom and one of my neighbors found me.
DAVE:	Did you ever remember that [the two aliens] after the incident?
JIM:	Never. Today's the first time I ever consciously remembered it.
RAY:	Sometimes they put you into a situation so when you do come to, from whatever they're doing, it looks like this is why you were missing time.

I went on to explain that after an abduction, aliens often camouflage the encounter by using or creating circumstances that will seem to account for missing time. For example, on the Allagash, they had placed the four campers back in the canoe. The canoe was then propelled to shore. When the campers regained their senses, they found themselves in the canoe. The last thing they remembered was paddling away from the glowing UFO. They thought they had paddled to shore, and had no conscious recollection of the abduction. The ruse would have worked, had it not been for the burned-down campfire. In the case of the sledding incident, the snowstorm and seemingly getting lost by taking a short cut was taken advantage of by the aliens to cover their tracks:

TONY:	They created the scene.
RAY:	They created the scene and then left. I was just wondering if there's missing time here. Maybe

they put you in the hole. But, that's...specula-
tion.

Jim had no further memory of what else may have happened. It would appear that the reliving of the sledding encounter had restored partial memory of the earlier incident.

These experiences, if taken at full face value, reveal that
Harry was certainly not a ghost. The apparent haunting of the
Weiner home was probably the visible tip of a covert alien sur-
veillance program.

With this new evidence in mind, I wondered: how many
other accounts of ghosts, poltergeists and paranormal phenomena could be traced to the same conclusion? This question is
faced in the next chapter, which chronicles the unveiling of other mysterious incidents experienced by the Allagash four.

CHAPTER 10

The Unveiling

Over three decades separate the earliest manifestations of Harry the Ghost and Jack and Mary's abduction from their mountain home. As mentioned, ongoing interest in abductees by their captors is a consistent element of the CEIV phenomena. This being the case, we were intensely curious about the lives of the Allagash four during those intervening years. Based on past research, we believed that other encounters must have manifested themselves during this interval of time; and with this in mind, we set out to examine the lives of each witness to see if this were so. We were not disappointed.

Encounter Profile—Charlie Foltz

Our probe into Charlie's life did not reveal any substantial evidence of childhood visitations by alien entities. However, the Allagash experience was not Charlie's first encounter with a UFO. He had witnessed a UFO while serving in the United States Navy between 1968 and 1972. The sighting took place in the spring of 1970. It occurred during a classified mission being performed by an atomic submarine tender. At the time of the sighting, the Navy vessel was located about 300 miles off the coast of Spain. Charlie and other members of the crew watched a glowing object approach the tender. It hovered for a while, as if observing the mission, then streaked off at an incredible speed. It is my opinion that the nature of the mission and the appearance of the UFO were related. However, Charlie felt that publicly revealing the nature of the mission would be a breach of national security, and he had taken an oath not to reveal such matters prior to his discharge. In fact, he felt conscience-bound to check with Naval Intelligence prior to his giving me permission to mention the incident. The Navy was highly pleased that he had checked the matter out with them first, and confirmed that Charlie could not reveal the substance of the classified mission. He could only refer to it as being of a highly sensitive nature.

Most likely, there is no connection with the Navy sighting and the Allagash incident. Charlie seems to have been a victim of circumstances on the Allagash. He had substituted for another person who had to cancel out on the trip, and Charlie had just been along for the ride. In the end, he got more of a ride than he had bargained for. However, his examination by the aliens and close association with the twins netted further interest in him by the aliens. The first hint of this came in a telephone call to me from Jack on November 22, 1989.

Jack phoned to tell me that Charlie had visited them over the Veterans' Day weekend and had planned to help Jack and Mary split wood for heating during the winter months. One morning, he appeared at the breakfast table, looking as if he had seen a ghost. He told Jack and Mary that he had a vivid dream. It had seemed so realistic that the images were still clear as day in his mind. In fact, he could not get the dream off his mind. I thought this strange as Charlie had told us, during his first hypnosis session, that he hardly ever remembered his dreams.

In short, Charlie dreamed that he had awakened in the night to see a group of alien entities outside the glass door. Two of them turned and walked towards the door, whereupon Charlie ducked back down in bed and went back to sleep.

I telephoned Charlie and asked him about the dream. He told me that it still bothered him. The dream was just as vivid in his mind as the night it happened. Not wanting to leave a stone unturned, I asked Charlie if he would let us examine his "dream" under hypnosis. Charlie complied and we set up a meeting after the holidays. The following are pertinent excerpts from this session.

Hypnosis Session #2—Charlie Foltz (January 20, 1990)

After Tony placed Charlie under hypnosis, he asked him the date that his dream took place:

CHARLIE: The eleventh or the twelfth.

RAY:	Of November, 1989?
CHARLIE:	Yeah.
TONY:	The events that occurred that night...what occurred?
CHARLIE:	(Starts to breathe heavily; blows out breath.) I was sleeping (pauses for a long time). And, ah, it's like I was dreaming that I sat up and looked out, ah, the sliding glass doors (clears throat). And saw (pauses) some (pauses) small beings looking toward the back of the house.
TONY:	How many do you see?
CHARLIE:	(Pauses for a long time.) Seven, maybe eight. They're all looking toward the back of the house, and one turns his head and looks at me (long pause) and then I think, "Oop! Nope!" And I lie back down; go to sleep.
TONY:	Say that one more time please—you lie back down?
CHARLIE:	I go back to sleep.
TONY:	Did it take you long to go back to sleep?
CHARLIE:	Um, um...
TONY:	It does not take long (pauses). Can you describe what they look like?
CHARLIE:	(Takes a very deep breath and blows out air heavily; pauses.) They're all short. Oval heads. Large dark eyes. They're all looking toward the back of the house.
RAY:	What are they wearing?
CHARLIE:	Looks like a, ah, black one-piece uniform. Dark, um, with a belt, light belt, narrow. They all have their hands at their sides, except for the one that turned and looked at me, that was pointing in the direction that they were looking.
TONY:	When he turns and looks at you, what else does he do?
CHARLIE:	(Pauses; smacks his lips.) Begins to come towards the house. That's why I go back to sleep.
TONY:	Why do you go back to sleep?

At this point, Charlie smiled, as we knew he was prone to do when under tension, and gagged. As he started to answer, he began breathing heavily:

CHARLIE:	I don't know. Just, ah (clears throat) just, saying, "Nope!" And just lie back down and go back to sleep.
TONY:	When you wake up in that morning, on that morning, what are your first thoughts regarding that incident?
CHARLIE:	It's strange. Strange dream. Vivid!
TONY:	How vivid?
CHARLIE:	It was like watching it. Seeing something.
TONY:	Do you usually have vivid dreams?
CHARLIE:	No.
TONY:	Do you feel that you can distinguish between a dream and a natural occurrence?
CHARLIE:	(Pauses for a long time.) I think so (sounds doubtful).
TONY:	How does your conscious mind react to that incident? Is it a dream, or is it an actual occurrence?
CHARLIE:	(Long pause; sighs.) It seemed more vivid than a dream (pauses) but I would think it would be that.

At this point, Tony placed Charlie in a deeper state of hypnosis and proceeded with a ploy designed to probe his subconscious memory:

TONY:	Give me a "yes" answer by making your right thumb twitch. Give me a "no" answer by making your left thumb twitch. And you are totally unaware—totally unaware of which thumb is doing what. Do you understand? Right thumb up for "yes." Left thumb up for "no."
TONY:	That's good. You're totally unaware. Is your first name Charles?
CHARLIE:	(Right thumb up—yes.)

Tony continued by asking unrelated questions, and Charlie continued to answer with his thumb. Then Tony sprung the following question:

TONY:	Was that incident a dream?
CHARLIE:	(Right thumb up—yes.)

Tony again eased Charlie into an even deeper level of hypnosis before continuing the questioning and asking the same queries again:

TONY: Did that incident actually occur in reality?
CHARLIE: (Puffs out air; both thumbs begin to quiver.)
TONY: Was that incident a dream?

Charlie would not answer. Both his thumbs continued to quiver back and forth as if reflecting an inner conflict between Charlie's conscious and subconscious memory. Tony asked the same question again, this time very forcefully. Finally, Charlie's right thumb won out and moved up for "yes." There had been a definite conflict between Charlie's thumbs. This should not have been if his memories were clearly a dream. From all signs, it appeared that the typical mental block we had encountered so many times in the past was strongly in place. Tony continued to edge Charlie into an even deeper state of hypnosis in an attempt to break through it:

TONY: Just relax, deeper and deeper.... What happened
             after the being turned and walked toward the
             door? How far did he get to the door? How many
             feet?
CHARLIE: (Pauses for a long time.) Four, five.
TONY: Can you see that one being when he turns? He's
             looking at the back of the house. And he turns,
             and he looks at you. Can you see that?
CHARLIE: He's pointing towards the back of the house. The
             others are looking towards the light.
RAY: What light?
CHARLIE: The light that's at the back of the house. Like the
             glow of the moon, but the moon's further for-
             ward towards the front of the house.
RAY: What did they say to you when you were up in
             Vermont? What did the beings say to you?
CHARLIE: Just looked at me.
RAY: When he looked at you, what did you think?
CHARLIE: "No!"
RAY: What do you mean, "No?"
CHARLIE: That's what I thought.
RAY: Why did you say "No" if he didn't say anything?
CHARLIE: I don't know. I just lay back down and went to
             sleep.

RAY:	What did you mean by "No?"
CHARLIE:	Not again.
RAY:	Not again what?
CHARLIE:	(Suddenly becomes agitated; begins to cough.) Just, "No, not again!"
RAY:	Not again what?

Charlie either would or could not answer because of his highly agitated state. He was gulping in more air than he could breathe out efficiently:

RAY:	You can—you can share this with us.
TONY:	Just relax, just relax.
RAY:	Not again what?
CHARLIE:	(Is highly agitated; does not answer.)
TONY:	Just drift back again, just drift back.
RAY:	It's okay to tell us. Not again what?

Charlie seemed to muster up all that was within him and, between deep breaths, managed to force out just two words:

CHARLIE:	No—more.
TONY:	No more what?
CHARLIE:	(Breathes heavily; forces words out.) Just—not—again—like—the—Allagash.
RAY:	Was it like the Allagash when you weren't supposed to tell?
CHARLIE:	(Does not answer; breathes heavily.)
RAY:	It's okay, if you won't tell us, but was it like the Allagash when you weren't supposed to tell?
CHARLIE:	I don't know.
RAY:	Why don't you know?
CHARLIE:	(Coughs and begins choking; does not answer.)
RAY:	Are you supposed to know?
CHARLIE:	I just went back to sleep.

Tony was determined to do battle with what appeared to be an induced amnesia. I watched, fascinated, as he successively brought Charlie into deeper states of relaxation between questions. Charlie continued to maintain that the event was a dream, but was becoming more and more agitated the deeper he sank into hypnosis. Then Tony employed another strategy often used in hypnotic regression to bypass mental blocks:

TONY:	When you say, "You went back to sleep," can you actually see yourself doing that?
CHARLIE:	(Coughs; seems agitated; does not answer.)
TONY:	If you had a camera running, recording this, what would it show you? When you woke up, did you sit up? Did you turn your body or did you just turn your head? What do you see yourself doing?
CHARLIE:	(Heaves out a big breath of air; pauses.) I see the dog [Jack and Mary Weiner's dog] coming downstairs (laughs) sniffing me.
RAY:	What does the dog do when he sees the beings?
CHARLIE:	It's morning.
TONY:	Let's go back to the night before. You got these cushions, these pillows ready, with the blankets on them or the sheets, whatever. You got into this makeshift bed and you fell asleep, is that correct?
CHARLIE:	Um-hum.
TONY:	Okay. Once again, let's go back to this [imaginary] camera that's running. What would it record—what would it show us if we could run it on a screen?
CHARLIE:	(Does not answer.)
TONY:	What I'm really asking, "Do you see yourself waking up?"
CHARLIE:	Yes.
TONY:	So, you sat—so, you sat straight up? You have to turn your head? Is that what you're saying?
CHARLIE:	To the right.
TONY:	To look out the sliding doors? Is that correct?
CHARLIE:	Um-hum.
TONY:	Okay. You're looking out the sliding doors.
CHARLIE:	Um-hum.
TONY:	You told us before what you see. And now what do you do?
CHARLIE:	I lie back down and go to sleep.
TONY:	Okay. Now, let me understand this. You may interrupt. If we were running a camera, say somebody left a camera running, forgot to shut it off, whatever—we would see you sitting up, turning your head slightly to the right, you're looking out

the sliding glass doors which had no curtains—
no shades of any kind—you lie back down—you
pull the blankets up to your chest—you leave
your arms outside the blankets—and you go
back to sleep. Is that essentially it?

CHARLIE: Yeah.

TONY: This is my question. And I want you to take your
time with your next answer. You see, if we left
the camera running accidentally all night. What
that camera should show is you lying in bed all
night. There should be no sitting up. There
should be no turning the head to the right.
'Cause you're telling us that this is a dream. And
yet when we ask you, "What would the camera
record?" You tell us that it would record you sitting up. You do see the discrepancy. So, again I
must ask you. And again, take your time—did
you dream this? So that the camera would show
us you lying there with the normal movements of
sleep, but lying there essentially all night. Or did
this occur [in reality] with the camera recording
you getting up—turning your head slightly to the
right—lying back down—pulling the blankets
up—leaving your arms out—and going back to
sleep? Can you explain that in any way that is
good for you, but that comes as close to the objective truth as it can possibly come?

CHARLIE: I remember sitting up. Looking out the window.
[Charlie was not dreaming!]

TONY: And?

CHARLIE: Seeing a group standing about ten feet from the
door, looking at the back of the house. The one
is pointing toward the back of the house at an
angle, then turned and looked at me.

TONY: And what did he do?

CHARLIE: When he looked at me, I just lay back down and
said, "No!" and pulled the covers up and went
back to sleep.

RAY: Why did you wake up?

CHARLIE: I don't know.

RAY: Did you hear anything?

CHARLIE: I don't remember hearing anything.

RAY: Did you feel anything?

CHARLIE: I felt a presence.

The tape ran out at this point. When I flipped the tape over,
I had put the recorder in the "record" mode, but somehow hit

the pause button and unfortunately missed the rest of the conversation. In any event, when I pressed Charlie about "feeling the presence" that had awakened him, he became very agitated and wrung his hands nervously. Essentially, we could get no further with this, other than what had been recorded. Charlie would like to think that this episode was a dream. However, an analysis of our findings concerning his so-called dream do not bear this out:

1. Charlie rarely remembers dreams. This dream was remembered distinctly. The details remain fresh in his mind today. In his own words, "It was more vivid than a dream."

2. The dream was peculiar, in that it was a dream about being asleep, waking up and falling asleep again.

3. Charlie's comments about the moon when dreaming that he was awake reflect reality. The sides of Jack's house line up with the four compass points. Charlie was facing due east as he looked through the glass door at the aliens. When he went to bed he described the moon as "lighting up the back yard [east]." This indeed would have been the case, since astronomical records reveal that on the night of November 11 and 12, 1989, the moon was near its full phase. When he dreamed that he woke up, he described the aliens pointing at a light coming from the back [north] of the house. In the dream, he described the light being, "like the moon, but the moon's further forward towards the front [west] of the house." This is precisely where the moon would have been late at night on either November 11 or 12. Thus, it would appear that Charlie was awake and "seeing," not dreaming what he saw that night.

4. Another anomalous event in the Weiner household during that weekend adds physical evidence of alien visitation.

5. Tony's use of the camera ploy during hypnosis revealed that Charlie really woke up and did not dream that he woke up.

Regarding item 5, Tony related the following in his analysis of the session:

Your tape will reveal the entire aspect of this session regarding Charlie's admitting to be "literal and precise"—yet, my question—if a camera had been, "left running all night, what would it have recorded?"

brought from Charlie the answer in the present tense—"I wake up, sit up, turn my head slightly to the right and see...." Of course, the trick here is that our very literal and precise Charlie should have responded (personal opinion) that the camera would have shown him lying and sleeping all night long. In fact, I still think Charlie should have responded each time we asked him...with something like, "I dream that I wake up, sit up, etc...." Even after pointing this out to Charlie under hypnosis, he still said, under hypnosis and in the waking state, "I wake up, sit up, etc.," and still did not say, "I dream that I wake up, etc."

I am also impressed with Charlie's recollection of this incident still being crisp and detailed and not having become hazy or fuzzy, as he admitted happened with other dreams of his—and as occur with almost everyone's dreams. Time effaces details, etc., but this incident is still as fresh as when it occurred.

Nevertheless, one question still remained—if what Charlie witnessed was grounded in reality: What did the aliens want? Charlie, even under deep hypnosis, gave no inkling of anything else happening to him. It would appear that the aliens approaching the door did not want Charlie, but their big, dark eyes seemed to mesmerize him. After his initial shock, he reacted uncharacteristically by going back to sleep. Physical evidence indicated that Jack was the target that night. These findings will be discussed later. In any event, other than the Navy UFO sighting, Charlie's UFO encounter profile started with the Allagash event and ended with the event under discussion. This was borne out during this second hypnosis session.

RAY:	When is the next time you see this being or the beings?
CHARLIE:	Just then [i.e. the dream].
RAY:	When was the time before that you saw the beings?
CHARLIE:	(Pauses for a long time.) Only on the Allagash.
RAY:	When was the time before the Allagash you saw the beings?
CHARLIE:	(Long pause.) I didn't.
TONY:	Do they look the same?
CHARLIE:	(Pauses.) Yes.

Encounter Profile—Chuck Rak

Chuck, like the twins, remembered childhood bedtime visitations by nonhuman creatures. In an autobiographical sketch that he prepared for our report, he briefly alluded to these visits.

> At age four to six, I had repeated experiences of a frightening but powerful presence invading my room at night.

During Chuck's first hypnosis session that covered his experience on the Allagash, I suddenly interjected questions about these childhood manifestations. At the time, Chuck had been describing the entities the four had encountered during the Allagash abductions:

RAY:	Um, these figures—these entities?
CHUCK:	Yeah.
RAY:	Had you ever seen them prior to this?
CHUCK:	(Pauses.) Oh—yeah.
RAY:	Where?
CHUCK:	Ah, there was something in my bedroom when I was little.
RAY:	How little?
CHUCK:	About four or five years old.
RAY:	Uh-huh. What happened then?
CHUCK:	There was something in my room.
RAY:	What something?
CHUCK:	It was a smaller form of these [Allagash] beings—much smaller.
RAY:	And what did he do? What did it do?
CHUCK:	It seemed to be just there, and I couldn't figure out what it was and why it was there.
RAY:	What happened?
CHUCK:	(Pauses for a long time.) I went into my parents' room.
TONY:	Why?
CHUCK:	Because it was a very unsettling feeling.
TONY:	Did you say anything to your parents?
CHUCK:	Yeah.
TONY:	What did you say?
CHUCK:	I said it reminded me of a rabbit.
TONY:	What did they say?
CHUCK:	They let me sleep between them.

RAY:	Why did it remind you of a rabbit?
CHUCK:	'Cause it was white.
RAY:	What else do you remember?
CHUCK:	I remember that experience that took place on Cape Cod [at the family's summer home].
RAY:	When was the next time you saw one of these figures or entities?
CHUCK:	It was, ah, in our other place in Waban.
RAY:	How old were you?
CHUCK:	About the same age.
RAY:	What happened then?
CHUCK:	It seemed like there was a saw coming through the floor...seemed like it could pass through like a membrane.... It reminded me of a buzzsaw. It was very frightening.

Chuck's description of the whirling buzz-saw-like entry of the entity sent a cool chill through me. About a year ago, someone had come by the house to buy one of my books. He related two personal adult UFO experiences to me as we chatted at the door. One was a daylight sighting of a domed disc. The other involved waking up at night to see an entity emitted from a beam cutting through his bedroom floor like a saw. He became paralyzed and remembered nothing more. I tried to find out more about Chuck's experience:

RAY:	What happened? Could you explain exactly what happened?
CHUCK:	Ah, (pauses) um, it scared me.
RAY:	Why did it scare you?
CHUCK:	It came close to me.
RAY:	And what did it look like?
CHUCK:	(Breathes heavily; blows out air.) It was the same way. It was the same thing.
RAY:	The same thing as what?
CHUCK:	That I saw at the Cape—only a little—it was—I can't, I can't really remember. I can't remember. I don't have a clear image.
RAY:	What did it do?
CHUCK:	It scared me.
RAY:	What else did it do?
CHUCK:	It, ah (pauses) it spent time in my room.
RAY:	Doing what?

CHUCK:	Scaring me.
RAY:	How long did it stay?
CHUCK:	(Pauses.) I can't tell.
RAY:	Did you both stay in the room?
CHUCK:	(Becomes very agitated.) Yeah.

It soon became obvious that we just could not penetrate the same mental block encountered so many times before in these cases. Session time was running out. This was our only opportunity to check Chuck's memory, under hypnosis, for other possible encounters during his life. I directed my questions to this end:

RAY:	So, it was the last time you saw it between that time and the Allagash?
CHUCK:	I think it was only those two times, when I was little. It might have been a third, but I can't—I don't have a clear memory.
RAY:	After the Allagash, did you ever see these figures again?
CHUCK:	No. Don't remember seeing them again.
RAY:	Is there anything else that you want to tell us?
CHUCK:	One night my wife woke me up. It was in the wintertime. And there was a bar of blue light coming through the north window. And we had plastic on the window. So, it wasn't a very clear image, except it seemed to be a bar of blue light. Our north window overlooks a valley with mountains in the background.
RAY:	When was this?
CHUCK:	It was a February...probably two years ago...at least. Maybe three [i.e. 1986 or 1987].... Kim was very, ah, scared—upset. She, she tried to wake me up.... Ah, I told her to calm down and relax. And she said, "What is it?" And I said, (nonchalantly) "Relax, it's only the aliens! Go back to sleep." And I just couldn't bring myself out of feeling heavy and slumberous.
RAY:	What did you do?
CHUCK:	I went back to sleep.

Shades of Charlie Foltz! Later, I questioned Kim about the blue bar of light. She told me that the light was hovering high over the valley. For some reason, she also did not react normally to its presence:

KIM: It was still there and um, for some reason...I
                turned over and went to sleep. Normally, I would
                be up half the night, scared.

We did not gain any additional information from Chuck. He
did briefly mention a strange incident that happened to him in
1981; however it was too nebulous to make any direct connection to UFOs. In short, while resting after mountain climbing,
he felt a large displacement of air swish by his head.

Unfortunately for us, Chuck is not a good subject for deep
hypnosis. There may be much buried in his subconscious. All
we know for sure is that he, too, had experienced bedtime visitations at age five or six, and that his next, and perhaps last,
UFO experience was the one he shared with his three friends on
the Allagash.

It was quite apparent that it was the twins who held an ongoing interest for the aliens. This was amply confirmed by the
following data, retrieved during the process of assembling their
encounter profiles.

Encounter Profile—Jim Weiner

Thus far, we have documented Jim's early childhood
hauntings by Harry the Ghost through his later childhood abduction while sledding. These events took place between 1955
and 1960.

Jim remembered nothing unusual happening between
1960 and the early '70's. At that time, he had no conscious
memory of his childhood encounters with aliens, and had no
idea that the manifestations by Harry were related to UFOs.

It wasn't until 1973 that Jim had his first consciously remembered UFO sighting. Significantly, 1973 had heralded the
largest wave of UFO sightings in history. Jim explains his sighting in a conversation recorded just prior to his first hypnosis
session that dealt with the Allagash encounter.

Mansfield, Pennsylvania (March, 1973)

RAY: What I'd like to do in this particular session is,
                ah, start at the very beginning. You had none of
                these experiences prior to 1976, when you had
                the experience in Maine—is that correct?

JIM: Well, the only, ah, I had, a, a sighting in 1973, in
                Northern Pennsylvania, with two other friends.
                Would you like me to tell you about it?

RAY: Just, ah, briefly, and then, I think, we'll move to
                the 1976 incident.

JIM: Well, that's when I was attending undergraduate school at Mansfield State College. It's now Mansfield University.... I was out one day with two friends...in the countryside...in March. We were driving home, and it was after dark 'cause the stars up there at night are incredible.... We were going through...a gigantic cow pasture [on a farm road]. And way on the end of the field...a half mile away...was a tree line. And we were driving along, and I noticed through my windshield that there was a "dipper" just above the tree line.... That's what caught my eye. These stars in a dipper shape...tumbling, end-over-end.... So, I immediately stopped the car. And we got out, and I said, "Look at that up there! What is that?" They looked like real, real bright stars. I couldn't tell if they were really big and way up, or whether they were not so big and close. Ah, I remember like five to seven lights...tumbling, end-over-end...across the sky from left to right...changing formation...tumbling...almost like a Slinky—when a Slinky walks end-over-end...they started coming down. It was coming closer to us. And then, this car came. Then they stopped coming lower and, and just maintained a constant altitude, going from left to right. And then the car went by. Then it came back. So, I had a flashlight in my car. And I said, "Let's signal the damn things and see what happens." So, we took the flashlight out of my glove compartment, and we blinked it a couple of times. And one of the lights just went off like a huge amber flashbulb. Just like went poof! And then, all of a sudden—I don't even recall them stopping—all of a sudden, they were going the other way again, as if just like instantly going backwards.... They just walked back up into the sky from exactly the same direction they came from.

TONY: Who was with you?

JIM: A friend of mine...named Craig Wofsy. And the other guy's name was Ray Donado.

Later, with Jim's help, I was able to locate Craig Wofsy. Ray Donado's whereabouts were unknown. I telephoned Craig and he confirmed the sighting:

CRAIG: Well I remember, ah, that he and I and another friend of ours at the time—his name was Ray Donado—ah, we were driving along the back

roads of...South Mansfield, Pennsylvania....
And, ah, we noticed, ah, some flashing lights in
the sky on the side of the road.... We got out of
the car...and we said to ourselves, "Those look
like UFOs!" So, we grabbed a flashlight and
flashed it at the lights and, ah, as I recall, they
sent out a signal back. It seemed to be like a—
I've always described it as being like a—when
you squeeze a tube of toothpaste. And, the, ah
the toothpaste comes out? That's the way the
light was. It came out. It seemed...like a tube of
amber light. [This is typical of other reports.]

RAY: Jim mentioned that, ah, there may have been a
              car or something that came by at the same time?

CRAIG: There were some headlights. The lights flashed,
              the signal light came out from...the UFO or
              whatever you call it, and right after that...a car
              approached us. And then the thing just took off.
              It did another 90-degree turn away from us and
              was gone!

After the experience in Mansfield, Pennsylvania, Jim's next
UFO sighting and consequential abduction took place in 1976,
on the Allagash. The following four years were quiet; however,
in 1980, strange things began to happen once again. Jim experienced a number of paranormal events between 1980 and
1988. Although Jim remembered these incidents consciously,
we decided to question him about it under hypnosis. Dave and
I felt that, by doing this, we might reveal more details. We were
correct.

The first incident took place in June, 1980, while Jim was
visiting friends in Austin, Texas. During his visit, Jim slipped a
disc in his back and had to spend some time bedridden until he
could walk again. His friends, Jim and Susie, let him use a
room in their home until he fully recovered.

Sherman, Texas (June, 1980)
Hypnosis Session #3B (March 10, 1990)

JIM: ...I went to bed one night and um, I woke up. I
              heard something outside of the window.... I had
              this feeling that there was a presence—threaten-
              ing.... I'm looking out the window, because the
              window is open, and it seems as if there's some-
              thing out the window, but I can't really make out
              what it is. Ah, a shape, that's all.

DAVE: Is there any light in the room?

JIM: No. No light in the room.

DAVE:	Or outside?
JIM:	No, just a very faint light coming from a corner street light.
RAY:	What happens next?
JIM:	Well, I, I, I remember telling myself, "This must be a dream. I'm dreaming or something."...I was looking at this thing outside the window and, ah, there's definitely something there. It was right there, outside of the window and...it was watching me.... It was really a frightening feeling.
TONY:	What floor was this bedroom on?
JIM:	It was on the ground floor. It was a ranch house.
RAY:	Did you ever see this figure up close?
JIM:	Not that night.
TONY:	Another night did you?
JIM:	Yes, yes! In Ojai, California.

We decided to have Jim tell us about the Ojai incident at a later time. Meanwhile, he continued to describe the Sherman experience. Jim felt that he must have been dreaming, and that the figure was an afterimage. He tried to go back to sleep:

JIM:	I, I, I lay down, and the very second my head touched the pillow—there was this noise—right next to my head on the sheets (scratches the side of the easy chair to simulate the sound). And I bolted up and turned the light on...and there was nothing in the room. But, there was this feeling that this—whatever it was—this threatening feeling—that something was in the room with me. Ah...I, I was wondering if I were going out of my mind or something. I kept thinking, "This is really strange. What the hell is going on here?"
DAVE:	When you turned the light on, did you look out the window [i.e., to see if the figure was still there]?
JIM:	Yeah, but I couldn't see anything. It was dark outside the window. So, I kept thinking, "Well, I must have...started dreaming." So, I turned the light off, and I lay down again and, sure enough, the second my head hit the pillow, this noise started again—right next to my head. So, I bolted up again. I turned the light on. Nothing again...except this feeling. So I thought, "All right. That does it. I'm going to turn the light off. I'm going to lie down again, and if it does this

sound again, I'm going to do it, too. Then we'll see what happens." So, I turn the light off. I lay down. And sure enough, the second my head hit the pillow, this scratching started next to my head on the sheets. So, I reached over and scratched with my finger. An instant—I mean the very instant later, I was being pulled off the bed! It was like something grabbed me. Ah, this, this same feeling that I had when I was a kid... when my body was about to explode [referring to his abduction and examination during the sledding experience]. And, and I could literally see myself being drawn towards the ceiling. I remember the ceiling rushing up towards me, and thinking to myself, "Holy shit! If I leave this room, I'm never coming back! I'm never coming back!" Then, something in my head snapped. It was like, ah, a little bomb went off inside of my head. Everything went like, "Whopft!" and I was back in bed again. And, I, I remember, I said, "That's enough of this shit!" And I got out of bed. I went into the living room, and I, I went to be on their sofa in the living room.

RAY: Did you ever see the bed from up there?

JIM: I seem to have a, a, a fleeting image of seeing the bed receding from me but only a flash.

RAY: Were you still on the bed?

JIM: No.

Apparently, Jim had not had an Out-of-the-Body Experience (OBE). We suspected that he may have been taken from the room at this point. However, Jim had no memory of this, nor did he know whether there was a period of missing time during the experience:

RAY: Did you notice the time when it first happened and the time when you were back in bed, by any chance?

JIM: No, I remember when I went into the living room, there was a clock that said 2:30 in the morning, but that's all I remember.

Ojai, California (May, 1982)
Hypnosis Session #3B (March 10, 1990)

RAY: Now in Ojai, why don't you tell us? You said it
                was similar to Sherman.
JIM: Yeah, it was the same thing. You see in Texas, I
                wasn't sure what that was, ah (pauses).

Tony stepped in and eased Jim into a deeper state of hypnosis:

TONY: Okay, Ojai, California.
JIM: Yeah, I was on the road then, working as a sales-
                man for this art gallery in Baltimore.

During an art show, Jim had leaned over to look at some
Japanese art that a couple wanted appraised. Again, his back
went out. The couple kindly took Jim into their home until he
recuperated. The following episode took place one night as he
slept in their guest room:

RAY: When you were in the room...what happened?
JIM: I woke up! I was in their daughter's room, who
                had died either that year or the year before of a
                brain tumor. She was young. So, they were let-
                ting me use her room. And I felt something—like
                a small animal walking on the covers of my bed.
                I remember it as clear as day. I remember the
                feeling of this thing. I thought it was a cat...And
                then, all of a sudden, I realized that I wasn't on
                the bed! That my head was on the bed, but that
                the rest of my body was floating off the bed like
                at a 45-degree angle. I could literally feel the
                weightlessness of my body. It felt like I was just
                going to float away.
DAVE: Was there any light? Could you see?
JIM: There was a, a light that came in through the
                door. They had a night light in their hallway, so
                there was a bare amount of white light coming
                through, coming into the room from the door-
                way. That was the only light.
RAY: You're suspended—part of you—what happens
                next?
JIM: Ah, I, this noise again, "Ah-wah-wah-wah," etc.
RAY: Okay, go on then.

JIM:	And, ah, when I realized—and I couldn't move. I couldn't move my body at all. And this noise was on the side of my head, "Ah-wah-wah-wah."
RAY:	Which side?
JIM:	The left side. And I moved my eyes over because I couldn't move my body, and there was—Jesus Christ!—there was this thing! I mean it was—and I knew—the second I saw it—that it was the same thing I saw in Texas. It had that same feeling.
RAY:	What did it look like?
JIM:	It was really strange. It was like a face that was coming through a shroud, and it was right next to my face, and there was something else. It was, it was, um, I got the impression that there was another dimension there. That, that there was some kind of cut in dimensions—that the dimension I was in was, was coexisting with this, this other dimension. This veil-type thing.... There was something else there. A tray. There, there are these utensils there. It's ah, a tray of these utensils that looked like, ah, like, ah, dentist's tools. That's what they reminded me of—dentist tools.
RAY:	What happened next?
JIM:	They, ah, after that, this thing—the whole time this was going on—this thing was doing this thing in my ear, "Ah-wah-wah-wah!" It almost hypnotized me. It was as if, ah, I just listened a little bit more, I could understand what it was saying. So, it almost drew me into it.... It was almost like a compulsion to listen to this thing.
RAY:	Okay, what did they do next?
JIM:	And they were doing something to my genitals on the bed. I remember my legs being up in the air, and there was something on the bed, because I could feel it shifting its weight. I could feel the bed shifting, and it was doing something to my genitals. I don't know what the heck it was doing, but the thought that went through my mind was that it was trying to have intercourse with me! And I thought, "This is absolutely crazy! I can't believe this!"
RAY:	Was this something alive, rather than an instrument? Are we talking about something alive, or something material that, that is touching your genitals?

JIM:	No. It was alive. Whatever it was, was touching me, was alive.
DAVE:	Could you see?
JIM:	No, I couldn't see what it was. I, I you know, I remember looking to the side and seeing this thing, and I think what happened was, was that when I saw that, I kept my eyes shut 'cause I didn't want to see what else was there. (Speaks with a trembling voice.) It was like, it was beyond just being a, a presence that was there...that just completely terrified me. And, I, I think I kept my eyes closed.
RAY:	Okay, what did you feel them doing to the genitals?
JIM:	I, I remember them doing something to my genitals, and the thought that went through my mind was that they were trying to have some kind of intercourse with me. And I thought to myself, "This, this is absolutely crazy. What is going on here? Am I dreaming this or what?" But I'd have sworn—I knew that I was awake.
RAY:	What happens next?
JIM:	That's all I remember. I don't remember anything else after that.
RAY:	Do you remember your legs going down?
JIM:	No, I don't remember being lowered. I don't, I don't even remember when the sound stopped. Then, the next thing I remembered was I, I woke up the next day. And, and, I never said anything to John and Bonnie [Jim's hosts] for obvious reasons...but I'll never forget it as long as I live.

Jim had experienced another procedure typically reported by male abductees—sperm sampling. Prior to hypnosis, he had recall of everything that happened at Ojai except this act performed by the aliens. They had blocked it from his conscious memory. More will be said about the aliens' motives for removing sperm from human males in another chapter. Suffice it to say that, most likely, the Sherman, Texas, and the post-Ojai bedroom confrontations dealt with this same procedure.

Boston, Massachusetts (1982-1988)

Between 1982 and 1988, Jim had many nighttime visitations. The following is a résumé of these experiences that he recorded on tape for our report:

Well, it was after I moved back to Boston, that, ah, these events started happening in my apartment. I would wake up at night...thinking I heard footsteps or movement in the living room.... I would always have the feeling that something...bad was out there. It was always the same feeling. And I would get out of bed...and turn the lights on in the living room to prove to myself that there's nothing there.... I could never fall asleep unless I came back to bed, locked the window, closed and locked my doors.... This went on for a long time.

There were times when I woke up and heard movement in and around my bed—same feeling of... something bad coming for me, and I didn't want it to be there, and I didn't like what was happening.

There were occasions, which I mentioned to you prior, about having awakened at night and seeing one of these creatures next to my bed. At one point, I remember, they put a long needle or rod or something into my chest cavity from the left side. And I remembered it was incredibly painful. I couldn't scream. I couldn't move. That's all I remember.

There was another occasion when I awoke and felt my lower body being levitated off the bed again, and something was in bed with me and doing something to my genital area, and again I couldn't scream. I couldn't move, and that's all I remember.

There was another time when I remembered them being on my right side, and I tried kicking and punching at them. And it was the strangest sensation because I clearly remember I put as much power into my punches and kicks as I could, but it was as if they were being stopped in midair—as if I would get halfway through with a punch, and it would just be stopped. I seem to remember that sensation and then nothing else.

It's these visitation nightmares, as I called them, that actually led me to come to see you...at the convention.

Ah, the most recent one happened just before Christmas [in December of 1988]. I was, I was lying in bed. I heard—I woke up and heard a noise outside my doors. The doors that go from my room into the living room. It's like French doors that open up, because my room used to be a dining room. And, um, what I thought was really odd was, my eyes felt like they weighed 50 pounds. And I remember fighting to keep my eyes up. And I was looking at the crack in my door, and there was this white light out there, and it wasn't the kind of light that you normally would see when our living room light's on. And, ah, I was fighting to keep my eyes open, and just out of nowhere, like, a thought came into my head, and it said, "Open your door, I want to come in." And I remember thinking to myself, "No way! You're not coming in here because last time you came in here you hurt me, and I don't want you coming in." And then that's all I remember. That, that was just shortly before Christmas.

During Jim's third hypnosis session, there was not enough time to deal with all of his Boston experiences. We decided to home in on this last and most recent happening. We were curious to see if, once again, hypnosis would reveal more of what had occurred. The following excerpt picks up when Jim received the telepathic command, "Open your door."

Hypnosis Session #3B (March 10, 1990)

JIM: I remember waking up. I heard a noise outside the door...and I thought it was a robber...but, that feeling was there—the same, exact feeling of this...threatening presence—so, I knew that it was those things. And in my head—it wasn't so much I heard—it was like a thought, "Open your doors Jim, we want to come." And I remember thinking back saying, "Oh, no. I don't want you coming in here. You stay away from me. If you come in here, I'm going to kill you!" And then all of a sudden, this whitish thing rushed right through the door. It didn't even open the door. It just came through the door. And, that's all I remember. I freaked. It's like, it's like I can deal with this to a certain point—these experiences— then I, I, I just blank, I just blank everything out.

RAY: So, you don't remember what this thing looked like or what it did?

JIM: It was whitish. It was whitish. It was, ah, it wasn't tall. It was fairly short, and the last thing I remember was that it just rushed into the room. I don't remember anything after that.

TONY: Did it have any shape to it?

JIM: It had a shape to it. It was shaped exactly like that—like the shape in [Sherman] Texas.

RAY:	Which was?
JIM:	It was this kind of anthropomorphic shape. And, and it was the shape that I saw in Ojai. It was a humanoid type.... I don't know how humanoid it was but, it had a slight ridge on the nose. It had a protruded chin, because I could see it, and it had a forehead, and it had eyes.
DAVE:	Like the ones in Maine?
JIM:	Well, it's ah, different, because the ones in Texas, I didn't get a really good look at. And the ones in Ojai, I got a good look at, but it was coming through something. So it wasn't, so it wasn't like I was looking at it, ah, right there.
RAY:	Same thing in Boston?
JIM:	Same thing in Boston.
DAVE:	Do you think that they were the same kind of beings that you encountered in Maine?
JIM:	The feeling was the same.... It's a threatening feeling.

We already knew that Jim was not alone in experiencing terrifying nightmares of alien visitation. His brother, Jack, and his sister-in-law, Mary, had similar dreams. We now turn to examine Jack's UFO encounter profile.

Encounter Profile—Jack Weiner

Jack, of course, shared the manifestations of Harry the Ghost with his brother Jim in the 1950's. However, the experience with the ball of light was unique to him. As far as we know, Jack's next UFO encounters were on the Allagash, in 1976. After that incident, the next anomalous event in Jack's life took place in 1981. It, along with one other event, provided physical evidence for alien visitation and will be discussed in the next chapter.

Between 1986 and 1988, Jack had realistic nightmares that reflected segments of his abduction on the Allagash. He had described these dreams in his initial report to me months before we engaged in the hypnosis sessions. Many aspects of these dreams tallied with what the Allagash four later relived while under hypnosis. One of his dreams was of him and Mary being startled by blue light flooding through the windows of their mountain home.

In May of 1988, he again dreamed of a blue light in the field adjoining their house and of his subsequent abduction with Mary. This abduction was vividly relived under hypnosis (as has been described in Chapter Seven). Since then, Jack had two more lifelike dreams of aliens, which we will examine at this point.

On October 28, 1989, Tony and I met to discuss the overall case with the Allagash four. One of the items discussed was a recent dream that Jack had experienced. It was very similar to Charlie's dream, in that Jack, too, dreamed that he was awake and saw aliens at his door in the middle of the night. The following is in Jack's own words from our recorded conversation:

Southern Vermont (Early October, 1989)

JACK: I heard the noise down at the door and I thought, "Oh, I got to take Iksley [the dog] out." So I got out of bed, and I put my pants on, and I turned the light on for the stairway, and Iksley was up-stairs.... So, I was about to turn the light off, thinking that I must have just dreamt this or something, when I heard a noise at the door again. I thought, "Well, that's odd. Here's Iksley. What's at the door?" The thought in my mind was that it was a porcupine, 'cause they're all over the place. So, I turned the light back on to the stairway and walked down the stairs, and I got down partway and I just looked under the overhang and at the back door are two of these things just standing side by side. I remember looking and thinking, "No way! I'm out of here!" And I just walked back up the stairs, turned the light off and went back to bed.

RAY: Two of these things being what?

JACK: In our house.... At our door! The aliens! These things. Two aliens. They were right there, and I, I looked and I went, "No, no! No way! Forget it. I'm not going to do this now."

TONY: You say this was a dream?

JACK: I walked up. I turned the light off. I went back to bed, and I just told myself that, "This is a dream." That's what I remember. I didn't want to deal with it, you know? I can remember saying to Mary that it was a dream.

MARY: That's the only part I remember—you telling me about the noise at the door.

JACK: I didn't think that there was anything to this... and so, I just wanted to forget about it. I, I, I thought of calling you and reporting it, and I thought, "Nah, it's just a dream."

RAY: Well, from now on when things like this happen—if they happen—I'm not saying they're going to happen—keep a little notebook and put the date, time and place and a brief description in it.

Tony and I cast a knowing look at one another. We were both thinking the same thing. Did Jack have a real experience but was programmed to forget it? It would seem that yet another hypnosis session was necessary to check out Jack's dream.

Like many other CEIV cases, the Allagash abductions seemed to be a never-ending story. We probed Jack's dream and other accumulated items of interest during our investigation's last hypnosis session. One of these items was another of Jack's bizarre dreams. The following are pertinent excerpts from that meeting. The conversation picks up where Jack came face to face with the aliens at the door:

Hypnosis Session #3A (March 10, 1990)

JACK:	And I went downstairs and I remember being halfway down the stairs, and I bent over to look at the door...and when I looked...it was those eyes. Those eyes were there! And I thought, "Uh-uh, No way!"
RAY:	Whose eyes, Jack?
JACK:	Their eyes! Four eyes.
RAY:	What were they attached to?
JACK:	Heads.
RAY:	Have you seen these people before?
JACK:	Yes.
RAY:	Where?
JACK:	The same—the same ones [Allagash aliens].
DAVE:	What were they wearing?
JACK:	They had shiny clothing.
RAY:	What color?
JACK:	It was light-colored—shiny, light-colored clothing, like a pearl. A pearl color that seemed to winkle or shine.... Their heads! It was them!
RAY:	What did they want?
JACK:	I don't know.
RAY:	What happened?
JACK:	I just walked up, got back in bed and put the cover over my head.

*Figure 25. Jack Weiner's illustration of the
entry of the Allagash aliens into his home, with
the blue beam behind them.*

At this point, Tony placed Jack in a deeper trance and brought him back to where he faced the aliens on the stairway. The questioning resumed:

DAVE:	Where were they standing?
JACK:	Right at the door.
DAVE:	Was the door open or closed?
JACK:	It was closed.
RAY:	Are they inside or outside the door?
JACK:	Right at the door [just inside].
DAVE:	How could you see them?
JACK:	There was a light behind them.
DAVE:	Behind them where?
JACK:	Outside.
RAY:	This is the glass door?
JACK:	Yes. (See Figure 25.)
TONY:	What color is the light?
JACK:	Blue [the familiar blue beam].
DAVE:	Could you see anything in the light? Any details?
JACK:	I, I didn't want to look.
RAY:	Did they tell you not to tell us about what happened that night?
JACK:	The eyes—that's what they said.
RAY:	That night they said that? While they were at the door?
JACK:	Yes.
RAY:	What did they say?
JACK:	They said, "Don't tell anyone (pauses). You must cooperate!"
RAY:	What weren't you supposed to tell us?
JACK:	What happens when they come.
RAY:	So, something did happen that night?
JACK:	I don't know.

Probably Jack didn't know, because of what he had just told us, "Don't tell anyone—you must cooperate!" The aliens' hypnotic-like command prevailed; try as he may, Tony could not get any further with Jack's memory of that night.

Apparently, the aliens were not pleased with Jack's ongoing attempts to tell us about their activities. Another warning was issued. This time it involved a real dream and an ominous threat. Jack phoned me about the dream shortly after it occurred, and I recorded the conversation. Pertinent excerpts follow:

Southern Vermont (January 6, 1990)

JACK: I was just working on a letter to you, on a dream that I had on January 6th. It was really a strange dream. At first, I tried to put it aside and forget about it, but it was such a strange dream that it has been impossible to forget about it.... The dream itself wasn't anything about UFOs...but four different times, during this dream, a figure would just kind of emerge out of thin air in front of me and would come right up to me.... It was exactly like the things that I recalled under hypnosis from the Allagash, except...it had a long, flowing garment that hid the rest of his body, and it had a hood.... All I could see was its face.... It kept repeating, over and over again—it was like a message that was going into my mind or something. It's hard to verbalize, but it's really strange, Ray. It kept telling me not to tell...and it kept on saying..."You will not tell. It is not the right time." And then it said that, um, that, I should not harm myself by telling. The last thing it kept saying was, "You will cooperate!" And then, after I get this message from it, it would just recede back into nothingness again, and it did this about four different times during the dream.... It made me feel like I wanted to completely, ah, surrender to its wishes. You know, it was almost like, "Yeah, I can understand that." It made me feel, even in my dream...like I was weak in the knees.

At this point, I wondered if Jack's imagination were getting the best of him. Was it just a nightmare, sparked by real warnings by the aliens? Was it a repressed memory of a real warning given by aliens during a mentally-blocked encounter? Was it a telepathic warning beamed to Jack while he slept? Whatever it was, we felt it deserved examination during our last catchall hypnosis session. The following is Jack's description of his dream while under hypnosis:

Hypnosis Session #3C (March 10, 1990)

TONY: You mentioned something about...a dream...of a cloaked, hooded alien who warned you not to talk about your UFO experiences. Do you recall that?

Figure 26. Jack Weiner's illustration of the alien entity that entered Jack's dream to warn him "not to tell."

JACK:	Yes.
TONY:	Was that a dream, Jack?
JACK:	It was a dream, but a funny dream. Not like a dream.
TONY:	How was that dream different from a normal dream, a regular dream?
JACK:	It came into my dream.
TONY:	A dream about what, Jack?
JACK:	Oh, it was a nice dream.
TONY:	About what Jack?
JACK:	Oh, Mary and I were in Boston, and we went to a show with Jim and Carol and Charlie and Pete in a theater.
TONY:	And what happened just before the dream was interrupted? Where were you in the dream when it was interrupted?
JACK:	I was in the last seat on the right aisle.
TONY:	In the show?
JACK:	In the theater, and there were people on the stage telling jokes and juggling.
TONY:	And then what happened?
JACK:	Right to my right, right next to me, there was a brown curtain. A thick brown curtain...like velvet material.
TONY:	And then what happened?
JACK:	And then the curtain had a face in it—like it was behind the curtain. And it was poking out—and the velvet was the face, and it looked right at me and then went away.
TONY:	Did it say anything to you?
JACK:	No. All it did was show itself. And then, there were people running outside the theater to find it. And they went in a building up the stairs to look for it. And I was on the sidewalk, wondering why they went in the building. And then the whole thing just came towards me. It just came into my dream like—like it wasn't part of the dream. And it came right up to me!
TONY:	What was that Jack?
JACK:	The thing!
TONY:	Describe it.
JACK:	It was just like those things with the big eyes and a shiny face with no nose and no mouth and a long hood over its head. But, I could see its face, and it just came right up to me—right up to

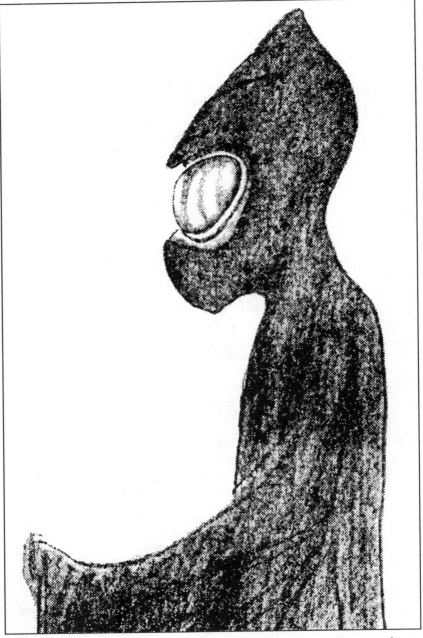

Figure 27. Jack Weiner's illustration of an alien entity that appeared next to him in a dream to warn him again "not to tell."

my face! And it would not let me move. It held me
there and told me not to tell—I "must not ever
tell! (See Figure 26.)

The dress and appearance of the alien were reminiscent of
the aliens that had abducted his brother, Jim, during the sledding incident. Tony asked him about the alien's clothes:

TONY:	Why was it wearing a hood?
JACK:	I don't know. I thought that was strange. And it had a loosely fitting cloak that covered its whole body—everything but its face. Those eyes! It wouldn't let me go.
DAVE:	Was it holding you physically?
JACK:	It seemed as if it was able to freeze me. I couldn't move. I felt weak, exhausted, and I felt like I had to do what it wanted.
DAVE:	Is this a dream Jack?
JACK:	Yes, in the dream—and then it floated away into a crack in the air and was gone.
TONY:	And then what did you dream about?
JACK:	And then I dreamt that I said to Mary, "Did you see that?" But she didn't. Then, we were on a trolley on Beacon Street at Coolidge corner, riding on the trolley, talking. And I was thinking about that face. And I was sitting in a seat.... (Suddenly becomes very agitated.)
TONY:	Just relax.
JACK:	(Speaks nervously.) And then there was something in the seat like clothing or a lump of clothing. And then—there it was again! It just took shape from the clothing, and it was right there again. (Becomes extremely agitated.) Those eyes! (See Figure 27.)
TONY:	Just relax now, just relax. It's okay. And after that, did you wake up?
JACK:	No. They told me again not to tell. Those eyes!
RAY:	What did you say to the eyes? Did you say you weren't going to tell? Or couldn't you?
JACK:	I said nothing. I—all I could think of was the message, not to tell, "You will not tell. It's not time."
RAY:	Is there going to be a time that you are supposed to be able to tell?
JACK:	Yes—I think—I think there is a time.

RAY:	What would happen? Did they tell you what would happen if you did tell?
JACK:	They told me, "You can be harmed. You can harm yourself if you tell."
TONY:	Did they say how?
JACK:	No.
TONY:	Did they say by whom?
JACK:	By myself.
DAVE:	Did they mention us or anybody else?
JACK:	No. No names.
RAY:	Was this the only time you had that dream?
JACK:	Yes.
RAY:	How did you feel when you got up in the morning?
JACK:	Awful, I felt drained—drained, weak, and, and anticipating. I felt that something would happen. That something was going to happen, and I felt scared.
RAY:	Did you feel like you wanted to tell?
JACK:	Ha! No. I felt like I wanted to do what they wanted me to do.
RAY:	How long did you feel that way?
JACK:	I still feel that way. I was scared.
RAY:	Did they ever—in any of these incidents—ever mention this investigation?
JACK:	(Pauses.) They didn't have to, because I know that they're talking about this investigation.
RAY:	Repeat?
JACK:	They know that they don't want me to tell you. I know that.
RAY:	How do you know that?
JACK:	It's just a feeling that they give me when they tell me that they know—that you're the one who wants to know—and I'm not supposed to tell.
RAY:	Did they ever tell you when you could tell and what the circumstances would be?
JACK:	(Pauses.) They said, "Now is not the time!"
RAY:	But, did they tell when the time would be and what the circumstances would be?
JACK:	Somehow it feels like I know. But I don't remember what it is or when I should remember or tell. But, I know, I know when, but I don't remember.
RAY:	Is it because they told you and then told you that you couldn't remember?

JACK:	(Pauses.) It's difficult to describe. It's something they did to us all in Maine—and—we know—but now is not the time to remember.
RAY:	Are they ever going to show themselves to people here openly?
JACK:	(Pauses.) I don't know. I feel that they are the only ones who can say. We know that they have shown themselves to us, but I feel that we don't know all of their motives.
RAY:	Were there any other times that you had relations with these things or beings where other people were involved other than, ah, Mary, Charlie, Jack, Chuck?
JACK:	No.
RAY:	Did you ever see Kim [Chuck's wife] in any of these experiences?
JACK:	No.
RAY:	Did you ever see these same beings before the Maine occurrence?
JACK:	One time when I was very, very little. I remembered being scared in our room where Jim and I used to sleep and I saw a face in my room that was like them.
DAVE:	How old were you?
JACK:	I was somewhere around five and one half.

This was a reference to Harry the Ghost. It brought us around full circle—Jack's UFO experiences were bracketed between the 1950's. and early 1990's.

The unveiling had continued our investigative process of adding still more strong anecdotal evidence for the reality of UFO abductions. As previously mentioned, it also added physical evidence because, in some cases, the aliens had left their calling cards behind.

CHAPTER **11**

Alien Calling Cards

Thus far, the data presented concerning the Allagash abductions has been strictly anecdotal in nature. A correlation of this data in the next chapter will provide the strongest kind of circumstantial evidence for the reality of the UFO encounters experienced by the Allagash four. However, there is yet another kind of evidence that needs to be discussed before a complete correlation of data can be satisfactorily accomplished. It deals not with the abductees' experience per se, but rather with the effects of the experience upon the abductee. These effects have been documented by a number of UFO researchers, including Dr. David M. Jacobs.

Dr. Jacobs is a professor of history at Temple University. His Ph.D. dissertation was published in 1975 by Indiana University Press as *The UFO Controversy in America*. Currently serving on MUFON's Advisory Board of Consultants, he defines the aforementioned effects to be the Post-Abduction Syndrome (PAS):

> A complex of physical and psychological symptoms that can have deleterious effects on its victims. Recognizing these symptoms is an important step in diagnosing abductions and providing the help that abductees need to overcome PAS effects.[1]

---

1. David M. Jacobs, Ph. D., "Post-Abduction Syndrome," *MUFON 1988 International UFO Symposium Proceedings, p. 87.*

The purpose of this chapter is to diagnose the abduction experiences of the Allagash four in the light of Post-Abduction Syndrome. Both physical and psychological symptoms will be discussed in some detail as they apply to each abductee.

Post-Abduction Syndrome
Physical Symptoms

Concerning the physical effects of Post-Abduction Syndrome, Dr. Jacobs remarks:

> Physically, the abduction experience can leave its victims with a wide range of aftereffects. Scars, eye problems, muscle pains, bruises, unusual vaginal and navel discharges, genital disorders, neurological problems, pregnancy anomalies, ovarian difficulties, and so forth, are just a few of...the physical problems associated with the abduction experiences. [2]

Our investigation revealed several of these symptoms present in one or more of the Allagash abductees: scars, bruises, muscle pains and neurological problems. The following summarizes our findings after an examination of each of the four percipients:

Jack Weiner

The apparent physical effects related to Jack Weiner's UFO abduction fall into two categories. One deals with an item not mentioned by Dr. Jacobs. The other would best fall under his category of bruises. Let us discuss each of these in turn.

One of several body locations that are of interest to alien entities is the area just above the shin bone called the tibia. This has been documented by myself and other abduction researchers such as Budd Hopkins and MUFON's Physiological Effects Consultant, Richard Neal, M.D. What is usually found in this area is, "a circular or scoop-like depression about one-eighth inch to three-quarters inch in diameter and maybe as much as one-quarter inch deep." [3] I, myself found such a mark on my right tibia after an abduction nightmare. A dermatologist told me that it looked exactly like a punch biopsy. My encounters with the UFO phenomenon are documented in my previous book, *The Watchers*.

---

2. Jacobs, "Post-Abduction Syndrome," pp. 87-88.
3. Richard Neal, M.D., "Generations of Abduction: A Medical Casebook," *UFO*, Vol. 3, No. 2, 1988, p. 22. (Credit: *UFO Magazine*, 1800 S. Robertson Blvd., Box 355, Los Angeles, CA 90035).

When Jack's leg was first examined in this area, a scar was noticed. He told us that it was from an operation which removed a strange tumor from his tibia. This information was significant, because Dr. Neal's research had revealed, in the cases of some abductees, that "questionable tumors (lipomas) have been noticed just beneath the skin." Of great interest is the fact that later on, after another abduction and a number of nightmares, a typical scoopmark resembling a punch biopsy appeared overnight just above Jack's operation scar. More about this later. First let us discuss the tumor.

Upon questioning Jack, I found that this certainly had been a "questionable tumor." It was also consequential because it was found in one of the body areas shown special interest by the aliens. Our conversation was recorded:

JACK: That thing they took out of my leg...they never did know what it was.

RAY: What was?

JACK: I had some kind of lump on my leg right here. See? There's the scar right there.

RAY: Oh, boy!

JACK: It was...as big as my thumb knuckle.

RAY: Okay, the first question I have is—when and how did you first notice this?

JACK: It was 1981 [January]. Um, I was just, ah, watching television with Mary and crossed my leg over and, ah, I felt a pain there.... I thought maybe something had gone through my pants into my legs that was stuck to my shoe or something. So, when I lifted my pant leg up and pulled my sock down, I noticed there was this peculiar lump on my foreleg down there near my ankle.

RAY: And that scar was caused basically by the operation.

JACK: Yes.

RAY: What did it look like before it was removed?

JACK: It was a bulge. There was no particular shape, you know—semi-spherical or something, you know, round.

RAY: Okay, and what did you do about it?

JACK: Well, um, I showed it to Mary, and then I said, "Geeze, maybe I bumped my leg at work or something." That's what I thought. That's what I hoped. So, I just kept an eye on it for about two weeks. We decided that if it's still there in a couple of weeks, I'll have it looked at. We did that,

	and in a few weeks, it actually got worse. I decided to go to the local doctor.... Her name was Dr. Wrigley.
RAY:	What did she say?
JACK:	She said it looked to her like it was a kind of ganglion, something under the skin, an infection of some kind.
RAY:	What did she do?
JACK:	Well, she stuck a needle directly into the lump to try to drain it.
RAY:	Could the needle go in?
JACK:	It went in, but nothing happened.... Nothing came out. She pressed and even tried to draw fluid out, and all she got was this kind of reddish, pinkish, clear kind of fluid.... She stopped right away and ah, she said, "Well this isn't what I thought it was." And she got a book out, and she started looking things up in books, and then she said, "Well, I don't know what it is for sure, so I'm going to send you down to a specialist in Brattleboro, at the Brattleboro Memorial Hospital."
RAY:	Okay, what did they do down there?
JACK:	Well, there, I went to Dr. Kinley's office...and he took a look at it and, ah, he said, "Yeah, there's something in there." And, ah, he thought right away that it should come out—to remove it surgically.
RAY:	Okay, when they removed it surgically, did you see what was removed?
JACK:	Yeah, it was about as big in diameter as a nickel. I don't remember that clearly. I was still feeling the effects of anesthesia.
RAY:	What color?
JACK:	Pinkish.
RAY:	Did you touch it?
JACK:	No, I don't remember touching it, but I remember the nurse...was surprised that I wanted to see it.... She had it in the palm of her surgical gloved hand.... It fit right in the palm there, this little pad of—like chewed-up bubble gum—pink bubble gum.
RAY:	Okay, now describe the follow-up with the doctor after they took it out.
JACK:	Well, the follow-up was lengthy.... He [Dr. Kinley] said, "Well Jack, our lab seems to think

there's a problem with this sample, and it reacted positively in our lab. And so, to be sure, we're
going to send it to the Center for Disease Control
in Atlanta, Georgia, and they're going to analyze
it a little bit more, just to be sure that there's
nothing to be alarmed about. But, I don't want
to alarm you. We're pretty sure that there's
nothing to it, but just to be positive, we're going
to send it out." And then I had to go back to see
him about once a week for the first few weeks because it was a lasting wound that was left
there.... To this day, it's a sore spot.

RAY: So, when did he tell you the results?

JACK: I kept seeing him. At one point, it must have
          been about two months into this thing...and I
          said, "Well doctor, have you heard anything?"...
          And he, he looked at me, and he seemed kind of
          nervous like he didn't want to talk about it, and
          in a side-handed way, he said, "Well, you know,
          I don't want you to worry, but sometimes with
          these rare cancers, it takes time to analyze
          them." Cancer! I was alarmed, and I said, "Are
          you telling me that I have some kind of cancer?"
          And he said, "No, no, I don't want to say that just
          yet, but it's been there for a long time.... The re-
          port isn't back yet, but it seems that it might be."
          At that point, I was getting pretty worried. And
          then, I guess it was another month or two, a re-
          port came back, and he had me come in, and he
          said, "Well, you know Jack, it looks to us like it
          was nothing to worry about, but we're not abso-
          lutely positive about that, so we're just going to
          keep an eye on it and if it comes back, we'll just
          take it out again."

RAY: Did you ever get a report on it?

JACK: They said they didn't know what it was. They
          gave up trying to figure it out. It seemed to be
          some kind of a cyst...or some kind of unusual
          [benign] cancer.

RAY: What you just showed me, you know, in this
          area, is one of the prime areas where things hap-
          pen.

JACK: Huh? Oh, no!...His exact words were, "We're re-
          ally not sure what that was." That's what Dr.
          Kinley told me.

Needless to say, Jack's lump corresponded exactly with Dr.
Neal's description of questionable tumors noticed just beneath
the skin of abductees. I asked Jack to obtain copies of his med-

ical records immediately for Dr. Neal's examination. He did, and the mystery deepened. The following is a transcript of Jack's description of his visit to the hospital to obtain records of his operation:

> I went down there and asked for them, and they called my record up on the computer. She got them out, and she said to me, um, "Were you in the military when this happened?" And I said, "No, I was working out of Unified Data at Cambridgeport." And she said, "Gee, they sent these [records] down to a Military Institute of Pathology.

Jack said he was shocked about this. He had been told specifically that the lump removed from his right tibia had been sent to the Center for Disease Control in Atlanta, Georgia, for analysis. Not only that, but the final pathologist's report was signed by a William R. Cowan, Colonel, United States Air Force. Colonel Cowan's title was Director of the Armed Forces Institute of Pathology (AFIP), Washington, D.C.

After making inquiries, Jack was told that the lump was sent to AFIP to save the hospital money since AFIP provided free service. This was puzzling, because Jack was fully covered by insurance. Others questioned at the hospital thought the procedure out of the ordinary unless Jack had sustained an injury while in the military.

> Soon after, I questioned the records clerk myself. She told me that she had nothing in her files that would indicate that the lump had been sent to the Center for Disease Control in Atlanta, Georgia. Furthermore, she could not locate any transmittal letter that would indicate why it had been sent to the AFIP in Washington, D.C.

> The pathologist's secretary said much the same thing. She could not find any transmittal correspondence on the matter. She stated that, at the time, it was the hospital's procedure to send such samples to outside consultants for a second opinion.

> This latest turn of events was of great interest to me because the United States Air Force has always been heavily involved with UFO research. When I phoned the AFIP about the matter, all I was told was that AFIP did occasionally provide services to civilian hospitals. I sent the records to Dr. Neal for his analysis. Later, he requested that X-rays of the lump be obtained and sent to him. When Jack asked for copies of the X-rays, he met with stiff opposition. He phoned to tell me about it. His recorded conversation follows:

JACK: It was a weird thing, Ray. When I went into the records department to get those X-rays, they said that you had to go to Radiology to get them. I figured that sounds reasonable, so I went up to Radiology, and I went up to the nurse there that was at the desk. I told her that I needed to obtain some X-rays. She was real nice to me and real accommodating. And she said, "Okay, what's your name and birth date?" And I told her. And then, ah, she called up the information on her computer monitor, and her computer spits out a card and she reads the card, and she gives me this real funny look. And all of a sudden, her attitude changed, ah, like, ah, between night and day. The first thing she said was, "Who wants these?" Just like that. And I said, "I want them." And she said, "No, no, no. What doctor wants them?" And I said, "Well, um, it's not a doctor that wants them." And she kept questioning me and questioning me about why I wanted them. So, I said, "Gee, this is really unusual because I've come up here and gotten X-rays before that I brought home to digitize when...for my wrist injury." Finally...she said, "Well, I can't give them to you 'till tomorrow." So I said, "Fine, fine, I'll come in tomorrow and get them." And then I went in the next day and got them.

The behavior of the radiology clerk was just another intriguing tidbit to add to the mystery of the lump. I decided to write to Dr. Kinley, in the hope that he might shed some light on these things. I also told him about the possible link between the lump and Jack's abduction experience. He would not comment and merely sent me duplicate medical records of Jack's operation.

Next, I sent the X-rays to Dr. Neal for his comments. Dr. Neal urged me to have Jack questioned about the origin of the lump under hypnosis. We all wondered how it could suddenly appear overnight in one of the aliens' primary areas of interest. Thus, the origin of the lump was one of the major subjects of interest covered during the last hypnosis session. Pertinent excerpts from this session are as follows:

Hypnosis Session #3D (March 10, 1990)

Tony initially placed Jack in a light state of hypnosis and asked Jack to tell us what he knew about the lump. Jack again summarized how he noticed it while watching television. He stressed how surprised he was to lift up his pant leg and see the protrusion above his right ankle. It had not been there the day before, nor had he felt any pain up until that point in time.

    Jack also described his trips to the local doctor and his referral to the hospital for surgery. After Jack had rehearsed all that he knew about the situation, Tony eased him still deeper into the hypnotic state. The questioning then resumed:

TONY: Do you know what caused that lump?

JACK: I don't really know. I know that it wasn't there because of something that I did, because I know that I didn't do anything to that spot that would have caused a bump or injury. I don't know how it got there.

TONY: I'm just going to ask you to relax even more. I'm going to ask that your mind just do the work for you—your unconscious mind do the work for you. What I would like you to do is just relax. I'm going to ask you to visualize a screen—perhaps a large TV screen—perhaps a movie screen. Can you do that Jack?

JACK: Yes.

TONY: Just divide the screen in half. Cut it in half from the top to the bottom. Can you do that, Jack?

JACK: Yes.

TONY: Just relax, you're doing very well. I'd like the right half to flash the word "Yes." Can you see that?

JACK: Yes.

TONY: I'd like the left half to flash "No." Can you see that?

JACK: Yes.

TONY: We can shut off both of those lights and any time that I ask a question, I'm going to ask you, which side of the screen lights up. The right half is "Yes"—the left half is "no." Right— "Yes." Left—"No." Do you agree with that Jack?

JACK: Yes.

TONY: Did the screen light up when I asked you that question?

JACK: Yes.

TONY: Did it light up "Yes?"

JACK: Yes.

TONY: So, whenever we ask a "Yes—No" question, the right half is "Yes", the left half is "No." I really want to talk to your unconscious, Jack. I just want you floating away somewhere: a hot tub— taking a walk—sitting on a beach—lying by a pool—do you know how that lump got there?

JACK:	(Does not answer.)
TONY:	Which side lights up?
JACK:	(Speaks very slowly and deliberately.) I—see—a— "Yes."
TONY:	Just relax. I know it is very pleasant. Just kind of drift off. In the few minutes that I speak to you, the world is off. It's so good. Is that lump there because of something you have done?
JACK:	No.
TONY:	Did the left side of the screen light up?
JACK:	Yes.
TONY:	That's good. And the more that you listen to my voice, the deeper you will relax because the more deeply relaxed [you are], [the more] you will have access to that filing cabinet that we call the unconscious. Every time you exhale, relax more and more deeply.

Jack's body slumped more and more into the chair as Tony slowly but surely placed him in a very deep level of hypnosis. Then he asked Jack the proverbial 64 million dollar question:

TONY:	Is that lump there because of what someone else has done?
JACK:	Yes!
TONY:	Just relax, just relax. Now push this all aside. Do you remember how that lump got there?
JACK:	I think I do. I remember (pauses) there was something that they did to my legs.
TONY:	Who are they, Jack?
JACK:	The ones we saw in Maine.
TONY:	Where in Maine?
JACK:	On the light—the light in Maine.... There were the things—the things [aliens].
TONY:	What did they do?
JACK:	They rubbed my legs (pauses) with (pauses) some kind of (pauses) thing that—I don't know what it was for. But, I can see them rubbing my legs, and they are going to do—they're doing something (pauses) down there.
TONY:	What are they doing, Jack?
JACK:	I, I don't know why, why they're doing—it's something they're looking at on my leg.
RAY:	The lump, Jack—do you think what caused the lump happened at that particular time?

JACK:	They did something to my legs with a thing that has a long thin [point] (pauses) like a needle (See Figure 28.)
TONY:	What did they do with it, Jack?
JACK:	First, they rubbed my leg with something that was small and smooth. (See Figure 29.)...I can't really feel what they're doing—but I can see two of them doing something to my legs with a long, thin thing and their eyes—I don't like their eyes!
RAY:	Did the needle just touch your skin? Scratch your skin? Enter your skin?
JACK:	It's hard to tell.
DAVE:	Do you feel any pain?
JACK:	No.
RAY:	Did you feel any numbness?
JACK:	I feel like I can't move.
RAY:	Before they rubbed your leg—and after they rubbed your leg—did it feel any different?
JACK:	Yes.
RAY:	How?
JACK:	I could not feel what they were doing.

It was just as we had suspected. The rubbing of Jack's legs with an instrument had anesthetized them. The session continued:

RAY:	Do you know what they're doing...?
JACK:	They're poking my legs with something in their hands, but I don't want to know (sighs and begins to breath heavily).
TONY:	Just relax, Jack. You're doing very well. Just relax.
JACK:	I know that there's something down there that they're doing like an operation—like a doctor—but I'm afraid, and I don't know why they are doing this to me.

The Allagash incident had occurred in 1976. The lump had appeared almost five years later, in the latter part of January, 1981. This caused me to wonder if the aliens had shown interest in the area from which the lump had been removed during Jack and Mary's abduction on May 20, 1988:

RAY:	When is the next time they look at that area?

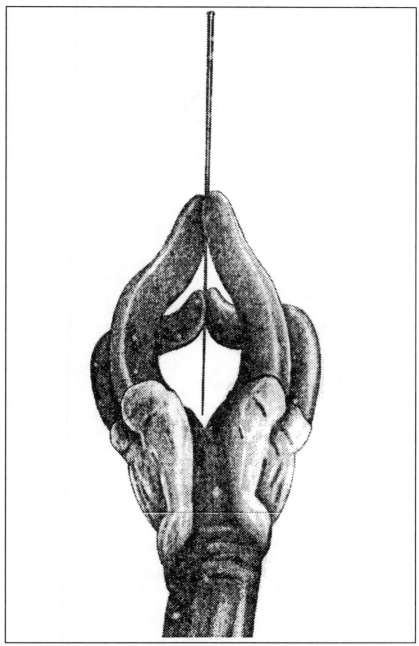

*Figure 28. Jack Weiner's illustration of the long
needlelike instrument that the alien entities
used to poke his leg.*

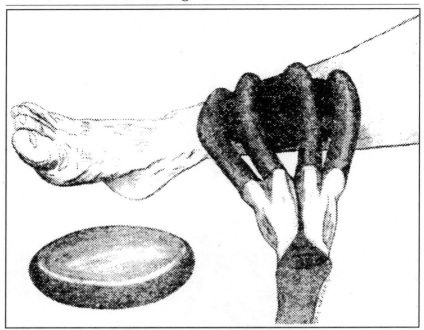

Figure 29. Jack Weiner's illustration of the alien entities working on his legs.

JACK: They used the same round, smooth ball to rub my leg and look there.

RAY: When was that?

JACK: When I "dreamed" that they were in our house [in Vermont] and came to the house. I remember they looked there. The same spot.

Was Jack referring to the 1988 incident, or another incident that we had missed? My next questions were framed to find out:

RAY: Can you go over when you first noticed them and tell us what happened?

JACK: They (pauses) were not interested in my fear. They seemed to only want to poke.

RAY: When did you first notice them? You were at your home in Vermont, right?

JACK: Yes.

RAY: Now, how did you know they were there? When did you first see them? Describe the circumstances surrounding the whole incident.

JACK: I remember it was the time that I got up out of
               bed to walk the dog and it was that time that
               they looked. I remember it was the time that I
               told you about.... It was the time where Mary
               and I were there.... That was the time that they
               looked at my legs and they spent some time at
               that spot [where the lump had been removed],
               and I didn't like their eyes!

It was clear that Jack was referring to the May 20, 1988,
incident when he and Mary were abducted from their home. He
had already relived this episode under hypnosis. It was discussed earlier in the book.

However on this occasion, as I listened to Jack, I wondered
what the aliens thought when they saw the scar and realized
something was missing! Perhaps the lump was originally a
small implant of living tissue used for alien genetics studies.
The rapid multiplication of cells indicates that something must
have gone awry with their experiment.

Since Jack had become very agitated during this discussion, Tony stepped in to calm him before resuming the questioning:

TONY: Where were you when they examined your leg?
JACK: I was in a room that was very bright.
TONY: Jack, just look around and tell us anything you
               can see in that room.
JACK: I see (pauses) very bright hazy light all around,
               and I am standing, but I can't feel how I'm stand-
               ing, and I can move my eyes. I see two of them
               [aliens] in front of me and beyond them, there's
               more space that's bright.
RAY: Where's Mary?
JACK: I don't know.
RAY: When was the last time you saw Mary?
JACK: In the [blue] beam—in the yard—was the last
               time I saw her face.

We interrupted Jack at this point because there were other
important items to discuss with him under hypnosis. Despite
the aliens' probable surprise at discovering Jack's scar, this
was not the last time they would examine his feet. The first clue
of this came to my attention when Jack had phoned to tell me
about Charlie's dream.

The dream, if you will recall, occurred when Charlie had
visited Jack and Mary to help split wood for winter fuel. He had

slept downstairs in front of the glass front door. In the early morning hours, he was awakened by the feeling of a presence. He raised himself up and glanced out the door. A group of aliens stood, bathed in a light which came from above. Two turned and looked at Charlie as they approached the door. Charlie took one long look and pulled the cover over him. This was all he could remember. This episode was fully discussed in the last chapter. Hypnosis failed to reveal anything further happening to Charlie. Charlie was an innocent bystander. Just as in the case of the Allagash, he was at the wrong place at the wrong time. As the hypnosis session revealed, Jack was the aliens' target that night.

When Jack phoned, he sounded worried. After discussing Charlie's dream, he paused and then asked me a question with a hesitant tone in his voice. The conversation was recorded. Pertinent excerpts follow:

JACK: Well, um, one of the things I wanted to ask you is, um, when this thing happened to Charlie, like about a day later...I noticed something on the bottom of my foot. And it's probably—it probably has nothing to do with any of this. But, I don't remember—I mean it was just there—one day it wasn't and the other day it was there.... It seems like all the skin on the bottom of my right foot was—I don't know what it—it, it, it's all coming off! I was wondering if you've run across anything that involved the bottom of people's feet [i.e., people who have had UFO experiences]?

RAY: No. Is there any pain?

JACK: It hurts. I've been putting on, ah, salve on it and stuff, because it's all cracked and sore. It's, it's almost as if I walked on either something extremely cold and froze my skin or burned it somehow....

RAY: What you might do is, ah, put down the date and the description...photograph it...and see a doctor because that's sort of serious. You have to walk everyday.

JACK: Yeah, I've been putting stuff on it and wearing a sock and everything and trying to stay off it as much as I can. I have no idea what would have caused that. I know that I didn't do anything.... It's just like one day it wasn't there and the next day it was.... I thought it was athlete's foot or something like that, but I never get that. I don't go to gyms. There's no place I can pick it up.... It was overnight, you know? I got up one morning

and my foot was all sore when I stepped on it. I
thought I had stepped on a piece of glass.

RAY: Well, do what I've mentioned and also perhaps
see a doctor about it.... Ah, When Charlie had
his dream, did you look around to see if there's
anything that ah—

JACK: Well, I did walk around the yard after he told me.
I mean, that morning at breakfast he was really
upset...

RAY: Okay, no footprints, no burn marks or tripod
marks or nothing like that at all?

JACK: It would be hard to see unless they were very
blatant, because this time of year...it's frost. The
ground's moving around.

RAY: Yeah...so if you can get a photograph of that.

JACK: Yeah, we'll photograph the bottom of my foot....
All the skin is coming off and it left these real
four deep cracks—crevices—all over the bottom
of my foot. (See Figure 30.)

I must confess that I had never heard of a UFO-related effect like Jack had described. But later, after hypnosis indicated
that Charlie's dream reflected reality, we decided that Jack
should also be questioned about his foot. If the house were visited by aliens that night, then the overnight appearance of
Jack's wounds may have been another example of their "calling
cards." The following is a transcript of pertinent portions of our
follow-up hypnosis session with Jack:

Hypnosis Session #3D (March 10, 1990)

RAY: Now, in November of 1989, Jack—this was after
your friend Charlie Foltz had a dream about
aliens standing outside the door?

JACK: Yes.

RAY: You woke up, either the day after or a few days
after, to find that the bottom of your right foot
appeared it had suffered either frostbite or a
burn or something. It was very strange.

JACK: I remember.

RAY: Maybe Tony can talk to you about how that happened.

TONY: Is there anything you want to tell us about that?
It's November, 1989.

JACK: I remember Charlie was visiting, and I remember
that he woke up in the morning and looked

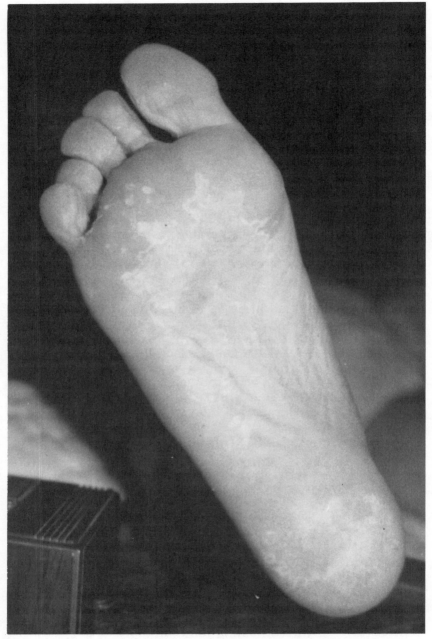

Figure 30. Skin deterioration of Jack Weiner's foot after aliens probed it with a round device.

	funny. He looked scared and tense (becomes agitated).
TONY:	Just relax, just relax.
RAY:	Okay, Charlie told us about that. Now, a day or so later, you noticed something wrong with the bottom of your foot.
JACK:	Yes.
RAY:	Do you remember how that happened?
JACK:	I remember waking up two days after Charlie was there, and walking down the stairs and noticing that my feet hurt. And I remember thinking that I stepped on glass or something, because it hurt like I stepped on glass.... I remember thinking how strange, because I knew that I hadn't stepped on glass or done anything to my feet that would make them bleed.
DAVE:	Is this just your right foot or both feet?
JACK:	My right foot was the worst, but both feet were chafed and cracked.
TONY:	Just relax Jack, just relax.

Tony placed Jack in an even deeper state of hypnosis. He then proceeded with the questioning, using the divided TV-screen procedure again. After asking Jack a number of non-related questions, Tony quickly sprung "the" question:

TONY:	The right is "Yes" and the left is "No".... Do you know what happened to the bottoms of your feet, Jack? Which side of the screen lights up?
JACK:	Yes [i.e., the right side lit up].
TONY:	Can you explain to us what happened?
JACK:	I (pauses) can't (pauses) tell.
TONY:	Is it that you do not remember?
JACK:	I don't remember why (pauses) I know that I'm not supposed to tell.
TONY:	How do you know you're not supposed to tell?
JACK:	Because I see the face—their eyes told me (pauses) not to tell.
TONY:	This is before or after that happened to your feet?
JACK:	After.
TONY:	Just relax, Jack. Just relax, just relax.

Tony calmed Jack and brought him to an even deeper state of hypnosis. He assured Jack that he was with an empathetic group of people who were there to support him:

TONY: I am going to ask that whatever happened will be clear to you so that you can tell us as clearly as possible what happened to the bottom of your feet. Just relax, just relax.

JACK: I see the face! Those eyes! I can see those eyes! And (pauses) I'm not—they are so big!

TONY: Just relax, just relax. Do you want to tell us what happened?

JACK: No.

TONY: Why don't you want to tell us?

JACK: I'm not supposed to.

RAY: Could someone else tell us? Look at that [imaginary] TV. Can you see it?

JACK: Yes.

RAY: Let's say that someone like a newscaster has been watching everything that happened. Why don't you have him tell us, and then you won't have to tell us.

JACK: (Pauses.) A face! Those eyes (pauses) are on the screen!

TONY: What screen is that, Jack?

JACK: The [imaginary] television.

DAVE: Where do you see the face, Jack?

JACK: Right in front of me!

RAY: Now, Jack, those same eyes, those same things [aliens] also told you not to tell us about the Allagash incident and other things, so it must be okay.

JACK: I know (pauses) why I'm not supposed to tell.

RAY: Now, did those feet get that way by accident? Did those feet get that way because they did it on purpose?

JACK: My feet were that way not by something that I did or happened for no reason.

TONY: Jack, you said a few minutes ago, regarding your feet, "I know why I'm not supposed to tell." Can you explain to us why you aren't supposed to tell?

JACK: Yes.

TONY: Okay, go ahead.

JACK: The eyes—the eyes told me not to tell.

RAY:	Can you see them doing that to your feet?
JACK:	(Pauses.) No.
RAY:	Can you feel what—when that's done to your feet?
JACK:	(Pauses.) I don't know how they did it.
RAY:	Did you feel anything?
JACK:	No.
RAY:	Why don't you know how they did it? Were your eyes open when they did it?
JACK:	(Pauses.) I (pauses) see (pauses) the faces (pauses) looking at that spot on my leg [where the lump was] and looking at me with those eyes! And they're saying, "You—will—cooperate!"
DAVE:	Where are they?
JACK:	At my feet.
DAVE:	Where? In your house or somewhere else?
JACK:	They are somewhere else.
DAVE:	Where is that?
JACK:	Where it's bright—very bright—and—I'm not supposed to (pauses) know.
DAVE:	Can you describe your surroundings?
JACK:	All I see are those eyes and heads and long, thin arms and funny hands at my feet.
DAVE:	How many are there?
JACK:	Two. Only two.
RAY:	Now—you've told us all of that, and the eyes told you not to tell us anything, so it's okay to tell us the rest now. What did they do with your feet?
JACK:	I (pauses) don't know what they're doing. It's something that I don't know why. I'm afraid.
DAVE:	We're not asking why, we're asking what are they doing?
JACK:	It's something they hold, and it's whitish and rounded, that they touch my skin with.
RAY:	What skin?
JACK:	On my feet.
RAY:	Where your feet were bleeding and chafed? Did they touch there?
JACK:	Yes.
RAY:	Did it hurt?
JACK:	No.
RAY:	Did they do anything to that area of your foot before they touched it with this other thing?

JACK:	They felt my feet with funny hands, first.
DAVE:	Could you feel their hands?
JACK:	No, it's like my feet are thick and numb, and I don't feel anything.
DAVE:	Were they working on both feet?
JACK:	Both feet.
DAVE:	Did they look at your legs?
JACK:	Yes.
DAVE:	What did they do to your legs?
JACK:	They rubbed my leg at that spot—where the scar [resulting from the surgical removal of the lump] is.
DAVE:	Rubbed your leg with what?
JACK:	The thing that was rounded (pauses). And they keep looking at me. (See Figure 29.)
DAVE:	Have you seen this rounded device before?
JACK:	Yes.
TONY:	Where?
JACK:	I see it—saw it—the first time they rubbed my legs [i.e., on the Allagash; apparently, this device was used to anesthetize Jack's legs].
RAY:	Can you remember that in detail and draw it for us? Is it that clear that you could draw it for us?
JACK:	I could.
RAY:	Okay, if you would remember to do that for us.
DAVE:	And any other devices that they may have used.

We found it impossible to extract any more from Jack about his injured feet. Time was fleeting by, and there were other items to discuss on the agenda. Suffice it to say, both Charlie and Jack saw the visitors that night. It seems only Jack was examined, but the aliens had mentally programmed him not to remember the incident. It was only through Tony's expertise that we were able to partially break through this induced memory block. It was enough to reveal that Jack's wounds were indeed related to yet another enigmatic confrontation with alien creatures.

During our examination of Jack's body, he showed us a faint scar remnant near his right shoulder blade. I did not place much significance in it, as there was no reason to believe that it was UFO-related. However, the day after Jack's and Mary's abduction on the night of May 20, 1988, the old scar made itself known. I'll let Jack describe what it did. Our conversation was recorded:

JACK:	Remember that time you checked that thing on my back?
RAY:	On your back? Right.
JACK:	Well, that really flared up. It was right after I had that dream in May was when it was worse. It was driving me nuts. Since then, it hasn't. I mean it seems to have gotten less and less bothersome since that time. I still have this area that seems almost like it has been shot with Novocaine, but it doesn't bother me as much as it did then.

It is possible that Jack's scar is related to one of the examinations performed by the aliens during an abduction. Although not as evident as Jack's lump and foot wounds, it is still worthy of mention.

Already mentioned is the scoopmark that suddenly appeared, overnight, just above the scar left by the removal of the tumor from Jack's leg. Just prior to its appearance, Jack had been waking up at night with feelings of sheer terror. He told me that he had a strong feeling of the aliens' presence. The scar is an exact duplicate of those found in the same area on other abductees' legs, including my own. A comparison of the punch-biopsy-like scar on my leg with the one on Jack's leg bears this out dramatically. The overnight appearance of this scar, concurrent with Jack's nighttime panic attacks, confirms that as of May 1, 1990, the liaison between human twin and phantom physicians was continuing!

Other members of the Allagash four also sport strange scars, marks and other reactions characteristic of the abduction phenomenon. Let us examine each of these in turn.

Charlie Foltz

I was very curious to see if Charlie had any residual scars located on any of the body areas where such marks are commonly found on abductees. Charlie, unlike the others, did not have a history of encounters with alien beings. However, he was not exempt from being examined by the aliens during the abduction on the Allagash. Charlie agreed to examine his body and report any strange scars to us. His response was recorded:

CHARLIE:	Ah, I've got a—on the inside of my left leg, ah...I have a, like a scar, depression, ah, I never ever—
RAY:	What is it shaped like?
CHARLIE:	Just a little pocket-like.
RAY:	Is it like a scoop...?

CHARLIE:	You could describe it like that. It's maybe half the size of my little fingernail.
RAY:	Have you ever seen a, ah, a punch biopsy?
CHARLIE:	Yes.
RAY:	Would it be an indentation like that?
CHARLIE:	Yep, yep.
RAY:	And how long has that been there?
CHARLIE:	I have no idea. In fact, I never even noticed it or paid any attention to it.
RAY:	Okay, this is on your left leg?
CHARLIE:	Left leg...on the inside of my thigh.

Again, I felt as if I had struck gold. This was yet another common area where a scar resembling a punch biopsy has been found on abductees. Dr. Richard Neal writes that both he and abductee researcher Budd Hopkins have observed scars:

> ...on the calf (including just over the tibia or shin bone), "thigh," hip, shoulder, knee, spinal column and on the right sides of the back and forehead.... Topographically, scars fall into two basic groups: A thin, straight, hairline cut, linear and about one-third inch long; and a circular or scoop-like depression, about one-eighth inch to three-quarter inch in diameter and maybe as much as one-quarter inch deep.[4]

Chuck Rak

Chuck had a mark on his back that he could not account for. It was located on the spinal column, between his shoulder blades. He had only noticed it recently, when we had inquired about anomalous scars. During a visit to my home, he showed it to me. Our conversation was recorded:

CHUCK:	I've got something in between my shoulder blades. I went to the doctor about it. He said, "Have you been out in the sun?" And I said, "Not without protection. I've worn protection there since I was 14 years old."
RAY:	What did he think had caused it?
CHUCK:	He said, implied, that it was some sort of ultraviolet thing from the sun.

4. Neal, "Generations," pp. 22.

No one can prove that Chuck's burn was related to one of the "calling cards." However, I would be remiss if I had not mentioned it. This is especially so, since Dr. Neal also refers to rashes and burns, found on various body areas of an abductee, that appear to be similar to "localized psoriasis." Chuck described the mark as, "A crusty area...of disturbed skin."

Jim Weiner

Jim had two possible physical manifestations that were characteristic of other abductees. The first concerned the typical area on the tibia. Both right and left areas just above the shin bone have clearly defined, elliptical areas devoid of hair. In a recent visit to his doctor, Jim pointed these areas out. The doctor offered no explanation for the marks.

Jim's second manifestation also falls into Dr. Jacobs' list of Post-Abduction-Syndrome effects, specifically in the area of neurological problems. Indeed, it was this very complication that ultimately was responsible for Jim seeking me out in the first place.

Two years after the Allagash incident, Jim had been involved in a home accident. Although he had felt recovered from his injuries at the time, soon after, he began to experience some painful symptoms, which he describes in his own words:

> While I was on the road out west [working for an art gallery], I was always feeling sick. I thought I had a heart problem, because I would experience a sudden loss of energy and a pain in my left side. My left side would get numb.

Jim's medical records indicate the following about the pains:

> These have occurred since 1978 or 1979, and he has been hospitalized and worked-up numerous times for his atypical chest pain. He has been seen at Massachusetts General Hospital by an internist and neurologist; at the New England Medical Center; in December of 1981 at the Allentown Sacred Hospital in Pennsylvania; in February of 1982 at McAllen Hospital in Mohave, Utah; in March of 1982 at the Marina Mercy Hospital in Marina Del Ray, California; and in March of 1982 at the Breckenridge Hospital in Austin, Texas. He was first seen at the Beth Israel Hospital, Boston, Massachusetts, in December of 1983.
>
> He has had numerous non-invasive tests, and was told it was either a neuritis over the rib cage, or it was all "in your head."

From 1983 to this present date, Jim Weiner has been involved with neurological testing and care provided by the Neurology Department at Beth Israel Hospital, Boston, Mass. Tests indicate that his chest-pain seizures are symptomatic of temporolimbic epilepsy (TLE).

During his treatment, Jim confided with his doctors about the bedroom visitations. He wondered if he were going out of his mind. At that time, he did not connect these childhood and adult phenomena with his UFO experience on the Allagash. It was only later that he began to wonder if there was a connection. This was in part instigated by Jack's dreams about alien entities and the realization that they might be connected with the missing time on the Allagash. However, his physicians entertained doubts as to whether Jim's strange experiences were a result of TLE. In fact, it was because of these very doubts that Jim's doctor suggested he seek help from UFO researchers.

In short, it cannot be established with certainty whether Jim's neurological problems are effects related to UFO experiences or to the home accident. It is true that some abductees do suffer neurological aftereffects. Nonetheless, it is important to document that there is considerable doubt, on the part of Jim's physicians, that the neurological problems have caused his UFO experiences. This should be quite obvious, because Jim's experiences with Harry the Ghost predate the accident that supposedly triggered the neurological problems by decades.

Jim's physicians have been very helpful in providing their professional opinions about the TLE/UFO question for our final report to MUFON. Their statements are as follows. The first letter is in response to a request made by Dave Webb:

Harvard University Medical School
Department of Neurology

September 5, 1989
David F. Webb
23 Eugene Road,
Burlington, MA 01803
Re: Jim Weiner

Dear Mr. Webb:

I received your correspondence of 8/22/89 and will respond. I have been Jim Weiner's neurologist over the past 4 to 5 years. He has a condition called temporolimbic epilepsy which can cause a host of psychic symptoms. Included among these are déjà and jamais vu, dissociative states with out-of-body experiences, unprovoked panic and chest pain, hallucinations. It is possible that Jim's reported nightmares and dreams may be TLE induced. However, this is not proven. It is extremely intriguing that his twin brother had the same close-encounter experience. The possibility that he [Jack Weiner] has TLE could be investigated, but the shared experience with same recall mitigates against TLE as the cause.

I hope this helps.

Sincerely, Bruce H. Price, M.D.
Behavioral Neurology Unit

Dr. Price's conclusion is further strengthened by the fact that both Charlie Foltz and Chuck Rak shared the experience with the twins.

The next statement is from Jim's personal health specialist at Beth Israel Hospital, Boston, Massachusetts:

March 15, 1989
To Whom it may concern:
Re: James Weiner

I have been following James Weiner at Beth Israel in conjunction with his neurologist, Dr. Bruce Price. I understand he has been undergoing hypnotic sessions with you; and information regarding his medical status has been requested. He is being treated with Tegretol for seizures. He has a variety of symptoms which have "thought" to be epileptogenic. However, extensive EEG monitoring about one year ago "failed to confirm the onset to his symptoms." Since he does respond to Tegretol, he has been kept on this. In addition he seems to be having sleep disturbances with frequent nightmares, during which he will awaken with many symptoms that sound like they could be seizures. There is no way to tell at this point whether these are actual seizures, or whether these symptoms could be related to "other phenomena."
Sincerely,
Patricia Osborne Shafer, R.N.
MN Neuro-Epilepsy Nurse Specialist

One can easily see why Jim's bedside visitations by alien creatures who allegedly examine him and extract sperm from him would be puzzling to his physicians. These stories/symptoms were a far cry from his earlier complaints about chest seizures. Jim told me that he knew when a seizure was coming on, and it was a totally different sensation than what he felt during the nighttime visitations by the aliens. However, to doctors and nurses not conversant with the UFO abduction phenomena, Jim's experiences, initially, would be evaluated within the context of the neurological effects of TLE. Only later, when Jim bravely told them about the Allagash experience, did his physicians open the door to the possibility that these manifestations might be UFO-related. This was especially a possibility in the light of the fact that some of Jim's symptoms did not fit the usual TLE paradigm. Jim's personal physician summed it up in the following letter:

August 22, 1989
Raymond E. Fowler
Woodside Planetarium and Observatory
13 Friend Court,
Wenham, MA 01984

Dear Mr. Fowler:

I am writing at the request of Jim Weiner, who has been a patient of mine since May, 1983. He has signed a written release authorizing me to be in touch with you. I know Jim through my capacity as psychiatric consultant at Beth Israel's Behavioral Neurology Unit. I gather you are interested in hearing from me about Jim's seizure disorder and his reliability and how these could affect his report of observing a UFO. His reliability to me is a straightforward issue: in all of my encounters with Jim, I find him to be honest, caring, reliable; there has never been any indication that he is an "attention seeker" or that he misrepresents the facts of any situation.

The question of his seizure disorder is more complicated. Depending upon where a person's seizures are physically taking place in the brain, symptoms may be such unusual experiences as visual hallucinations, auditory hallucinations, a feeling or experience of a "presence" or a connectiveness with God or a higher power, loss of time....Seizures are characterized, however, by their repetitive, stereotypical pattern. That is, a given person may even have several different kinds of seizures, but the seizures tend to be recurrent, occurring in exactly the same manner over and over again. Jim tells me that his experience occurred not only to him but to others in his company; seizure activity could not account for this, of course, and further, there is no correlation between suggestibility and seizure disorder.

I hope that what I am telling you is useful to you. I would be glad to answer any further specific questions or provide more information if it would be helpful, and of course, how could I not be fascinated and curious about your work and the results of this particular investigation!

Sincerely,
Jonathan Weinberg, M.D.

The physical effects just discussed are only part of the Post-Abduction Syndrome. There are also a number of reported psychological problems that apparently affect UFO abduction victims.

Post-Abduction Syndrome
Psychological Symptoms

In his paper on Post-Abduction Syndrome, Dr. Jacobs writes:

It is these problems that have the most destructive effect on the course of people's lives and on their relationships with others. Abductees usually suffer the impact of psychological problems caused by abduction experiences long before they are fully aware that they have been victimized by them. These unaware abductees have characteristic adverse psychological symptoms...ranging from minor to debilitating psychological effects caused by unrecollected abduction experiences. [5]

Dr. Jacobs lists a number of psychological symptoms suffered by abductees. I have reviewed all of them in the light of the experiences of the Allagash four. Several symptoms seem to apply: sleep disturbances, panic disorders, bleedthrough memories, and missing time. Dr. Jacobs discusses each of these in turn. It is not difficult to see their relationship to the experiences of the Allagash four:

---

5. Jacobs, "Post-Abduction Syndrome," p. 88.

Sleep Disturbances

The most common of all post-abduction-syndrome problems are sleep disturbances. For the average adult, sleep can be something to look forward to
for relief from the anxieties and tensions of the day.
The abductee often views sleep as a fearful event, filled
with terror and distress. They desperately need sleep,
but they cannot close their eyes because of some great
indefinable fear. Sometimes they are afraid that someone will come into their room or they are frightened
something will happen to them while they sleep. To al-
leviate the fear, many abductees can only sleep when
either the lights, the radio, the television or all three
are on. They have their spouse check the house to
make sure there are no intruders. The door to the bedroom and to the closet have to be closed. Even after
this ritual victims still have terrible bouts of insomnia.
Closing their eyes floods their mind with terrifying images of hideous beings with large horrible eyes. The
image so jars and frightens abductees that many stay
awake as long as possible rather than chance seeing
it. When they do fall asleep, abductees often have difficulty staying asleep, waking up many times during
the night frightened that something is going to happen
to them. [6]

What better description could there be of the psychological
side of Jim's bedside visitations at Austin, Texas and Ojai, California, not to mention the many incidents in his apartment in
Boston. It is no wonder that he sought medical help. He
thought he was going insane. Little did he know that such bizarre experiences were the common lot of hundreds of other abductees.

Dr. Jacobs continues:

Sleep can bring vivid and disturbing dreams. They
dream of lying on a table, being surrounded by small
large-eyed creatures, "operations" being performed on
them, seeing strange-looking babies, there might be a
horrifying sexual component to these dreams. [7]

Both on-going and past abductions can be half-
remembered as very frightening, extremely vivid and
lifelike dreams. They do not have the unreal, jumpy,
often nonsensical quality of normal dreams. When the

---

6. Jacobs, "Post-Abduction Syndrome," p. 88
7. Jacobs, "Post-Abduction Syndrome," p. 88

victims wake up in the morning after having an abduction experience that is now relegated to a dream they
are shaky and nervous—a feeling that might last for
one or more days. They feel exhausted even though
they presumably got their normal amount of sleep. [8]

As I read the above paragraphs, I think immediately of
Jack and Charlie's vivid dreams, which hypnosis revealed to be
actual experiences remembered as nightmares and, of course,
the horrifying sexual component was quite evident in Jack's
"dreams" of the Allagash and Jim's bedroom visitations. Yet,
there are still more PAS symptoms applicable to our four abductees:

They may develop strong and seemingly irrational
fears of their bedroom and sleep in another room from
then on, all the while telling themselves that they are
foolish or stupid to act this way. They sometimes find
that they can go to another person's house and sleep
soundly but when they return to their own room the
sleep disturbances begin again. Often boys and girls
and even young men and women living at home prefer
to sleep on the floor next to their parent's bed, even
though they may be embarrassed to do so. Being in the
room with their parents gives them a feeling of safety
that they cannot get in their own bedroom. These sleep
disturbances can be extremely disruptive to their lives
but they learn to cope as best they can trying to get
along on as little sleep as possible.[9]

This research gives an apt description of the twins' reaction
to Harry the Ghost and Chuck's reaction to his nighttime visitors when a child.

Panic Disorders

Dr. Jacobs lists many types of panic disorders exhibited by
abductees. The following symptom is characteristic of one of
Jim's neurological problems supposedly caused by TLE:

Very often abductees have generalized anxiety but
when this anxiety becomes acute, panic disorder can
plague the victim. Abductees may be seized with a
panic attack at any time with no recognizable stimu-
lus.

As panic overcomes them their hearts race, they
breathe rapidly, they become flushed, and they may

8. Jacobs, "Post-Abduction Syndrome," p. 89
9. Jacobs, "Post-Abduction Syndrome," p. 88.

hyperventilate. A life-threatening fear overwhelms
them. [10]

How many other abductees have PAS symptoms diagnosed
as TLE? Some might say that TLE is responsible for the abduction phenomena. Are we to say that the hundreds of abductees
from all over the world all have TLE? One problem with this theory is that TLE does not cause the typical scars, tumors and
burns suffered by abductee claimants. TLE could not cause the
shared experience of The Allagash abduction.

The author of *Communion*, Whitley Strieber, experienced
similar PAS symptoms after his UFO-abduction experiences.
He, like Jim, thought he was going insane. Whitley himself un-
derwent extensive neurological testing because it was suspected that he was suffering from TLE. The results were negative.

Bleedthrough Memories

> Apart from obsessions, phobias, and panic at-
> tacks which seem to materialize out of nothing, un-
> aware abductees very often have bleed-through
> memories of strange and unusual events happening to
> them. [11]

The above description was especially true when we initially
probed the twins and Chuck for possible evidence of UFO encounters prior to their experience on the Allagash. Things kept
popping back into their minds that had long ago been forgotten
but now seemed relevant to the investigation. Indeed, they
were.

Missing Time

Dr. Jacobs treats an abductee's reaction to missing time as
one of the psychological symptoms of PAS. He states:

> Budd Hopkins has discovered the diagnostic im-
> portance of puzzling missing time episodes in abduct-
> ees' lives. They are unable to account for a lost period
> of time which may be as short as an hour or two, or as
> long as a day—or much longer. Trying to understand
> the origin of the missing time can torture the victim. It
> makes no sense. There is no explanation, and yet they
> know it happened. [12]

---

10. Jacobs, "Post-Abduction Syndrome," p. 90.
11. Jacobs, "Post-Abduction Syndrome," p. 91.
12. Jacobs, "Post-Abduction Syndrome," p. 92.

All of the Allagash four agonized for years about the lost time on the Allagash. When they got together, it was often a topic of discussion. Jim also could not account for lost time during two events remembered from childhood. He had no remembrance whatsoever of being lost in a snowstorm and found in a hole by his older brother and a neighbor. He also had no recall of time lost during a sledding incident. Prior to recovering portions of the lost time under hypnosis, which revealed alien encounters, he told me:

> Those are a couple of events that happened in my childhood which to this day I am unable to explain, and I've always wondered, ah, what happened.

There is little doubt in my mind that Jack, Jim, Charlie and Chuck each exhibit key symptoms of Post-Abduction Syndrome. Such alien calling cards add overwhelming physical and psychological evidence to support the complementary, credible testimony of the Allagash four.

At this point, we will establish the final link to the growing chain of evidence for the physical reality of the UFO abduction experience. This shall be accomplished by demonstrating that an extraordinary interrelation of similar data bits exists between hundreds of recorded UFO-abduction cases and the incredible UFO experiences of the Allagash four.

CHAPTER 12

Correlations

A landmark comparative study of more than 300 UFO-abduction reports was published in 1988. The 642-page, two-volume work, is entitled *UFO Abductions: The Measure of a Mystery.*[1] It was commissioned by the Fund for UFO Research.[2] The author is Dr. Thomas E. Bullard, a folklorist, who wrote his doctoral thesis at the University of Indiana on UFOs and their correlates as a folkloric theme.

One volume analyzes the sequence of events in abduction stories from capture to aftermath, categorizes the mental and physical effects associated with the experience, explores the various descriptions of the aliens and their craft, and examines the validity of the extraterrestrial and psychological interpretations. Volume Two is a catalog and summary of each case used in Dr. Bullard's sample. Each is rated according to the reliability of the witness and the investigation. In summary, Dr. Bullard writes that the reports, which he calls "stories," show a great number of similarities, both major and minor—too many, in fact, for them all to be hoaxes or random fantasies. Dr. Bullard cannot explain why they are so similar, but notes that his study is:

> An act of literary criticism, an effort to reconcile an adverse collection of details into a hypothetical unity.

---

1. Bullard, Thomas E., *UFO Abductions: The Measure of a Mystery* (Mount Rainier, Maryland: The Fund for UFO Research, 1987).
2. P.O. Box 277, Mount Rainier, Maryland 20712

Making sense of such different parts of the story requires many assumptions and oversimplifies the evidence, but one inescapable conclusion is this: Clues of
many kinds from all through the story converge on one
general interpretation. Dissimilar parts of the story in-
terlock into the same meaning. Few narrators would
have the foresight to organize their stories with all
these implications in mind, and no familiar psychological phenomenon installs a multifaced image of
aliens...into many individuals. Reality best explains
where this unified picture of purposes and motivations
originates.[3]

It is not my intent to attempt a summarization of Dr. Bullard's massive work in this chapter. However, his study affords
a unique opportunity to compare the story content of *The Allagash Abductions* with several hundred other UFO-abduction reports. Thus, in this chapter, the many-faceted and intriguing
elements of the events experienced by the Allagash four will be
the catalyst for a correlation with the benchmarks arrived at by
Dr. Bullard's thorough survey of the UFO-abduction phenomenon. In order to accomplish this, we shall use a general outline
of the Bullard study as our template for comparison. The number, gender, occupation, recall, age and geographical location of
witnesses are addressed first in the Bullard study. It was found
that out of 309 cases comprising 400 witnesses, there was only
one witness in 76% of the cases, and more than one in 24% of
the cases. There were 2 witnesses in 49 cases, 3 in 12 cases and
more than three in 12 cases. However, the multiple-witness
cases often included children who were too young or otherwise
unable to testify. Furthermore, the additional witnesses in
some cases refused to cooperate. Thus, the maximum number
of adult witnesses who have testified independently in a single
well-researched case is three. This makes the Allagash case
unique in the annals of UFO history.

The gender of the witnesses in Dr. Bullard's case study was
64% male and 36% female. Occupations encompassed the complete gamut of society, including unskilled laborers, farmers,
housewives, doctors, nurses and professors. However, the cases sampled revealed a disproportionate number of occupations
that involved people who spend time outside at night in remote
areas, such as soldiers, policemen, traveling salesmen and
truck drivers. Dr. Bullard makes a further statement that is directly applicable to the abduction of the Allagash four (italics
are mine):

---

3. Bullard, Thomas E., "Abductions in Life and Lore," *International UFO
    Reporter*, Vol. 12, No. 4, 1987, p. 17.

This trend enlarges with inclusion of witnesses taken during recreational activities like hunting or "camping," or people simply exposed while doing something as everyday as crossing an open field at night. In this light abductions appear as opportunistic events, or at least *dark and lonely conditions* seem to favor the experience.[4]

Needless to say, the above paradigm is perfectly echoed in the circumstances surrounding the Allagash abduction. The four campers were plucked from the Allagash Waterway, one of the darkest and loneliest areas in New England.

Concerning the witnesses' recall of the abduction event, Dr. Bullard states:

> Hypnosis has become a recognized tool to unlock the memory of a witness, but also a controversial issue in the investigation of abductions. In 97 cases [31%] the investigators used hypnosis at some point. At no time in any of the reports on record has an abduction appeared out of nowhere to someone undergoing hypnosis for unrelated reasons. All abductees have some inkling of a disturbing event or else they would not submit to further investigation. The degree of awareness an individual may have varies greatly from case to case: Steven Kilburn felt a nagging uneasiness for years.... Sara Shaw knows of a light outside followed by an inexplicable time loss.... Patty Roach...and Betty Andreasson...retained vague but unusual memories from the peripheries of their experiences.... The Hills maintained a state of mental and emotional upset and Betty [Hill] relived the abduction in a series of nightmares.... In cases where some sign of the experience lingers on...hypnosis serves to recover the hidden abduction. In other cases the witness may recall some or even a great deal of the abduction proper, and hypnosis serves only to firm up those memories and clarify occasional vague points.... Only a minority of cases include hypnosis in their discovery and investigation. For 212 cases [69%] the reports include no mention of hypnotic probes.[5]

The Allagash case reflects all of the above patterns. All four percipients experienced sighting the glowing sphere, unexplained time loss, and nagging uneasiness. Jack relived a segment of the Allagash event in a series of nightmares. He, Mary and Charlie reflected follow-on encounters through vivid

---

4. Bullard, *UFO Abductions*, p. 35.
5. Bullard, *UFO Abductions*, p. 35.

dreams. Jim's mental and emotional reactions led to medical treatment.

The Bullard study revealed that the ages of abductees, in some cases, ranged throughout the course of their lifetimes. Statistically, abductions reach a peak when witnesses are in their twenties and drop drastically beyond the age of 40. Some witnesses experienced abductions from childhood to adulthood, as if being monitored by the aliens over a period of time. Thus far in their lives, Chuck and the twins seem to fall in this latter category. Charlie seems to have been a victim of circumstances with no prior history of abductions.

Geographically, 142 of the Bullard case sample occurred in North America. A total of 51 cases took place in European countries. South America hosted 66 cases and the rest took place in other parts of the world. It is apparent that the location of the abductions in his sample is directly related to the availability of such cases through known investigative sources. Thus, no accurate distribution pattern can be accurately extracted from his listing.

Let us now turn to the heart of the Bullard study, which deals with the types of UFO abduction. His definition of "story type" is as follows (italics are mine):

> Story type refers to a recognizable pattern of events recurring among different narrative texts. The names and places may change, details may differ; but whoever the actors may be, if they perform the same actions or experience the same events in the same order in two different narratives, these narratives tell the same story. Both stories belong to the same type.... The abduction report...tells a story of action and events, often several episodes long, and offers a narrative pattern with enough complexity to identify a kind of story as *uniquely as a fingerprint* identifies its owner.... If two complex narratives bear extensive resemblance of form and content, *change becomes implausible* and only an origin shared in common explains the resemblances in a convincing way. Extensive similarities among abduction reports would force a conclusion that diverse witnesses were telling the same story.
>
> All true abduction stories fit within a *single type*. One conclusion follows from this fact alone—abduction stories are remarkably consistent. That is not to say that they are all alike...but rather each story corresponds to an ideal pattern or portion of it with little or nothing left over.[6]

---

6. Bullard, *UFO Abductions*, pp. 47,48.

Dr. Bullard discovered that the ideal pattern for UFO abductions breaks down into eight parts. He emphasizes that not every story contains all possible parts. In fact, the only account in his sample that contains all eight parts is the Andreasson affair, which I have been investigating for over a decade. The eight parts are:

1. **Capture.** Witness is caught and taken aboard a UFO.
2. **Examination.** Witness is subjected to an examination.
3. **Conference.** Witness talks with aliens for a period of time.
4. **Tour.** Aliens allow witness to see parts of the ship.
5. **Otherworldly Journey.** Witness visits strange place.
6. **Theophany.** Witness has a religious experience.
7. **Return.** Witness is returned and departs from ship.
8. **Aftermath.** Aftereffects and other unusual events.

Concerning the above eight parts, Dr. Bullard states the following (italics are mine):

A narrative counts as true to form if episodes follow the order of the prescribed pattern; that is, the conference follows the examination, the tour follows the conference, and so on. Not every potential episode has to be present, but an episode present must take its proper place in the sequence. To show significant relationships a narrative must contain at least two episodes.... An impressive majority of abduction stories describes the same order of events [72%].

The greatest number of orthodox narratives consist of just two episodes, usually *capture and examination...capture and aftermath...or capture and return....* Three-episode cases comprise nearly one third of the total, four episodes [18%], and five episodes [10%], while even six and seven-episode cases are present, all true to the same pattern.[7]

The abduction from the Allagash Waterway echoes the content of the greatest number of orthodox narratives in the Bullard study. The witnesses experienced the most common four of the eight episodes: capture, examination, return and aftermath. Let us examine each of them in the light of Dr. Bullard's findings:

7. Bullard, *UFO Abductions*, p. 52.

Capture

The typical sequence reported during the capture consists of the following four specific events. Each will be defined and then a correlation will be made with the Allagash event.

Alien Intrusion

An initial observation of a UFO is the common denominator for 71% of the cases in the study.

Obviously, the Allagash incident correlates perfectly with this subset of capture. The very first milestone of the abduction experience was the sighting of a large glowing UFO.

Zone of Strangeness

Prior to entering the craft, the witness seems to enter a twilight zone, where natural laws fail to work or work in unnatural ways. This was experienced by Jim and Jack just after they were engulfed by the light beam from the UFO:

JIM: It's not normal!
JACK: Something happens. Something changes. I
                feel—the feeling changes. There's something dif-
                ferent—it's—something's happening.... I don't
                feel like I'm here (pants). I don't feel like I'm sup-
                posed to feel.

Neither Charlie nor Chuck could verbalize their entering this zone of strangeness. Both were highly agitated and had to be calmed by Tony at this juncture. Dr. Bullard states:

> 77 cases...include the zone of strangeness inci-
> dent. Of these...66 cases locate the incident at the
> point following the initial intrusion.[8]

Again, the correlation between the above findings and the capture sequence on the Allagash is obvious.

Time Lapse

The third subset during the capture represents a change in the relationship of the witness with the abductors. Dr. Bullard writes:

> So far the witness has merely observed external
> happenings. Now he exchanges his seat in the audi-
> ence for a part in the action—and a key part it is, be-
> cause the action focuses on the witness from this point
> onward. Where before the witness has kept control of

---

8. Bullard, *UFO Abductions*, p. 60

his mind and body, his mental and physical states
now change. Conscious memory of a period of time
may lapse and be recovered only under hypnosis,
physical paralysis or lethargy may set in, actions may
become involuntary or uncharacteristic and the witness has no idea why. One of these possibilities or several may cluster together as the witness loses his will
to escape and memory of what happens.[9]

No doubt, the reader remembers that this is exactly what
the Allagash four experienced. As far as they could remember,
one moment they were canoeing away from the UFO and the
next moment they were on shore, unafraid and watching the
UFO. Their actions at this point were certainly uncharacteristic:

JIM: I have a sense that there is something I should
                remember, but it's almost like I—a block.

JACK: It's right behind us, and I'm paddling with my
                hand.... Then—then—we're at the beach.

CHARLIE: We were paddling toward our camp...then I re-
                member standing by the canoe in, ah, in the wa-
                ter right at the shore.

CHUCK: It started moving towards us.... And then a
                panic ensued.... And then we got back to shore.
                We're at the shore! I don't even remember how
                we found ourselves at shore.

Dr. Bullard elaborates further concerning this typical time
lapse that occurs during the capture phase of a UFO abduction:

What the time lapse amounts to then is a period
of memory excised from consciousness and the two
ends of normal recall sutured together to give the appearance of a normal continuum, often with dubious
success. The time lapse does not mean actual uncon-
sciousness or semiconsciousness, because the witness remains more or less aware of what happens....
Dreams, spontaneous recall or hypnosis later demonstrate that the memories were present in the unconscious all along even if inaccessible to conscious
recall. Time lapse acts to blanket the whole experience
as a retroactive effect, a gradual fading of recollection.[10]

A total of 188 cases in the Bullard study contain the time-
lapse phenomenon. Bullard points out the fact that 177 cases

9. Bullard, *UFO Abductions*, p. 60.
10. Bullard, *UFO Abductions*, p. 178.

and 94% of narratives containing this incident locate it in the prescribed place, affirming the less-familiar truth that events in the capture episode are consistent to a high degree. The event on the Allagash correlates perfectly with the findings of this aspect of the Bullard study.

Procurement

Alien intrusion, the zone of strangeness and time lapse prepare the way for the final sequenced subset of the capture episode. This is the actual acquisition of a human being by the aliens. A total of 185 cases in the Bullard study reflect the event of procurement. Dr. Bullard states:

> In the previous parts of the capture episode a single event likely often represents the recurrent element, but procurement events are likely to be several in number and successive in relationship, so that this portion of the story lengthens into its own sub-episode. Some 16 events with fixed positions recur among the procurement accounts though the frequency varies considerably. The truly common elements reduce to eight.
>
> 1) A beam of light strikes the witness,
>
> 2) a drawing force pulls him toward
>
> 3) beings who then appear, and
>
> 4) converse with the witness, usually to reassure or instruct him.
>
> 5) Physical and mental controls follow, as the witness feels pacified or paralyzed, loses his will or lapses into an unconscious or semiconscious state.
>
> 6) The beings escort the witness, often touching or holding him,
>
> 7) so that he floats toward the craft, and then
>
> 8) enters with a temporary memory lapse, or doorway amnesia. [11]

Let us examine the Allagash incident in light of each of these eight sub-episodes of procurement.

The Beam

Dr. Bullard states the following concerning the beam:

---

11. Bullard, *UFO Abductions*, p. 61.

How light beams...relate to the craft remains vague, but the importance of their roles in abductions is clear. In 61 cases the witness reports that a light strikes or engulfs his person, car or bedroom. This light may beam directly from the craft or from a be-ing.... The usual position of the light incident is early in the story during capture, where a beam functions to deprive the witness of mental and physical freedom. The witness loses consciousness as soon as the light strikes or soon thereafter.[12]

Again we see a perfect correlation between the abduction incident on the Allagash Waterway and the statistics reflected in the Bullard study. The glowing UFO did emit a hollow, cone-shaped beam, which engulfed the four campers in their canoe. It indeed deprived them of their mental and physical freedom.

JIM: All of a sudden this beam came out of the—this thing.... It's on us.... It's around us.

JACK: There's a beam. A beam of light comes out of it.... The beam. It's got us! It's there. We're in it!

CHARLIE: And a shaft, or beam of light with a bluish cast...came straight down.... It seems, ah, time—doesn't—seem—to—be—moving.

CHUCK: The thing sent down a cone-shaped beam of light.... It's right over.

The Drawing Force

Dr. Bullard states the following concerning the drawing force associated with the acquisition of the abductees by aliens (italics are mine):

In 40 cases some sort of force draws the witness toward the UFO or beings. This element holds the same relative position in 32 cases and initiates pro-curement in 25 cases. In 5 instances the force follows or has some *connection with the beam*.... Beams of light may serve other functions, most notably to *float or draw the witness toward the craft*.[13]

The drawing force is also mirrored in the Allagash incident. The four campers were drawn into the hovering UFO through the hollow beam of light emanating from it.

JIM: I see the inside of the tube.... It's moving...the walls move...they're not there [Charlie and

---

12. Bullard, *UFO Abductions*, p. 199.
13. Bullard, *UFO Abductions*, pp. 61-62.

	Chuck].... [I'm] in a room [Jim is now aboard the UFO].
JACK:	The beam.... We're in it.... It's got something in it moving.... Chuck's gone.... Something is happening.... Oh! Lights in front of me and there's Jim [Jack is now aboard UFO].
CHARLIE:	Geez.... The canoe!... It's in the water—it's underneath us [Charlie finds himself in the UFO].
CHUCK:	It's [the beam] right over.... It's like a tunnel.... Getting drawn towards it.... A room [Chuck finds himself aboard the UFO].

The Beings Appear

Under this episode, we find a typical deviation which also shows up in the Bullard study. A number of abductions have the beam of light strike the abductee and draw the victim toward the beings, who then escort the abductee to the waiting UFO. This is not so within the framework of the Allagash incident which reflects a sequence even closer to the norm. Bullard states:

> A far more common course of events has the beings appear at the *end* of the capture sequence, after *the UFO brings them* and various changes in the outer world and the witness's consciousness prepare the way.... Sometimes the account may be fragmentary or the witness may awaken to find *beings* already in the room. [italics mine][14]

Thus, in the Allagash case it was the beam from the UFO that brought the Allagash four into a room aboard the craft where the aliens awaited them. This leads to the fourth segment of the sequence of events involved in procurement.

The Beings Converse

The first communication from the aliens takes place soon after the first confrontation between the abductors and their captors. In some cases, this takes place when the abductee is first confronted by the aliens outside the craft. When this is so, the aliens usually reassure the witness and ask that the witness come away with them.

When the witness is drawn directly into the UFO first, the communication takes place soon after the first confrontation with the aliens on board the craft. The Allagash incident follows this particular sequence of events. In either case, the conversa-

14. Bullard, *UFO Abductions*, p. 59.

tion is usually one-way and consists of either reassuring or instructing the witness. The Allagash four experienced both reassurance and instruction through what would be best described as mental telepathy. This mode of communication was employed by the aliens in the majority of cases within the Bullard study.

> Of 124 cases with the means of communication specified, 98 [79%] involve telepathy, thought transference, or the witness being able to understand or hear the beings without their mouths moving or any apparent auditory input. [15]

Let us now examine the Allagash incident in the light of these statistics:

JIM: They, they got my shirt off. They made me take it off.... I just got the impression that if I didn't do that, I was going to be in trouble.

JACK: They're saying things...with their eyes...in my head...they're saying, "Don't be afraid.... We won't harm you.... Do what we say."

CHARLIE: It was almost like he said it with his eyes.... "Don't be afraid. Relax."

CHUCK: It's like they're directing us.... We just know to do all these things. We just know.

Once more we note the fascinating affinity that exists between our case at hand and other abduction reports on record. The harmony continues as we move to the fifth aspect of human acquisition by the aliens.

Physical and Mental Controls

As we have seen, the Bullard study reveals that an abductee usually suffers debilitating effects before direct confrontation with the beings. However, once on board the UFO, the aliens exert further physical and mental influences in order to make the abductee acquiesce to their every demand. The techniques used are often ascribed to the aliens' hypnotic eyes or to actual physical contact with them.

In 71 cases from the Bullard sample, the aliens make some effort to control the witness. Pacification, paralysis, rendering the abductee unconscious or semiconscious, and somehow taking control of the will and behavior of the victim are the techniques usually employed by the aliens. Such control was certainly exerted by the aliens upon the Allagash four. The

---

15. Bullard, *UFO Abductions*, p. 109.

following excerpts from the hypnosis sessions demonstrates this quite convincingly.

RAY:	Why didn't you help Jack?
JIM:	I don't know.... All I could do was watch.... I feel like I'm dulled...very difficult to maintain awareness.... They poked me with something to make me go down there. Bastards!
JACK:	I'm paralyzed.... I can't move.... I feel like they're [his legs] far away.... They make me move.... They're saying, "It's not so bad," and I'm saying, "Okay, it's not so bad."
CHARLIE:	I feel like I want to look around but I don't want to look around.

[At this point, Charlie is both physically and mentally under alien control. He stands immobilized after being drawn into the UFO. Later he finds himself lying down but doesn't know how or why he is doing so at first].

TONY:	Why are you lying down?
CHARLIE:	I dunno.
TONY:	Are your eyes open while you're lying down?
CHARLIE:	I don't want to open 'em. I keep 'em closed.... I sit up.... The one behind me helped me sit up.
TONY:	What did it feel like when he helped you sit up?
CHARLIE:	Like I was tired.

Chuck's experience was similar:

TONY:	Can you move as you stand there?
CHUCK:	Not really.
TONY:	Can you look behind you?
CHUCK:	No.
TONY:	Do you notice anything about yourself?
CHUCK:	Almost like I'm drugged.... They're leading me to a bench.

In essence, the Allagash four had little or no control over their behavior. For the most part they behaved like zombies, doing exactly what the aliens wanted them to do.

Escort

This sixth element of procurement only applies to cases where the witness is confronted by the aliens outside the UFO. At this juncture, the abductee falls under control of the aliens and is escorted by them to the UFO. In the Allagash incident, the four campers were drawn into the UFO by the hollow beam of light. Shortly after entering the UFO, they were confronted by the aliens, who then placed them under their control and escorted them.

Talking about Jack:

JIM:	They're taking him [Jack] over in this other place.... They're kind of ushering him...one on each side.... I think it's my turn...but I don't want to go over there.... There's two of 'em...one on either side, and they're holding me up.... I feel like, ah, I'm going to faint.
JACK:	They just take my arms and move me.... I'm walking but I don't feel like I'm walking.
CHARLIE:	They take us away from the window.... We followed the person that brought us in and two others...that person that brought us in the room.
CHUCK:	They're ushering me...almost like I'm drugged.... They're leading me to a bench.... They lead [Charlie] over to the...table.... We're following him ["an alien"].

Floating Effect

Soon after a witness is confronted by aliens outside a UFO, he or she is often then "floated up" to the hovering craft. In the Allagash incident, as mentioned, there is no initial alien confrontation on the ground. Instead, the four are apparently floated through the hollow beam of light to confront the aliens who are waiting for them in the hovering craft. As mentioned earlier, they find themselves enclosed by the beam. Then, a variety of physical effects are felt, as each suddenly arrives on board the UFO enclosed by the beam. The fact that only Chuck remembered exactly how this happens has to do with the eighth and last constituent of the procurement segment of capture.

Doorway Amnesia

Dr. Bullard explains this last event of the procurement cycle as follows:

A funny thing happens on the way to the spaceship as the witness undergoes a memory lapse as he enters the ship, then recovers consciousness once inside. Why or how this brief hiatus takes place remains unknown, but it appears in 32 cases and 28 of them station this incident as the last significant event of the procurement sequence.[16]

16. Bullard, *UFO Abductions*, p. 63.

This phenomenon is very pronounced in the Allagash case, as the following quotations from the hypnosis sessions attest:

TONY: What happens two minutes after the light [beam] enveloped you?

JIM: I can't remember. [Jim then finds himself aboard the UFO.]

JACK: It's all around the canoe. Everything is lit up. It's so bright.... Something changes...I don't feel like I'm supposed to feel. [The next thing Jack knows is that he is no longer in the canoe. He is aboard the UFO!]

CHARLIE: [Charlie remembers the beam of light overtaking the canoe. His next remembrance is being aboard the UFO looking down at the canoe in the water.] The canoe!...It's in the water—it's underneath us!

CHUCK: [Only Chuck remembers being drawn up the tube through a barrier and into the UFO.] It's over us.... It's like a tunnel.... Something's at the end of the tunnel.... It's almost like a barrier... seems solid.... Getting drawn towards it.... Passing through a barrier.... A room.

Before we move on to the second episode of the typical abduction, it is worth mentioning one more event that sometimes takes place during the procurement cycle of capture. Dr. Bullard lists several less common events that recur. He states:

> None of these events count as significant from the standpoint of frequency, but they have a certain inherent interest and rate mention because they hold to a fixed order.... The most memorable of these scarcer incidents occurs when the witness resists his captors. Fourteen cases contain this occurrence. The witness feels an ambivalence about his situation, or more properly, the controlling effect temporarily wears off ...and the witness grows anxious over his predicament.... Then the witness's anxieties boil over into action and the beings suddenly have a fight on their hands.[17]

Jim's anxieties certainly boiled over and nullified the pacifying effect at one point during his abduction. It occurred when the aliens tried to lead him into another room on the craft.

JIM: I'm not going in there! No! No f---ing way! Uh, just leave me alone!...Eh? They poked me—they poked me with something to make me go down there. Bastards!

---

17. Bullard, *UFO Abductions*, p. 63.

For most abductees, the next major episode of the abduction story type appears to be the very reason for their capture.

Examination

Dr. Bullard makes the following opening statement in the section of his study that deals with what he refers to as "The Heart of the Matter:"

> A bizarre and unpleasant ordeal awaits the captive once he enters the ship. Beings usher the witness into an inner room of uniform lighting and hospital cleanliness, then subject him to a systematic, thorough and often painful medical examination.... In fact, abduction reports unroll a litany of callousness, mistreatment and torture perpetrated by the captors on their victims, so that abduction becomes a prospect to dread.... The number of abductions, the beings' disregard for human suffering and preoccupation with reproduction hint that something more than scientific curiosity motivates the examinations, and lends weight to alternative views that aliens are gathering genetic raw materials.... In any case a wealth of clues about the character and purposes of the beings as well as the nature of the abduction experience itself make examination the most revealing episode in the abduction story. Strictly from a standpoint of literary appreciation, no other episode grips the attention so firmly or raises hairs on the back of the neck so dependably as this conversion of humans into guinea pigs....

The examination events follow a regular course of action with the following steps:

1) **Preparation.** The beings make the witness ready for examination.

2) **Manual Examination.** The beings touch or manipulate the witness's body by hand or use handheld instruments.

3) **Scanning.** An eyelike device scans the witness's body.

4) **Instrumental Examination.** Instruments probe the witness's body.

5) **Samples.** The beings take samples of blood or other body materials.

6) **Reproductive Examination.** Tests concerned with reproduction or genital organs follow.

7) **Neurological Examination.** Attention turns to the head, brain and nervous system as the

beings explore the mind, brain and nerves of the witness.

8) **Behavioral Examination.** The beings test behavior and ask questions of the witness.[18]

A number of cases in the Bullard study contain one or more elements of the manual examination; 24 cases provide only one event; 41 cases show two events; 15 cases have three events; seven reflect four events and one has 5 events. The study reveals:

> Examination episodes are little better ordered than capture episodes.... The beings can resort to as full a repertoire of techniques as the job demands.... If one examination event changes place with another, it never strays far from its place or loses meaning in the context of associated events. Taking sperm, for example, relates to the reproduction exam but may fall more conveniently within the activities of sample taking. For the beings to rearrange the order of events to take advantage of this opportunity simply demonstrates that the course of events is flexible in favor of efficiency, rather than mechanically rigid.[19]

Based on our study, we have found the examination of the Allagash abductees involved at least five of the typical examination events.

Preparation

Eighty percent of the cases analyzed in the Bullard study describe some form of preparation comprised of three constituents. The most common element (57%) is a table, on which the witness lies or finds himself lying. The second most common element (26%) is the removal of all or part of the abductee's clothing. Only 7% of the cases describe a third constituent, which involves the cleansing of the abductee.

Dr. Bullard states that there is no strong pattern of order among these three constituents. Sometimes the witness may simply stand for a brief examination. The witness may undress or be undressed before lying on a table. Conversely, the witness may lie on the table before undressing. The Allagash case reflects the two most common elements of preparation:

The Table

JIM:.   There's a table.... They got me on the table.

---

18. Bullard, *UFO Abductions*, p. 82.
19. Bullard, *UFO Abductions*, p. 90.

JACK:.	I'm lying down, and I don't know what they're doing.
CHUCK:	They put [Jack] on a table.
CHARLIE:	I looked at it when I was lying on the table.
CHUCK:	They put me on the table.

Removal of Clothing

JIM:	They got my shirt off. They made me take it off.... I get the impression that I'd better take my pants off.
JACK:	My feet, my toes! I'm naked.
JIM:	They're taking down his [Jack's] pants, or rather, he's doing it.... They've got him completely naked!
CHARLIE:	His [Jack's] clothes....he took them off.
RAY:	How did you get your clothes back on?
CHARLIE:	I must have put them back on.
CHUCK:	I see my midsection.... They're rolling down my pants.

Manual Examination

According to Dr. Bullard's analysis of this early phase of the alien examination (italics are mine):

> The beings touch, feel or use handheld instruments to inspect the witness in a general, apparently preliminary way in 16 cases.... In other cases the beings simply touch the witness, poke at some point like the base of the spine, or feel the head or some other part of the body. Handheld instruments independent of connection to any larger device may play a part in this examination...like a *penlike device or chrome pencil*. The small device may emit a *beam of light* to illuminate or probe somehow the witness's body....
>
> An offshoot of the manual examination involves more vigorous experiments with the witness's body, where the beings *flex or twist limbs* to the point of causing pain.[20]

Each member of the Allagash four was subjected to this same type of preliminary manual examination. Several examples extracted from the hypnosis sessions follow:

| JIM: | [Describes aliens examining Jack in a standing position.] They're looking at his throat. They got his head way up and looking at his throat, and |

---

20. Bullard, *UFO Abductions*, p. 84.

they're touching it with their hands like they're, ah, studying the musculature.... They've got instruments.... One is a kind of a prod or some sort.... Ah, thin, long, eight to ten inches... touching his eyes with it...like a little flashlight...blinking...looking at his genitals, feeling his testicles and his penis and the insides of his thighs...looking at his knees...making him rotate his feet...looking at his toes.... They hurt Jack...moving his arm.... It's my turn.... They're doing the same thing...looking at every single one of my ribs...doing the same thing with my arms... checking out my genitals.

JACK: On my wrist, my left wrist it touched me.... They lift my arm.... One of them has something... metal...shiny...like a pen.... They touch me... under my arms...feels like a scrape...scraping my legs...inside my calves...backs of my knees.

CHARLIE: [Has no memory of the manual examination. He remembers suddenly finding himself standing in a room. The next thing he remembers is finding himself lying on a table.]

CHUCK: [Has no memory of the manual examination. He also only remembers being led and made to lie down on a table.]

One might speculate that Jim and Jack were singled out for this preliminary phase of the ongoing examination because they were twins. Each received the exact same treatment. With this in mind, it is interesting to note Jim's immediate impression as he watched his brother Jack going through the first manual examination:

JIM: They, they know that Jack and I are the same— that we look alike and the other two [Charlie and Chuck] don't, and that's what they're interested in.

Later on during the examination, Charlie got the same impression.

CHARLIE: It's like they're interested in why they [Jim and Jack] look the same.

Instrumental Examination

A number of instruments are often described by witnesses. Dr. Bullard mentions one type that seems similar to that described in the Allagash incident, "devices lying on their chests."[21] Chuck, sitting on a bench, watched the aliens place something on Charlie's chest as he lay on a table:

CHUCK: He's prone...some sort of device on him...sil-
                very...got curves on it...[placed] on his midsec-
                tion.

[handwritten margin note: ? XRAY machine to see his heart]

Charlie wanted to keep his eyes closed, but once in a while he peeked to see what was going on as he lay on the table:

CHARLIE: It's on the thing above my chest...like a tray or a
                panel or something.

Charlie could not see what was being done to him at this juncture, but later watched the aliens place the same device over Jim's chest, and was able to describe what was being done to him.

CHARLIE: They have a panel or tray...above his chest....
                They're taking things from it and putting things
                back on it...touching Jim.... (Sighs.) I don't want
                to watch.

Neither Jim nor Chuck could remember this type of instrument being placed above their chests. When they placed Chuck on the table, he found it hard to focus on his surroundings and stated that he felt "almost like I'm drugged." Jack, however, did mention something being placed above his chest when they placed him on what he described as a machine which hummed:

JACK: They put something on me...on my chest.

Samples

Concerning this phase of the alien examination of human beings, Dr. Bullard writes the following:

> In the course of an examination the beings collect
> specimens of bodily materials from the witness in 29
> cases.... The favorite material is blood, gathered in at
> least 16 cases.... Other bodily fluids like...eye fluid...
> sperm...urine...gastric juices and spinal fluid.... Solid
> as well as liquid materials attract attention...hair...
> nails...ear wax...scraping provides the skin.[22]

Again, this procedure was employed by the aliens with members of the Allagash four. The aliens scraped Jim's skin from various parts of his body prior to his being placed on the table. While on the table, Jim was made to ejaculate sperm into a silver container:

---

21. Bullard, *UFO Abductions*, p. 85.
22. Bullard, *UFO Abductions*, p. 86.

JIM: They want a sperm sample.... They have some
                  kind of a container...silvery metal...they're gon-
                  na let me ejaculate in it...that's what I'm doing.
                  I'm giving them their damned sample.

Jack, on the other hand, was made to provide a urine sample via an instrument placed over his penis:

JACK: They're touching my penis.... They put some-
                  thing on it...like a bell, and its got a tube. And
                  the tube (pants) the tube (speaks slowly and em-
                  phatically) goes—to—a thing—a bottle. And I
                  can feel it. It's going in. I don't like it!.... It's hurt-
                  ing! I'm peeing into it. I can't stop.

The primary thing Chuck remembered about his examination was the apparent removal of sperm:

CHUCK: They're examining me.... They just seem very in-
                  terested in that part of my body. [His genital
                  area].... They're looking at it intensely. They put
                  more light on it.... It's almost like something
                  fluttering...coming down on...my penis...then I
                  can't remember...it was something oozing, ah,
                  from my penis.

Charlie, perhaps because he was the newcomer to abductions in that he had no recall of previous visitations, seems to
have experienced the whole gamut of specimen taking. When
asked if the aliens had taken anything from him, he replied:

CHARLIE: Skin, s-some samples of fluid from my mouth,
                  some blood...skin scrapings...urine and feces,
                  some hair, fingernail clippings, toenail clipping-
                  s...they probed...my testicles with something
                  they have in their hand...sort of like a—like a mi-
                  croscope type of device.... They put it down and
                  clamped, and then they looked and they discon-
                  nected it.

After examining his testicles with the device, they hooked
Charlie's penis up to something that entered the urethra. Charlie slurred his words at this point and said, "I don't know if
there were moisture or not. Swabbed it." Again, this could have
been the removal of a sperm sample via a similar device to the
one used on Chuck.

Reproductive Examination

This phase of the examination involves the aliens' specific
interest and examination of the genital area, which as we have
seen, involved all four of the Allagash witnesses. In the case of
female abductees, a needle is often inserted into the naval to examine the reproductive system and remove ova. Other cases

allegedly involve actual male abductees being forced to have sexual intercourse with alien beings.

The four episodes that follow the examination were not experienced by the Allagash four according to our findings. There was no conference held with the beings. All conversation was one-way in the form of commands from the beings to the abductees. There was no specific tour of the craft given to the four campers. They experienced neither an otherworldly journey or a theophany. These episodes seem to be reserved for specially chosen abductees like Betty Andreasson. Betty was given preferential treatment and a message to give mankind. The Allagash case is closer to the norm. Dr. Bullard reiterates that "The internal episodes of conference, tour, journey, otherworldly journey and theophany are rare...in occurrence."[23]

We now move on to the third major episode highlighted by the Bullard study. It involves when and how the abductees are released by their captors.

Return

The abduction experience ends with the abductee being brought back to familiar surroundings and the normal activities that were being pursued at the time of the abduction. Dr. Bullard states:

> How the witness reenters the everyday world often reflects a mirror image of capture...111 cases refer to it.... Fewer still detail the experience in any clear and substantial way. The distinctive consistencies of the episode are as follows:
>
> 1) **Farewell.** The beings give their captive some final messages and bid him farewell.
>
> 2) **Exit.** Doorway amnesia returns as the beings escort the witness and he floats out of the craft.
>
> 3) **Departure.** The craft takes off while the witness watches.
>
> 4) **Reentry.** The witness takes up normal activities while memory of the abduction fades out.[24]

The events comprising the return of the Allagash four correlate well with each of the above consistencies.

Farewell

In the preamble to this section, Dr. Bullard makes the following introductory remarks (italics are mine):

---

23. Bullard, *UFO Abductions*, p. 104.
24. Bullard, *UFO Abductions*, pp. 64.

Indistinctiveness rather than a clear-cut bound-
ary marks the beginning of return. *Redressing* after an
examination...may provide a point of departure. Not
long before the witness leaves the craft occurs the first
distinctive event—the beings, or a least one of them...
bids the witness farewell...and leaves the witness with
positive impressions.... A compromise version begins
when the beings say that *now is the time for the witness to leave*...and finally the beings ask, advise or ad-
monish the witness to *forget*, at least for now, about
the abduction.[25]

Jim remembers redressing and being surrounded by the
aliens just prior to leaving the craft.

JIM: They let me put my clothes on.

Doorway amnesia began early for Jim. When I asked him
how he left the craft, he could not remember.

JIM: I got no recollection at all. It's almost as if every-
                thing just went blank.

Jack, on the other hand, remembers the four being re-
grouped and spoken to by the aliens. This took place after the
examination and just prior to redressing. He recalled them all
being escorted to a machine that looked like the opening to a
tube in a wall.

JACK: And then they tell us—they say, "Don't be afraid.
                Don't be afraid. We're almost done."...And then
                they help us put our clothing on.... They move
                us to a machine...a tubelike glass.

Charlie put his clothes on and remembers being escorted
to what he referred to as a door or opening.

CHARLIE: We followed the person that brought us in....
                There's the wall behind him...a door... The
                wall...sort of shimmered, speckled, sparkled like
                tinsel or something in light...then there is an
                opening there.

Chuck remembers getting up from the bench with the others and being escorted by the aliens to what he referred to as a
portal in the wall.

CHUCK: We're following him.... It's like a portal.

Exit

Members of the Allagash four experienced their exit from
the craft in different ways from each other, but, their experience
shares a common similarity with cases in the Bullard study.

25. Bullard, *UFO Abductions*, p. 64.

The differences, as we noted above, relate to when doorway amnesia takes effect. Dr. Bullard states the following about this mental lapse. (Italics are mine):

> A reversal of procurement accounts for most of the action in the return episode. As the witness leaves the ship he experiences a mental lapse in 55 cases, ...the highest proportion of any event in the episode.... In 25 cases, a period of amnesia at the *end* of the abduction provides a narrative with its *only point of contact* with the return episode.... Even when the beings plant a seed of forgetfulness as the witness leaves the craft, their influence sometimes grows to full effectiveness only after he experiences several other events. Most common are the alien escort to the door of the ship and sometimes beyond (24 cases), and *flotation* from the ship to the ground (22 cases). In six cases a *beam of light* also takes part in the process.[26]

It was difficult to break through doorway amnesia as we attempted to extract a clear description of how the witnesses left the ship. We failed totally with Jim.

DAVE: How did you get in the boat?

JIM: I don't remember.... It's like one instant we were in there [in the craft] and then all of a sudden we were in the boat.

We fared much better with Jack, but it meant putting him through some very harrowing trauma:

JACK: The tube...it starts to move...coming towards us...makes me feel like I'm coming apart! I'm going to be sick...happening so fast.

TONY: Do you feel like you're coming apart? Do you get the sensation that you're coming together again?

JACK: Yes...in the canoe.

The incredible physical and visual effects relived by Jack when he and his friends entered the tubelike machine are another first in the annals of UFO history. Watching the expressions on his face and listening to the tone of his voice while he was experiencing this under hypnosis was literally an unearthly experience for all of us.

Charlie also was able to describe the sensation he felt after entering the shimmering, sparkling opening that suddenly appeared in the wall.

CHARLIE: It was like an escalator type thing. Somehow we were like escalated down to the canoe.... I just

---

26. Bullard, *UFO Abductions*, p. 65.

remember having that sensation of escalating down.

Chuck referred to the opening as a portal. He noticed that it opened just after an alien activated some instruments on the wall:

CHUCK: The figure's doing something with his hand... raising his arm...seems to be manipulating some kind of instruments...the portal opens.... It's like a membrane...we go out through the portal...we walk to the edge...floating...like a ski tow...going backwards down the mountain instead of up.

Chuck described seeing the lake first and then the canoe. One should bear in mind that each of the witnesses was more or less affected by the tranquilizing and memory lapse imposed by the aliens during the exit. Each described their entrance from the craft from their own mental ability and perspective. It would appear that the opening in the wall was the upper end of the hollow beam of light that originally drew them up into the craft. The area below the craft was illuminated by its glowing rim as they were being lowered through its hollow center. As in most cases, their method of exit was the exact reverse of their original capture.

Departure

The Bullard study contains 20 cases that describe the UFO taking off from the ground or flying away after dropping off the captive. All cases insert this event between the time witnesses were returned to earth and before they resumed normal activities. Suffice it to say, without needless repetition, all members of the Allagash four watched the departure of the UFO from shore before resuming their normal activities. Typically, they were placed in exactly the same situation that they were in just prior to their capture. The abduction experience was no longer part of their conscious memory. As far as they knew, they had just fled to shore in the canoe when the UFO had approached them with its sweeping beam of light.

Reentry

Dr. Bullard gives the following description of this facet of the return (italics are mine):

Once back on earth the witness resumes his normal activities, but sometimes unusual effects shadow the return. Drivers recover in a particularly notable way. Their car may lower to the highway and drive itself for a while, or the witness may drive in a state of unawareness until he passes some barrier and becomes conscious of what he is doing once again. Ten cases include this element.... Once the driver or other witness recovers normal consciousness, all memory of an abduction may have disappeared, so only discovery of *missing time* clues him that something extraordinary happened to him....

Comparison of capture and return affirms a general symmetry between the two episodes, since the UFO comes and goes, vehicle effects set in and leave off, the witness loses mental control then regains it, and the beings take him in and turn him out....

The message which accompanies the farewell often enlists the witness into a sort of cooperative relationship with the beings. They may entrust the witness with secrets or promise him important work to do. *He has to forget* but only for a while, only with regret and *for his own good.*[27]

The factor of missing time was realized by the Allagash four when they reached shore to find their huge bonfire almost out. It had been blazing as they fled towards shore from the approaching UFO. Other clues would follow in the aftermath, but this was their first suspicion, to put it in Dr. Bullard's words, that something extraordinary had happened.

The aliens' farewell message to the Allagash four may have been much more detailed than what we were able to extract. One thing is certain. It contained the all-too-typical reinforcing injunction to forget the abduction:

CHARLIE: They helped us into the canoe...and said we were okay and that there was nothing to be afraid of and to go back to our place...not to remember...don't be troubled.

Once reentry has been completed, the next and last of the eight episodes characteristic of an abduction experience begins involving the long-term aftereffects that often plague the abductee. Dr. Jacobs dubbed these effects as the Post-Abduction Syndrome. Dr. Bullard refers to them simply as Aftermath. We shall briefly summarize Dr. Bullard's findings for the sake of comparison where there is overlapping of data. I will only mention those directly applicable to the Allagash incident. Other items not covered in the last chapter will be dealt with in more detail.

---

27. Bullard, *UFO Abductions*, p. 66.

Aftermath

The Bullard study breaks down this episode into three categories: Immediate, Intermediate and Long-term Aftereffects.

Immediate Aftereffects

Twenty cases involve cuts, scrapes and punctures. Both Jack Weiner and Charlie Foltz have scoopmarks resembling punch biopsies in the exact location where such marks have been found on other abductees. After waking up with a feeling of sheer terror, Jack found that a scar had appeared above the scar left by the removal of the lump. This incident will be discussed under Intermediate Effects. Chuck's scoop mark appeared after the Allagash incident and is located on his thigh.

Another set of injuries suggests exposure to ultraviolet light. Burns of various kinds appear on the skin in 23 cases while itching sensations occur in a couple more, and some of these injuries may be traced to ultraviolet radiation as well. Possible remnants of these effects have been found on the bodies of the Allagash four. Other consequences highlighted in the study were psychological in nature. These include sleep disturbances, which may be applicable to Jim Weiner's problems in this area.

Intermediate Aftereffects

Some intermediate physical effects noted in the Bullard study again are similar to Jim Weiner's medical problems: recurrent chronic blackout episodes, disorientation and the urge to flee, accompanied by paralysis.

Another effect mentioned is pertinent to Jack and Mary Weiner. Dr. Bullard states that some:

> ...recurrent effects become chronic for witnesses who periodically...hear a buzzing sound.[28]

Both Jack and Mary concurrently began hearing a humming sound sometime during the month of January, 1990. At first, Jack attributed the sound to local sources and didn't even mention it to Mary. Mary, too, did not mention the sound to Jack until he finally asked if she heard it. I'll let Jack describe what happened in his own words:

> It started the last couple of weeks that I worked at Mount Snow this winter...the latter part of February or the beginning of March [1990].... The first thing I thought was it was trucks, and then I thought it could

---

28. Bullard, *UFO Abductions*, p. 149.

possibly be the pumps at Mount Snow that pump water to make snow.... Mount Snow is about 20 miles distant.... On a quiet night we might hear those pumps.... They don't run them anymore.... Mary and I were convinced that it had to be something in the house making noise, like the refrigerator or the pump or something like that....

I went and turned off everything in the house that could possibly run on electricity, including the outside pump, and it's still there. It's in both Mary's and my head because wherever we go, we can hear it. It doesn't matter where we are. We can be down in Deerfield in somebody else's house and we can both still hear it.

We can hear it over in Chuck and Kim's [house], um, out in the woods, walking down the road—it doesn't matter where we are. I even heard it in New Hampshire. So, it seems like it's something that we're carrying with us.... It's not painful, and it doesn't keep me awake, but I notice it. If I just stop and if I turn off the radio and go somewhere where there's no background noise, I can hear it as plain as day.... I said to Mary, I was so concerned about it that, "I'm going to go and get my hearing checked or something. What if I have a tumor growing in my head or something?" And she said, "Well, why do I hear it?" And that's the whole thing that keeps bothering me. It would be one thing if just I could hear it, because then I could say it was hearing damage or whatever, but the fact that she can hear it—and you know it's funny—like when we were in New Hampshire this weekend, visiting our friends, and we went to sleep, there was no sound in the house, and we were lying there in the guest bed, and I could hear it as plain as day. And, ah, I'm so tired of saying to Mary, "Hey Mary, do you hear it now?" I wasn't even going to mention it to her and Mary said, "Jack, do you hear it?" And I said, "Yes," and she said, "I hear it, too."

In the mental realm, the Bullard study lists 42 examples in which the nightmare or abduction dream counts as one of the most common of all aftereffects. Jack especially experienced such dreams about the Allagash incident. A more remote mental effect in this middle phase of the aftermath is: "An excessive reaction to some harmless and ordinary situation with similarities to the forgotten abduction." Again, Jack has suffered this type of reaction after his post-Allagash abductions from his house in Vermont.

One of the incidents occurred on the night of March 26, 1990. This was five months after Jack had been awakened by a noise at the glass door downstairs. If you recall, he thought it was a raccoon or his dog. When he went down to investigate, there were two alien beings standing at the glass door. On this particular night in March, Jack was having trouble with his back. He had found it too painful to climb stairs, so he slept on the first floor in front of the glass door. Jack woke up when the dog began barking at a raccoon that had gotten into some garbage just outside the door. When Jack sleepily glanced at the glass doors, something terrifying happened. I'll let him describe it in his own words:

> For absolutely no reason, ...this wave of absolute terror came over me. And it wasn't that I was afraid of the dark...it was there. Something was in my head and it was like they, these beings or these entities or something were, were out there. They were coming. It was almost like my behavior was out of control. It was absolutely unwarranted. There was nothing at the door. There were no lights outside.
>
> There were no sounds, just this overpowering feeling of absolute terror. It was so intense that I couldn't even look at the door, which I was sleeping right next to—four feet away.

This certainly was what Dr. Bullard refers to as an excessive reaction to a harmless situation that reminded Jack of a largely forgotten abduction.

Long-term Aftereffects

Dr. Bullard lists a number of happenings that have been reported by abductees over the long term. Those applicable to some members of the Allagash four concern the so-called Men-in-Black, instances of telephone tapping, mystery helicopters, apparitions, personality changes and, last but not least, subsequent UFO experiences.

Men In Black

This term is applied to any strange man or men that the abductee may encounter under strange circumstances. It would seem that Chuck Rak may have met such persons a few weeks after his second hypnosis session. Chuck lives in a very isolated situation, where unexpected visitors would be extraordinary to say the least. He surprised trespassers on his property on October 12, 25 and 26. On October 27, his house was buzzed by a black, unmarked helicopter. The first two intruders claimed to be out joyriding. The second intruder just drove off. The third is the most interesting. Chuck, Kim and Jack caught him by surprise and challenged him. The following is a recorded conversation with the Allagash four:

CHUCK: Was it Wednesday, Jack— that we saw the metal detector?

JACK: Oh, yeah, the guy on your property. Very, very suspicious character.

CHUCK: Yeah, Jack and Kim and I were out getting a load of manure at a nearby place, and when we came back, we saw this fellow coming out of the driveway, and he had a—like a pickup or a Chevy Suburban, Blazer or something.

JACK: Blazer. A late model Blazer. It wasn't an old one.

CHUCK: Right—and it was sort of a clean-cut looking fellow.

JACK: Very clean cut. Short cropped hair.

KIM: Clean shirt.

JACK: Real nice, dressy shirt, um, he seemed like, you know, he was on his way to visit somebody or something. (Turns to Chuck.) He told us that he was what?

CHUCK: Um, [using] a metal detector. He was investigating "class six roads." He used that term. I never heard of it before.

JACK: I never did either.

CHUCK: We were concerned that he was casing us for a robbery or something.... I noticed that the license plate looked just like a Massachusetts plate, but when I was very close to it I saw the words New Hampshire. But it had the style and everything of a Massachusetts plate. As a result, I think it was probably some kind of an official plate, because they're a little bit different than usual.

JACK: He was definitely in a hurry to get out of there. He didn't want to—he seemed very nervous about us stopping him and asking questions. He wanted to get going in a hurry.

CHUCK: And then the next day, Kim was down in Brattleboro, this was Thursday now...and I was coming back from scouting painting locations about, ah, oh, it must have been about 2:00 in the afternoon. And I was almost to the house when one of these helicopters came and buzzed overhead.

RAY: Did you see any markings on it at all?

CHUCK: No markings. It was an olive-black Sikorsky.

RAY: Do you often see helicopters in Wardsboro?

CHUCK: No.

KIM: Never.

JACK: Never.

There was no way to check out the excuses given by the first two intruders. Also, attempts to identify the ownership of unmarked helicopters had proved time-consuming and fruitless in the past. The third intruder was a different story. He had made a specific statement that could be checked for accuracy. He said that he was investigating class six roads with a metal detector.

I telephoned the Vermont State Division of Transportation and Maintenance and spoke to their legal department. I was told that there was no such thing as a "class six road" and that the state would not be checking any roads with a metal detector by someone driving a car registered in New Hampshire. I then contacted the Wardsboro Highway Department and was told the same thing. Now, it could be that the person unknowingly used wrong terminology in his description of the mountain road. Perhaps he was an archeology buff looking for some kind of artifacts. But, questions still remain.

Why would a man from New Hampshire, dressed in nice clothes, be on Chuck's remote property? Why did he mention using a metal detector when no metal detector was seen in his truck? Why did he act so nervous and want to leave in a hurry? Another puzzling thing was the man's accent. Chuck has traveled extensively and has made it a habit to study accents. He told me that he usually can tell a lot about where people were raised, what kind of socioeconomic class they come from, etc., by their accent:

> The man in the official New Hampshire Blazer had no accent whatsoever. There was not the slightest diphthong or speech cadence or rhythm that betrayed anything about his background. This is unusual, because most official state jobs are given out in the context of political structures and are notorious for their particular socioeconomic niche and use of regional accents. I have never come across a police officer, registry official, etc., whose speech was not earmarked by those attributes, except for the man in the Blazer.

One could get paranoid about this incident. Was his mention of a metal detector a cover story for the use of a similar instrument like a Geiger counter? Did his closely-cropped military appearing haircut indicate that he worked for the government?

The sudden and rare appearance of Chuck's intruders and the helicopter overflight could easily be explained as coinci-

dences were it not for other strange incidents that have occurred involving intruders. Recently, Chuck and Kim house-sat
for his sister on the island of Martha's Vineyard, in Massachusetts, between February 17 and April 1, 1990. Chuck told me:

> During that time, Jack Weiner checked up on our
> place from time to time. On his second visit, he noticed
> that a piece of plywood that we had put in front of our
> corner hutch (an antique full of valuable glasses, etc.
> that we didn't want to be seen through the windows)
> had been moved aside. Nothing else had been dis-
> turbed and nothing had been taken. When Kim and I
> returned, we noticed the hutch had been moved for-
> ward from its normal position. We went through all
> kinds of explanations of how this could have occurred,
> and decided there must have been someone in the
> house.

I then called Jack and asked him about it to see if he had
more information about the incident. He told me the following:

> The first time I went up there and checked—they
> have a hutch in the corner where they keep all their
> good dishes and stuff. And the first time I checked,
> they had a board that was pushed in front so that you
> could not see it at all. You could go up on their porch
> and look in the window and all you could see was this
> board there. And the first time I checked, that board
> was in the way. You couldn't see anything. You
> couldn't even tell that there was a hutch there.... And
> a couple of weeks later, I went back and checked on
> the house again and I got up on the porch and looked
> in the window and the first thing I noticed was that
> board had been moved off to the side and I went, "Oh,
> oh, this is bad!" And also that time, the upstairs slid-
> ing doors were opened. I went in and checked around
> the whole house. Nothing seemed to have been taken.
> There was nothing taken from the hutch, but this
> board had been moved aside and left up against the
> wall there. And the upstairs door was open. Now
> there's usually a board that they have down so that
> the doors can't open. That was up and the door was
> open seven or eight inches. I have no idea of how it was
> unlocked or anything. The first time I was up there, I
> remembered putting birdseed near the upstairs doors
> and I remembered locking it. I have no idea how it got
> opened.

Telephone Tapping

Earlier, a similar type of intruder had entered Jack's house, while he and Mary were away visiting his mother in Pennsylvania. Jack described what happened to me:

> When we got home from Mom's...there was white stuff all over the rug in the bathroom [the bathroom window was not locked], and I couldn't understand where it came from, because it wasn't there to begin with. And then I realized...we had a pile of sheetrock out back that I'd thrown out the window when I did the upstairs. And apparently, whoever broke into the house walked over the sheetrock and got plaster on their shoes, and when they jumped in our bathroom window, the got it all over the floor.

Later, after getting settled in, Jack went upstairs to his studio. He picked up the telephone to place a call and the telephone came apart in his hands! Someone had taken it apart. All the long bolts holding it together were in place but not screwed in. It appeared that someone had started to do something with the telephone but for some reason had to leave in a hurry. Jack sent me the telephone just as it was. I examined it thoroughly but could not find anything visibly different with the telephone. Several weeks later, Jack received a strange telephone call:

> I was sitting up in my studio working on a computer, and the phone rang and it seemed like it was dead. That happened four times in a matter of ten minutes. Finally the phone rang again, and I picked it up, and it was this guy on the phone and he said, "Are you John Weiner?" And I said, "What do you mean, trying to find my line?" And he said, "I work for the phone company, and I'm trying to find your line because it needs to be replaced." And I said, "Well, I haven't called. We haven't had any problems with our phone. It doesn't need to be replaced." And he said, "Oh no, it has nothing to do with you. This is a standard thing that we do." And I said, "Well, don't you know where the line is?" And he said, "Well, the guy who usually is in charge of your route is sick and I'm lost." And I said, "Well, don't they give you a map—where to go—if you work for the phone company?" And he was like, well, you know, "I didn't have time." He had all these excuses as to why he didn't know where our line was. And so I said, "Do you want the pole number?" And he said, "No, I just want to know what road you're on." So I said, "All right," (and told him the road we live on). "Do you want me to run down and get the pole number?" And he said no, I'll find it." And he hung up.

Again, this was another incident that could be checked. I phoned the New England Telephone Company. A check of their records indicated that no repair or work had been done on the telephone lines in Jack's area for over a year. There was no repair work done on his personal line. Who was the man that called Jack? Has some agency installed a monitoring device on his telephone line?

It is interesting to note that neither Chuck nor Jack have had problems like this prior to our investigation. Nothing was stolen from either house. In one case, the telephone was actually physically tampered with. Who were these mysterious intruders and what were they looking for? Other abductees such as Betty Hill and Betty Andreasson have experienced similar intrusions and telephone problems.

Apparitions/Subsequent UFO Experiences

Needless to say, the Allagash four have had their share of both of these aspects of the aftermath episode in the form of bedtime visitations and follow-on abductions. Since these experiences were discussed in detail earlier, it is unnecessary to repeat them here. However, there is an aftermath effect that has not been covered previously and which deserves our attention now.

Long-term Aftereffects: Personality Changes

In his original written report to me on the Allagash abduction, Jim mentioned the following effect on his personality that seemed to coincide with his UFO experience:

> At the time of our trip to Maine, I was attending Boston University's program in Artisanry—working toward a Certificate of Mastery in Ceramics. Prior to our encounter, my style of pottery design was fairly traditional in nature. Following the encounter, my pottery underwent a sudden and dramatic change to a direction of investigation that involved a very esoteric and sophisticated design paradigm that incorporated process-oriented construction and firing techniques. The concept for this new direction came as sudden insight in its entirety.

Both Jim and Jack experienced a sudden change in their attitudes toward science, math and computers after the Allagash encounter. Jack's artwork reflected this in a dramatic way. I talked to the wife of his business partner during my character reference check. She brought up the reversal in Jack's artistic style without any solicitation on my part:

He was showing me a lot of his early artwork, which I really love. It's very classic looking. And then all of a sudden I noticed that there's a big change in his artwork. And I said, "My God, what's happened to you? You've gone from a really beautiful, classic-looking, flowing-looking style to this, ah, very linear, very geometric style. It's like you're going into dots and this weird geometric stuff." And he said, "It's so funny, I was always lousy in math, and I could never figure things. I could never paint like this. I didn't do stuff like this. And then, after I had this experience, all I could do was this stuff." And he said, "Now the computer absolutely fascinates me, where before, I never really cared about it." I found this very interesting. It was such a difference! You know? It's like almost like a cutoff mark. I also draw and paint. It's like something dramatic happened to him because to make such a big switch is like—I mean it's like almost changing your whole perception.

This completes the correlation of the Allagash incident with the eighth and final episode of the typical abduction story type in the Bullard study. Similar correlations also exist between the Allagash four's other UFO experiences and the Bullard study's ideal pattern for UFO abductions. However, one more set of striking correlations should be examined before bringing this chapter to a close. The correlations relate to the abductee's description of the alien occupants in the Bullard study.

The Occupants

The Head Region

Shape and Size

Dr. Bullard makes the following summary statement regarding the most typical descriptions given to this area of the alien's body:

> A standard humanoid possesses a large hairless cranium and narrow chin.... Witnesses use metaphors like egg, light bulb or pear to portray the general effect.... In overall effect the being looks fetal.[29]

Jim, Jack, Chuck and Charlie gave these descriptions:

JIM: Their heads are egg-shaped.

JACK: Large round heads...nothing on top.

CHARLIE: The head is...like egg-shaped.... No hair.

---

29. Bullard, *UFO Abductions*, p. 242.

CHUCK: Looks like an embryonic chicken head.... Cranium almost looks like a duck...bulbous.... Can't see hair.

Eyes

The Bullard study reveals that the aliens' eyes capture the attention of the abductee like no other bodily feature. Almost half of its sample population refers to the eyes. They are described as large in 42 cases. Words used to describe their shape include elongated, almond, walnut, slanted, teardrop, wraparound and catlike. References to eye color in the study are scarce, but the eyes are generally said to be unusually dark and uniform.

The Allagash four said:

JIM: Bugging-looking eyes.... They're dark.... Temporally located.

JACK: Large eyes on the sides of their heads.... Funny-looking...like eggs.

CHARLIE: Like large Asian, almond eyes.

CHUCK: Dark eyes...elliptical. They're black.

Mouth, Nose and Ears

In striking contrast to the aliens' eyes, one finds that the abductees in the Bullard sample describe almost nonexistent features in these three areas. Adjectives like small, lipless, hole and slit mouths predominate. The aliens' noses are so diminutive that witnesses often report that the nose is practically not there. This is also true of the ears, which are tiny or simply holes in the head.

JIM: Something like a mouth.... They don't have ears, just, ah, holes.... They don't have noses, there's something, ah, there.

JACK: Like turtle mouths...no nose...no ears.

CHARLIE: They don't have like a mouth—like if your lips were sealed.... An Asian nose...small compared to mine—ears smaller...lays close.

CHUCK: [The mouth is] like chicken lips.... Can't really make it [the nose] out.... Can't really see much...[of the ears] just suggested.

Body Build

Dr. Bullard remarks that 25 out of 39 given descriptions of standard humanoid aliens describe them as frail, thin, without muscle-tone or definition, sickly, thin-necked, narrow-shoul-

dered and "like a skeleton." He states that sketches made by
abductees often confirm these descriptions:

> Illustrations often confirm this...by making the
> beings look top heavy and precarious with the huge
> heads balanced on thin necks and the rest of the body
> all out of proportion with skinny limbs and sunken
> chests.[30]

JIM:	Bony...an exoskeleton.
JACK:	They're small and thin. I can't see their joints.... Thin...arms
CHARLIE:	Slight build...petite.
CHUCK:	They're bony...slender.

Clothing

The following is a composite description of the clothing
worn by alien beings from the Bullard study.

> The...alien wears a one-piece suit of some kind in
> 82 out of 105 cases. These suits usually cover the en-
> tire body except for the hands and face, and show no
> signs of buttons, zippers, seams or separation into
> pants and shirt.... The most common adjective used to
> describe these suits is tight or close-fitting.... Some-
> times the clothing is so tight the beings seem naked. [31]

According to our four campers:

JIM:	Suits or something on—kinda skiers—tight-fit-ting.
JACK:	They're covered.... It's a suit.... No buttons...no wrinkles...no seams.... Like a skier racing in a suit.
CHARLIE:	Clothing...smooth...close-fitting.
CHUCK:	It's tight-fitting.

This chapter has dealt essentially with the remarkable similarities that exist between the data elements in the Allagash
abduction and those contained within the sample of abduction
reports in the Bullard study. A similar comparative study of elements from other experiences of the Allagash four and the
Bullard study would probably yield similar results. The implications posed by these extraordinary correlations provide the
subject matter for the next chapter.

---

30. Bullard, *UFO Abductions*, p. 246.
31. Bullard, *UFO Abductions*, p. 249.

CHAPTER 13

Conclusion

The Bullard study reveals that an extraordinary symmetry persists throughout the hundreds of abduction reports now on record. As Dr. Bullard so aptly puts it, "The similarities are so obvious that you could train a monkey to pick them out."[1] The remarkable correlations that exist between the Allagash abduction and the Bullard study attest to its kinship with the overall UFO abduction phenomenon.

Why UFO abduction reports are strikingly similar remains the 64 million-dollar question. Bullard offers several reasons for their similarity: a shared psychological mechanism that gives rise to similar subjective experiences, a tradition of transmission that establishes itself as people tell stories like those they have heard before or a similar objective experience. Let us first examine those theories that involve a shared psychological mechanism.

Subjective Experiences

Imaginary Abductions

Advocates of this theory preselected individuals for their investigations who were generally unaware of the content of UFO abduction reports. These individuals were then hypnotized and asked to describe a situation in which they are being abducted

---

1. Bullard, "Abductions in Life and Lore," p. 18.

by a UFO. Each one of them described an imaginary abduction. While there were parallels between these imaginary abductions and alleged real abduction reports, there were significant differences. Unlike alleged real abductees, the imaginary abductees:

- were told to imagine their abduction.
- usually controlled their emotions and merely described their fantasy.
- displayed no physiological effects or reactions
- had no conscious recall of a real UFO sighting followed by amnesia.
- did not describe the typical aliens reported by real alleged abductees.
- did not believe that their experiences were real.

I am of the opinion that if the same individuals were preselected and asked to sit back and, without hypnosis, imagine being abducted by a UFO, similar results might be obtained.

Fantasyprone Personality

This hypothesis suggests that UFO abductees must belong to the four percent of the population who have been classified as "fantasyprone personalities." These individuals, usually from childhood, have secretly indulged in a parallel fantasy life. Such a personality might be the catalyst for vivid dreams. Living in a make-believe world, believing in fairies, having imaginary companions, seeing apparitions, and believing oneself to possess occult powers are all characteristics of this type of personality. Outwardly, these people appear to be socially aware, normal and healthy.

There is no doubt that such people could easily fantasize, report, and relive a UFO-abduction experience under hypnosis. They would really believe that such an event occurred and could easily pass a lie-detector test.

I have met several people who could fall into this category during my long years of UFO investigation. However, such persons, if undetected by UFO researchers, would not prove that all of the hundreds of abductee reports originate from fantasyprone personalities. It is a bit much to state categorically that all abductees fall into this small percentage of our population. Indeed, many abductees, including Betty Andreasson Luca, have been psychologically screened by competent professionals and have taken psychological profile tests which do not reveal fantasyprone personalities. Dr. Leo Sprinkle, Director of Counseling and Testing and retired professor of Counseling at the University of Wyoming has subjected well over 200 abductees to a number of psychological tests. The test results did not support the hypothesis that abductees are experiencing neurotic reactions.

Psychosis

This hypothesis is similar to the fantasyprone personality hypothesis. Advocates would assert that UFO abductees are persons who are experiencing neurotic or psychotic reactions. The same arguments applied to the fantasyprone hypothesis are also applicable to this position. Psychologists and psychiatrists who have tested a number of alleged abductees would be quick to say that the results of psychological testing do not support this theory.

Birth Trauma

Adherents to this hypothesis would suggest that hypnosis awakens the subject's subconscious traumatic memories of their birth. Abductee accounts of tunnels, womb-shaped rooms, cervix-like doors, bright lights and of being probed by aliens with instruments all would correspond to the birth experience of a fetus. The fetus moves through the birth canal (tunnel) into a bright room (hospital) containing strange creatures (doctors and nurses) who prod and poke with instruments. This hypothesis also attempts to account for the fetus-like appearance of reported alien beings.

A number of objections can be leveled against such a possibility. Many nonabductee witnesses have consciously seen and reported fetus-like creatures in association with UFOs. Many abductees remember part or all of their experience without the aid of hypnosis. Two studies reveal that between 29 and 33 percent of 232 cases involved abductee recall of their experiences without hypnosis. I might also add that abductees born via cesarean operations would not experience that alleged imagery associated with normal births. Lastly, most embryologists would totally discount the theory that a fetus would have the ability to see its own image.

The Collective Unconscious

Noted psychiatrist and analyst Carl Gustav Jung pioneered the idea of a collective unconscious that somehow links all of mankind since time immemorial. Jung, although not denying the extraterrestrial origin of some UFOs, also theorized that they might have a psychological origin. He suggested that UFOs are archetypal images shared by us all. Some UFOs, according to Jung, are psychic projections that enable mankind to bring wholeness and serenity to a fragmented and violent world.

Those who hold to this hypothesis would also include other concepts detailed within UFO-abduction accounts as being generated by the collective unconscious. These would include the shapes of UFOs, visions of being in a tunnel and OBEs (out-of-the-body experiences). Adherents of this view would state that such a collective unconscious explains the similarity between modern UFO abductions and the abduction motif found in human's folklore, which tells of dwarfish entities with supernatural powers who kidnap human beings, who need human assistance in giving birth, who are interested in genetics, and who can control time.

Thus, Jungian theorists would dismiss much of the UFO phenomenon and its abduction subset as nothing more than a new mythology instigated by the collective unconscious. But, Jung himself admitted that he would be challenged to place radar-visual, physical trace, and photographic cases in this category. Nonetheless, some Jungian extremists would insist that the powers of the collective mind could produce such physical effects, including the scars found on abductees. This, of course, cannot be demonstrated scientifically. Concerning the Jungian view of scars and other physical effects on abductees, D. Scott Rogo writes the following (italics are mine):

> My biggest problem with the fantasyprone proponents is that it cannot explain the physical dimensions of the abduction phenomenon.... If you study the literature on the psychosomatic effects of suggestion, you will find that these effects represent *transient* physical changes on skin tissue, body functions and so on. *What we find on persons claiming UFO abductions are permanent scars or lesions.* Nowhere in the literature on suggestion is there a precedent for such a phenomenon.[2]

D. Scott Rogo is a lecturer in parapsychology at John F. Kennedy University and a prolific writer on paranormal phenomena, including UFOs.

Hoaxers

There will always be those who attempt, sometimes quite successfully, to perpetrate a hoax when it comes to UFOs. Some do it for notoriety. Others do it to fulfill some deep psychological need. A few hoaxes are merely intended jokes that somehow get out of control. Surprisingly, statistics compiled by military and civilian researchers alike, indicate that genuine hoaxes comprise only a small percentage of any kind of UFO reports.

---

2. Rogo, D. Scott, "Letters (fantasyprone theory)", *International UFO Reporter,* Vol. 13, No. 4, 1988, p. 20.

Let us now move from psychological theories for abductions to another alternative offered by critics—abductions are just stories.

Traditional Narratives

Adherents to this theory maintain that the well publicized 1961 abduction story involving Barney and Betty Hill is the catalyst for all subsequent abduction reports. Other abduction stories are merely the retelling of the same script by different actors. Folklorist Dr. Thomas Bullard admits:

> People of perfect good faith may consider themselves all but eyewitnesses to an event they never saw and that never happened for anyone to see—such is the persuasive power of tradition.[3]

A variation to this theory is that the cultural tradition effected by the Hill case influences other abduction reports so that similarities exist between reports. In his comparative study of UFO abduction cases, Dr. Bullard acknowledges that some abductees come to their experience with innocence lost because of being exposed to other abduction accounts in the media. However, in spite of this, Dr. Bullard concludes from his overall study:

> The possibility that abduction reports emerge out of a story tradition fared none too well in comparative analysis. Impacts from well-publicized cases and changes over time indicative of story development failed to materialize.[4]

Another test for the traditional narrative theory is whether or not the similarity between abduction reports exists worldwide. If abduction reports show deviances based upon geography, it would indicate that they might reflect the cultural traditions of a given location. If certain characteristics cluster in reports from one area and are absent from another, it could be said that abductions exhibit a significant property of traditional narratives. However, Dr. Bullard states in his analysis of the reports in his study:

> Perhaps the most remarkable thing about a geographical comparison of cases is that any similarities exist at all. The fact that similarities account for 65 out of 85 possibilities (78%) means that witnesses tell a pretty consistent story wherever they come from, and national versions are not obvious and striking outcomes of this experiment in comparison. Even where differences occur, they are of degree rather than of

3. Bullard, *UFO Abductions*, p. 366.
4. Bullard, "Abductions in Life and Lore," p. 18.

kind, a little more or less of the same thing and not something new.[5]

I would simply add that some of the arguments presented against the alternatives discussed under Subjective Experience would equally apply to the Traditionally Narrative hypothesis.

Dr. Bullard comes to no definitive conclusions on what UFO abductions represent. He presents a far-reaching, detailed study and comparative analysis of hundreds of abduction reports. He then presents the pros and cons of the major theories offered to explain them. His analysis of the theory that UFO abductions are real events, together with my personal observations, form the basis for the next and final alternative hypothesis: UFO abductions are real events grounded in physical reality.

Objective Experience

Dr. Bullard notes the following concerning the objectivity of UFO abduction experiences:

> One of the strongest arguments comes from witnesses who assert that the abduction experience was as convincing as any other real event. These witnesses represent a broad cross-section of society and include many individuals of sound reputation. Psychological tests show no hint of mental illness. In any other matter these people would be credible enough for their testimony in court to land you in jail. Sometimes multiple witnesses participate in the same abduction, and each witness usually describes similar events—a pretty good practical definition of objectivity.[6]

In the Allagash abduction we definitely have multiple witnesses who describe similar events. Jim Weiner does have a physical problem as a result of a home accident, which has been tentatively diagnosed as a form of epilepsy. However, we have documented the fact that this impairment is not a causal factor regarding his UFO experiences. It was his doctor who suggested that Jim seek help from a UFO investigator.

Other than this, all of the Allagash witnesses are of sound mind and reputation. They not only tell essentially the same story, they relive it with all the trauma and emotions that would be expected of a real physical event. Any variances within their overall testimony can easily be attributed to the vantage points and mental states of each individual.

---

5. Bullard, *UFO Abductions*, p. 320
6. Bullard, "Abductions in Life and Lore," p. 14.

It is important to take into consideration the initial shock and alien-induced, somnambulistic state suffered by the Allagash four and other abductees during the abduction process. In this state, abductees are certainly not thinking about the list of questions that UFO investigators will ask them later on. The number of digits on an alien's hand, the exact size of eyes, ears, nose, mouth, etc. are not items of particular interest to the abduction victim. Sketches of the aliens, their craft and instruments used during an examination are impressions, not photographs. Abductees are confused, bewildered and terrified by the situation in which they find themselves. In addition, they are usually given a strong posthypnotic command not to remember the experience.

These are the obstacles that a UFO investigator is confronted with during the probe of an abduction report. It is indeed a wonder that so many similarities exist under such conditions. This very fact undergirds the premise that their experience was physically real.

Dr. Bullard continues:

> A comparison of investigators gives no persuasive evidence that they make a difference in the contents of reports. Hypnosis has been used to break through time-lapse amnesia since the Hill case.... A subject under hypnosis can be guided deliberately or innocently by the hypnotist...but (a) comparison of cases spontaneously revealed with those revealed by hypnosis shows few differences in content, however. These findings weigh against hypnosis as a causal agent in forming the abduction story. When arranged in chronological order by date of report, abductions present the same characteristics holding essentially steady over time. Well-publicized cases like the Hill, Pascagoula or Walton cases proved to have little impact on subsequent reports. Such historical consistency is the signature of real events, not developing oral narratives or mythologies.[7]

I would add that during our investigation of the Allagash abduction, great pains were taken not to ask any leading questions of the witnesses during the hypnotic regression sessions. They were encouraged to recall and relive their experience. Questions were asked of specific information that we were looking for, but in such a way that it would not corrupt their testimony.

It should be noted that leading questions also can influence persons who are not under hypnosis. A person could lie

---

7. Bullard, "Abductions in Life and Lore," p. 14.

under hypnosis, but it is also equally possible for a person to lie during a non-hypnotic cross-examination. Hypnosis in and of itself is neutral. It is how hypnosis is used that is the important factor. An honest person who would not lie in a non-hypnotic state will not lie under hypnosis.

During an examination of my own abduction experiences under hypnosis, I had no desire to lie. My staunch Christian ethics still prevailed while under hypnosis. In fact, I found myself exceptionally careful to be painstakingly accurate in everything I said. During my investigation of abduction cases, including the Allagash case, I have noticed that the hypnotized person often corrects the hypnotist if inadvertently or intentionally (as a test) misquoted.

During hypnosis, I found myself back in time, reliving my abduction experiences. I felt the overwhelming emotions, the literally overpowering alien-induced mental blocks and the stark-naked fear of these previously suppressed memories.

It is quite apparent to me that the accuracy of memories hypnotically retrieved by a skilled hypnotist is directly related to the psychological and moral makeup of the subject. If the subject is of sound mind, is a good hypnosis subject, and has strong ethics, then I believe that hypnosis will probably be successful in retrieving true and accurate memories.

Our witness background checks and personal observations leave no doubt in our minds that each member of the Allagash four passes such a test of character with flying colors.

In his comments, Dr. Bullard emphasizes that both the initial abduction and subsequent physical examination follow a complex order with surprising fidelity. In the last chapter, we observed the amazing correlation that exists between the data content of the Allagash abduction and the complex order and description of events uncovered by the Bullard study. Dr. Bullard remarks:

> What matters most about this order is its arbitrariness.... No demand or act locks narrators into one sequence. Yet that sequence appears time and again, as if witnesses gave an honest account of a real experience. The descriptive details of reports also grow monotonous with familiarity.... The beings are seldom finished with a witness after just one abduction.... Aftereffects tantalize researchers with evidence bordering on physical confirmation of the abduction story. Abductees report sunburn, eye injuries, gastrointestinal upset and puncture wounds as immediate results of the experience, followed within a few weeks by anxiety and nightmares as hidden memories begin to surface. A symmetry of cause-and-effect here, since each

aftereffect usually traces to a cause during the abduction, even though witnesses may remember nothing of the abduction itself until long after they have noted the consequences.... The economy of a physical reality best accounts for these events.[8]

After taking these and other significant aspects of the abduction experience into consideration, Dr. Bullard concludes:

Not a long tally of individual points but a broad overview of the abduction story argues the most persuasive case for an objective experience. This higher perspective considers the pattern of meanings and purposes afoot in the reports. What we find are pieces of evidence coming from every quarter with a portion of the same message, all parts of the same puzzle.[9]

In my estimation, the moral character of witnesses and the extraordinary correlations between abduction reports provide overwhelming circumstantial evidence that UFO abductions are indeed objective experiences. I say this apart from my own experiences, documented fully in my last book, *he Watchers*. I have tried very hard not to prejudice the conclusion of this book with my personal experience. Thus far, it has been sufficient to use the Bullard study, along with the quadruple and other abduction experiences of the Allagash four to provide an objective litmus test for the physical reality of the UFO- abduction phenomenon.

However, there is another kind of evidence, which when coupled with the strong correlative evidence, constitutes physical proof that UFO abductions are real. This is where I feel compelled to talk about my own UFO abduction experience. I am referring to the physical aftereffects suffered by abductees.

In August of 1988, I was the recipient of one of the typical aftereffects mentioned by Dr. Bullard. It appeared overnight. It was a scoop-like scar. A small circular chunk of flesh had been removed from just above my right ankle. I had seen such marks before on abductees. Strangely, I could not remember anything out of the ordinary that had occurred on the night of August 16, 1988. However, later on, I received two dramatic flashbacks of memory related to that fateful night.

Both flashbacks erupted just two weeks after a second hypnosis session was used to probe abduction experiences that stretched back to my early childhood. The first took place on the night of September 22, 1988, as I lay talking to my wife. My recall was instigated by a simple remark that she made to me, "You can always fall asleep at the drop of a hat." Instantly, two

8. Bullard, "Abductions in Life and Lore," p. 16.
9. Bullard, "Abductions in Life and Lore," p. 16.

forgotten events burst forth from the recesses of my mind, sending a cold chill pulsating up my spine.

The first memory concerned the night of August 16. How could I have forgotten that eerie, sleepless night? Until then, I remembered only coming home from giving an astronomy lecture at a nearby club. What I had forgotten was that I was kept awake into the wee hours of the morning by a strange, uptight, electrical feeling. On the following morning, I had discovered the scar.

My second flashback was of a dream that I had the night before my wife had made her innocent remark about my sleeping ability on September 22. During the night of September 21, I had a frightening nightmare. It was peculiar in that people usually visualize things in a dream; in this instance, I dreamed that I could not see. I felt myself being moved somewhere. When I opened my eyes to see what was happening, all I could see was black. I knew that I was dreaming and tried to wake up but I could not. Later, when I did wake up, I abruptly sat up in bed and almost blurted out loud, "They are operating on my leg!"

As I lay recuperating from this nightmare, it dawned on me that perhaps it had something to do with my scar. I wondered if what had happened back in August had leached out of my subconscious in the form of this nightmare. I told myself that I must remember this dream. I started to reach for the Kleenex box to put on my bureau which would remind me in the morning, but that was the last thing I remembered. Later, under hypnosis, it was discovered that I had been programmed by my abductors to forget the incident.

In *The Watchers*, I documented this and other UFO incidents experienced by myself and members of my family. Such incidents were traced back to a CEI by my mother in 1916 or 1917 and a CEIII by my father when he was serving as a Navy operator. Both events took place on Mount Desert Island in Maine.

Although not covered by the Bullard study, another intriguing paradigm that crops up again and again in UFO abduction research is that it is a family phenomenon. Concerning this, Dr. Neal surmises that, "There is some type of ongoing genetic manipulation that is occurring within various family generations." He theorized that such experiments would bring about, "new genotypic individuals in proceeding generations." Dr. Neal further conjectures that "each family is subjected to a different or comparable type of experimentation by the alien."[10]

The incredible thing about the scoopmark that appeared overnight on my leg is that it was put there during my writing

10. Fowler, *The Watchers*, p. 299.

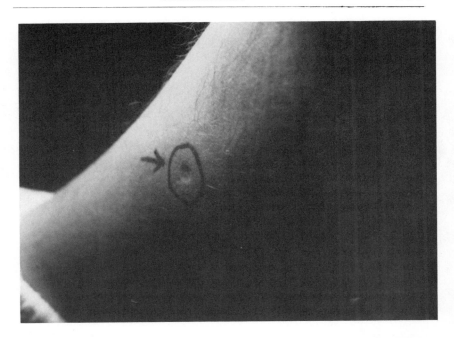

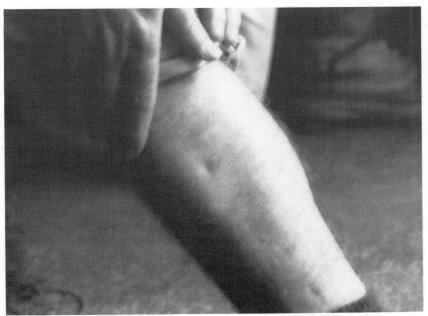

Figure 31. Typical scoopmarks resembling punch biopsies on Ray Fowler's right leg (top) and on Jack Weiner's right leg (bottom).

of *The Watchers*, just when I desperately wanted proof concerning the incredible things that were being revealed during an investigation. An equally incredible thing about the identical scoop mark that appeared on Jack Weiner's leg is that it also happened overnight, after a series of nightmares and during the writing of this particular book.

These scars, and those of other abductees seen by myself and other researchers, are identical to each other. The scars are located in the same areas of the body. They are prominent and look exactly like the remains of surgically removed tissue samples. In fact, when mine was examined by a local dermatologist, he commented that it looked just like a punch biopsy, but could not be because I hadn't been operated on by a doctor. Needless to say, I didn't tell him about its true nature. He may have thought I was crazy, had I done so.

Photographs of my scoopmark and Jack's have been included for comparison. (See Figure 31.) What other explanation can be given for these and other identical scars that appear in typical locations on an abductee's body?

When such physical effects are combined with the overwhelming evidence presented by our comparative study of the Allagash abduction with hundreds of other cases, it should leave little doubt, to an unprejudiced mind that UFO abductions are real!

CHAPTER 14

Witness Update

I have kept in close contact with the Allagash four since the completion of the ten-volume 702-page report on their experiences. In the future, I may reopen the investigation to examine some old and new experiences not covered during the primary inquiry. What are the four abductees doing now, as this book goes through its editing process? How did their experiences affect their lives? Recently I asked each of them these two questions. The following are their responses:

Charlie Foltz

In as much as how the Allagash experience has affected my life, I have no real way of imparting such an observation of myself. I am doing what I came to New England to do. That is, I came to educate myself in the art field. At first, I sought a teaching degree so I might return to my native Ohio and pursue a teaching career. I have, however, become employed as a medical illustrator, working with medical researchers, educators and scientists in the biotechnological field. I also work as a volunteer at Children's Hospital here in Boston. I have endeavored to continue to educate myself in my field as well as other related areas and creative art fields. I still pursue my hobbies that I did in my youth, and hope to continue doing so throughout my life.

This is just what I would have expected Charlie to say. His quiet manner and easygoing temperament seem relatively unaffected by the UFO experience in an outward sense. However, I feel sure that inwardly he does a lot of thinking about what happened on the Allagash Waterway during that fateful camping trip. He now reads books on UFOs to become better acquainted with the subject and to see how his UFO experience relates to those of others.

Chuck Rak

Chuck continues to be self-employed as an artist. He performs as a caricature artist in shopping malls and at special events and does portrait work privately. He shows his pastel and oil paintings at the Vermont Art Center at Manchester, Vermont.

His UFO experiences are much on his mind to the point that he has collaborated with Jack on a pictorial account of his experience. (See last page of this book.) He, unlike the others, finds the abduction segment of the Allagash experience harder to accept as real. After he had come out of hypnosis, he was bewildered about where these memories had come from and wondered if he were really under hypnosis and if he somehow made the account up himself. We assured him that he was under hypnosis. We informed him that it is common for a hypnotized subject to have doubts about having been hypnotized after coming out of hypnosis. Chuck reiterated this in a recent letter to me:

> The abduction segment of my UFO experience is still quite nebulous. However, the object and its beam is forever and indelibly etched into the fabric of my memory. The sensation is similar to how well I remember where I was when I found out Kennedy had been shot in Dallas. It is vivid.
>
> I remember clearly the stark terror of an alien presence in my bedroom when I was a little boy. I don't know if this is related but I have had a lifelong fear of invasive medical procedures.

In addition to reading UFO books, attending UFO symposia and drawing a pictorial account of the Allagash experience, Chuck has an even deeper interest in the subject. His experience has motivated him to organize a CEV group in Vermont, patterned after a national organization dubbed CSETI that seeks to observe UFOs and attempt overt communication with their occupants. CSETI is the acronym for the Center For The Study of Extraterrestrial Intelligence.[1] Chuck summed up his feelings in the following way:

---

1. Steven M. Greer, M.D., headquarters at P.O. Box 15401, Asheville, NC 28813

In general, I feel the UFO phenomenon is beyond our ken. One of the dimensions that I believe is connected with it is psychic force and telepathy. These seem to me to be a prerequisite or a result of our UFO experience. I remembered feeling compelled to make sure Jack and Jim experienced the Allagash [camping trip]. In instigating and organizing that trip, I knew that the bizarre haunted those twins. If I could get them up there, I knew I could be part of something unusual.

The latter part of Chuck's statement was a new revelation to me. It would seem then, as in a number of other abduction cases, that their experience on the Allagash was not a random event. It may have been planned. Chuck may have been unknowingly controlled by alien influences to plan and expedite the camping trip with the twins. Charlie had literally gone along for the ride. Little did he know what kind of a ride he was to be in for!

Jack Weiner

As mentioned, the UFO encounter on the Allagash Waterway has instigated Jack to work with Chuck on a pictorial account of their experience. Prior to this, they met often to discuss, compare and draw what they could remember of the event. This proved to be cathartic for both of them. However, the Allagash event and my subsequent investigation revealed earlier and follow-on UFO experiences in Jack's life. The full impact of bringing memories of them to his conscious mind has had a number of other effects on Jack's life. Jack responded to my request as follows:

Your request for a short statement concerning how my abduction experience has changed my life is totally justified, but not an easy one to fulfill. Naturally, being abducted by possible beings from outer space is not your average experience. Even after all I've been through, I still can't provide solid answers to all my questions concerning the abduction experience. However, I do have some thoughts on the matter. So, I'll do my best to communicate some of them to you. I hope that you'll be patient and understanding if my statement seems a little mixed up or vague.

It is important to say that my abduction experiences have verified, for me, that extraterrestrial life certainly does exist. There's no longer any doubt whatsoever in my mind about that. But, the question of who they are and where they originate from is still an unsolved mystery for me. Also, why they have chosen me as an object of their scientific study is still a total enigma. I don't consider myself special enough, other than being one of a set of identical twins, to qualify me to be chosen as a subject for study by extraterrestrials. But, my abductions by the aliens have certainly caused some changes in my thinking and the way I look at life now.

Ever since I was a small child, I have always been an artist and interested in creating pictures to help express myself. I have always felt a particular delight in being able to create rather then destroy. While I was in art college, before the Allagash abduction experience, my main focus was fine art—in particular, drawing and painting still life and landscapes. I considered myself a very orthodox artist, with my interests steeped in the art that had come from many artists before me. I had no interest whatsoever in science, mathematics, geometry, engineering, computers, etc. In fact, I considered myself incapable to the extreme when it came to comprehending any of the sciences, especially mathematics and geometry.

Immediately after the Allagash abduction, my interests changed completely. I lost all interest in creating traditional art. I became obsessed with new technologies. My new interests suddenly included science, mathematics, engineering, architecture, geometry, and, curiously, everything I could find out about the ancient Mayans of Central America.

I began to spend all of my time investigating all of these subjects, To this day, I can't seem to get enough reading done concerning these topics to satisfy my curiosity. As for my artwork, virtually all of my present artwork is done using a computer as my medium. I taught myself this with the help of my twin brother, Jim.

I absolutely know that the changes in my interests were directly connected with my abduction experiences. But, I still cannot answer why. I do suspect that the radical change in my artistic expression is simply a response generated by my exposure to the alien technology that I encountered while on the extraterrestrials' spacecraft. I have actually seen a totally alien technology—a science that is extremely different from our own. I suppose I'm still trying to figure it out.

Unfortunately, unlike some other UFO abductees, I did not receive any messages for mankind from the aliens. Nor do I feel that I was chosen to fulfill any special purpose toward the advancement of the human race. In fact, I was left feeling that I was simply nothing more than an object of scientific study. I was an organism to take samples from, be tagged, and then set free to be monitored until they have the information that they seek. This will probably be for the rest of my natural life. I really do believe that the aliens are simply extraterrestrial scientists doing their job to study life forms on this planet—nothing more. Whether or not their investigations are for the benefit of mankind, I simply cannot answer that question.

I'm not obsessed with trying to figure it all out. My life is still very typical. My time is spent doing all the normal things that people everywhere must be concerned with in order to survive from day to day. However, I do know that this study isn't over yet. They will be back from time to time to check up on me and collect more data, of that I feel certain. I wish I knew when they were coming again. I'd prepare a list of things I'd like to ask them. But, they don't seem interested in how I feel about them or their agenda here on earth. So far, they haven't asked for my opinion on those matters. I really do wish they seemed friendlier, though.

Curiously, I don't feel that I will ever have all the answers to my questions concerning my abduction experiences and I'm not really all that disappointed about that prospect. Whenever I go out in my back yard on a clear, star-studded night and look up at the countless stars overhead, I know that I have encountered something from out there. And, I know that we are not alone in this vast universe. Maybe sometime later in my life, all my questions about them—the whys and what-fors—will be answered. Until then, all I can do is cast my gaze upon those beautiful stars and wonder.

Jim also wrote and shared how his UFO experiences have affected his life.

Jim Weiner

Jim is still employed on the faculty of the Massachusetts College of Art in the Computer Arts Learning Center. Basically, he teaches students computer art and how to become computer-creative. He related the following, concerning how the UFO experiences had changed his life:

How the abduction experience has changed my life is a bit more difficult to answer in just two or more sentences. It has only been the past four to five years that the abduction memories themselves have become an accepted part of my conscious thought processes.

I often wonder how the unconscious/repressed abduction experiences from childhood on, have affected the development and evolution of my present belief system. Do I attribute my present beliefs to possible programming by the aliens? Or, do I believe the things I do in spite of the aliens? Just what kind of beliefs are

we actually looking at, and from when in terms of
gradual or sudden onset/reversal?

These are questions that I don't have precise answers to. I do however, have definite feelings about
certain aspects of my abduction experiences. I know
that each time I have an encounter, I feel a strong aura
of malevolence emanating from the beings.

At first, I attributed this feeling to the neurophys-
iological effects of Fight/Flight Syndrome and it could
well be just that. However, I can't help but consider the
possibility that my feeling may be an accurate reflection of my body's intuitive senses.

I think my intuition is telling me not to blindly assume these beings are benevolent, or that their biolog-
ical-engineering agenda is, ultimately, for my own or
humankind's benefit. Their methodology is, in my experience, intrusive and abusive. We put people who
treat their children like that in prison.

In another vein, I have increasingly come to believe that the U.S. government and the military are lying about their lack of involvement in the abduction
phenomenon. I feel both are deeply involved at levels
too frightening to contemplate.

On a totally different level are beliefs which en-
compass peculiar or esoteric interests. In my case—a
sudden, inexplicable interest/obsession with ancient
temple architecture and its relationship to Ley-Lines,
the earth grid and something more. Something about
architectural volume and its effect on acoustic energy-
resonance as a model of macro-computer technology.
This began immediately after the '76 Allagash abduction and continues to this day.

I feel like I'm searching for something extremely
important, yet I really can't say exactly why I feel this
way or how I initially became interested, or if I truly
understand any of what I'm looking at. I feel like Richard Dreyfus in Close Encounters who's trying to find
meaning in his mashed potatoes!

Well Ray, there you have it—a small portion of my
belief puzzle.

I would add that Jim has joined a UFO abductee support
group. It meets weekly at the home of a Harvard Medical School
professor, Dr. John Mack. Dr. Mack has recently become involved in UFO abduction research. Not too long after Jim had
joined the group, the other attendees elected him group leader.

In closing, I believe that these remarks by the Allagash abductees are probably just the tip of the iceberg regarding how
their lives have been changed by the UFO experiences. These
encounters began early in life for Chuck and the twins. Who
could begin to guess how the repressed memories of their expe-

riences had already affected their lives thus far. Who knows what untapped memories still lie within their subconscious minds and how they will affect their future? And, speaking of their future—one of the things that we have learned about the abduction phenomenon is that many times it does not end for an abductee—it can be a never-ending story!

Figure 32. From left to right: Jack and Jim Weiner, Charlie Foltz and Chuck Rak, 1993.

List of Figures

Index

A Bold Decision

Coincidentally, each of the Allagash Four is an artist. Therein lies both an opportunity and a danger.

The opportunity is manifested in this book and in the associated docucomic. In each there are original illustrations, more telling than any photograph, prepared professionally by the men who were abducted. These illustrations are unique and can be sold at market prices.

But therein lies the danger, too. Any appearance of profitability to any of the abducted artists will be sure to be used by desperate debunkers to support a hoax theory. They will surely say that these men made up this story in order to make money.

They did not. The Allagash abductions really occurred.
The extraterrestrial presence is among us.
This is not a hoax. The evidence is ironclad.

All of the Allagash Four make their living as artists. Their artwork is a natural extension of their life experiences. Their artwork has been affected by this experience, and they have devoted much of their time since recreating what they saw. It is natural for these men to sell their artwork to interested people.

So the question is posed: should these men be allowed to benefit from their experiences, at the risk of being easy targets for debunkers?

Wild Flower Press, after much deliberation, supports the theory of the free market in this case. The case for the Allagash abductions is so secure that debunkers will not be able to shake it based on artists selling their work. Further, it would be a restraint on free trade to try to forbid these artists from plying their trade.

Consequently, Wild Flower Press is pleased to announce that customers can purchase original hand-done illustrations and limited edition color computer prints by the Allagash Four.

See opposite page for ordering details.

Related Materials

The Allagash Incident (in docucomic format)
by Jack Weiner & Charles Rak
Published by Tundra Publishing,
Northampton, MA.
This 32-page black & white docucomic has full-color covers. It covers the Allagash abductions in fully illustrated style, featuring original artwork by the abductees. Not just for children.
$2.95 plus $1.00 shipping and handling.

Original Artwork by the Allagash abductees, suitable for framing. Subject matter relates to the Allagash abductions:

•Hand-done *original* illustration by Chuck Rak.
$75.00 plus $3.00 shipping and handling.

•Limited-edition color computer print by Jack Weiner.
$40.00 plus $3.00 shipping and handling.

•For additional information on artwork, sizes, media, etc., write for a free brochure.

Resources for abductees/contactees (experiencers) and the professionals who work with them:

•*Contact Forum*, an interactive newsletter for experiencers and professionals.

•G.R.A.A., Group for Research and Aid to Abductees

To contact either of these groups or to get descriptions and ordering information for additional UFO titles, please call or write for one of our free catalogs.

Wild Flower Press
P.O. Box 230893
Tigard, Oregon 97281
1/800/366-0264

Update on Witness Polygraph Results

As this book goes to press in June of 1993, two of the Allagash Four have successfully passed polygraph examinations. Results for the remaining two are unavailable at this writing.

The polygraph examinations were carried out by Secret Services Associates of Dedham, Massachusetts, Ernest C. Reid, Certified Stress Analyst, C.P.E., presiding.

Charlie Foltz was given three polygraph examinations on May 21, 1993. "On the basis of the analysis by this Examiner," writes Mr. Reid, "we must conclude that he is not being deceptive with regard to the facts surrounding his confrontation in August of 1976; we do not believe that he is lying or being deceptive with regard to conspiring with anyone to lie about the incident of August, 1976; and finally we do not believe that he was lying or being deceptive with regard to having any monetary gain or publicity from the incident. On the basis of our analysis of the charts, we conclude that he is being truthful in all areas where questioned."

Jim Weiner was similarly examined May 24, 1993. He related the experience of August, 1976, in some detail, and Mr. Reid formulated a twelve-question examination that was repeated three times in different orders as a validity check. Mr. Reid reports, "The...facts of the incident are, with extremely slight limitations made by the observations of the observer, in direct correlation with the story related to us by Charles Foltz, on whom we conducted a previous examination." He found Mr. Weiner to be "...truthful and showing no signs of deception."

The fact that these two witnesses passed the polygraph examinations provides even more weight to the conclusion of this book: alien abductions are real, and it is time for thoughtful people to formulate informed opinions about the phenomenon.